Road to Nowhere

Historical Studies of Urban America

Edited by Lilia Fernández, Timothy J. Gilfoyle, and Amanda I. Seligman
James R. Grossman, Editor Emeritus

RECENT TITLES IN THE SERIES

Ruby Oram, *Home Work: Gender, Child Labor, and Education for Girls in Urban America, 1870–1930*

Stephen M. Koeth, *Crabgrass Catholicism: How Suburbanization Transformed Faith and Politics in Postwar America*

Daniel Wortel-London, *The Menace of Prosperity: New York City and the Struggle for Economic Development, 1865–1981*

A. K. Sandoval-Strausz, ed., *Metropolitan Latinidad: Transforming American Urban History*

Alexander Wood, *Building the Metropolis: Architecture, Construction, and Labor in New York City, 1880–1935*

Leslie M. Harris, *In the Shadow of Slavery: African Americans in New York City, 1626–1863*, With a New Afterword by the Author

Tim Keogh, *In Levittown's Shadow: Poverty in America's Wealthiest Postwar Suburb*

Nicholas Dagen Bloom, *The Great American Transit Disaster: A Century of Austerity, Auto-Centric Planning, and White Flight*

Sean T. Dempsey, *City of Dignity: Christianity, Liberalism, and the Making of Global Los Angeles*

Claire Dunning, *Nonprofit Neighborhoods: An Urban History of Inequality and the American State*

Tracy E. K'Meyer, *To Live Peaceably Together: The American Friends Service Committee's Campaign for Open Housing*

Mike Amezcua, *Making Mexican Chicago: From Postwar Settlement to the Age of Gentrification*

Arnold R. Hirsch, *Making the Second Ghetto: Race and Housing in Chicago, 1940–1960*, With a New Afterword by N. D. B. Connolly

A complete list of series titles is available on the University of Chicago Press website.

Road to Nowhere

How a Highway Map Wrecked Baltimore

EMILY LIEB

The University of Chicago Press
Chicago and London

The University of Chicago Press, Chicago 60637
The University of Chicago Press, Ltd., London
© 2025 by The University of Chicago
All rights reserved. No part of this book may be used or reproduced in any manner whatsoever without written permission, except in the case of brief quotations in critical articles and reviews. For more information, contact the University of Chicago Press, 1427 E. 60th St., Chicago, IL 60637.
Published 2025

34 33 32 31 30 29 28 27 26 25   1 2 3 4 5

ISBN-13: 978-0-226-84436-7 (cloth)
ISBN-13: 978-0-226-84438-1 (paper)
ISBN-13: 978-0-226-84437-4 (ebook)
DOI: https://doi.org/10.7208/chicago/9780226844374.001.0001

Portions previously adapted from " 'White Man's Lane': Hollowing Out the Highway Ghetto in Baltimore" by Emily Lieb from *Baltimore '68: Riots and Rebirth in an American City*, edited by Jessica Elfenbein, Thomas Hollowak, and Elizabeth Nix. Used by permission of Temple University Press. © 2011 by Temple University. All rights reserved.

Library of Congress Cataloging-in-Publication Data

Names: Lieb, Emily, 1973– author
Title: Road to nowhere : how a highway map wrecked Baltimore / Emily Lieb.
Other titles: Historical studies of urban America
Description: Chicago : The University of Chicago Press, 2025. | Series: Historical studies of urban America | Includes bibliographical references and index.
Identifiers: LCCN 2025017475 | ISBN 9780226844367 cloth |
   ISBN 9780226844381 paperback | ISBN 9780226844374 ebook
Subjects: LCSH: African American neighborhoods—Maryland—Baltimore—History—20th century | Highway planning—Social aspects—Maryland—Baltimore | Eminent domain—Social aspects—Maryland—Baltimore | Discrimination in housing—Maryland—Baltimore | Race discrimination—Maryland—Baltimore | Rosemont (Baltimore, Md.)—History—20th century
Classification: LCC F189.B16 R67 2025 | DDC 307.3/36208996073097526—dc23/eng/20250716
LC record available at https://lccn.loc.gov/2025017475

Authorized Representative for EU General Product Safety Regulation (GPSR) queries:
Easy Access System Europe—Mustamäe tee 50, 10621 Tallinn, Estonia, gpsr.requests@easproject.com
Any other queries: https://press.uchicago.edu/press/contact.html

For Luke
Thank you.

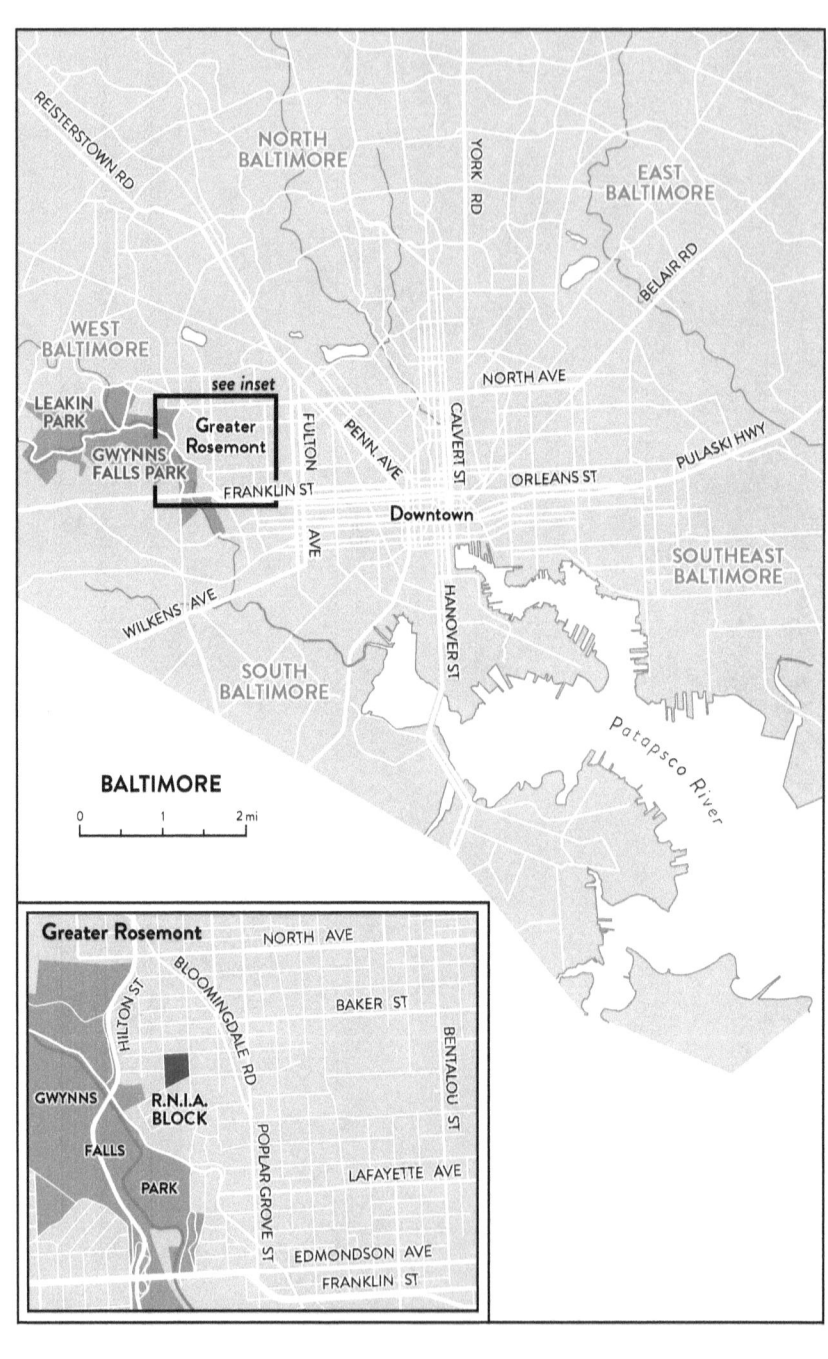

Contents

Introduction: Mary Rosemond's Rosemont   1

PART I The Neighborhood

1   "Gone White to Negro": How Jim Crow Made Rosemont (1910–1952)   15

2   "The Gigantic Conspiracy": How Rosemont Made Blockbusters Rich (1950s)   29

3   "Elected to Be the Sacrificers": How Rosemont Saw Its Future (1957)   44

PART II The Highway

4   "As Bad to Us as a Bomb": How the Highway Got Its Map (1957)   57

5   "Crime in the Street": How the Highway Robbed Rosemont (1967)   75

6   "If You Are Dead, You Are Dead": How the Highway Stalled in Rosemont (1968)   92

PART III The Aftermath

7   "The Rosemont Dilemma": How Baltimore Reinvented Rosemont (1968–1971)   115

8   "Ripped Off": How Rosemont Paid the Price (1972–1975)   131

Conclusion: Roads to Nowhere   151

Acknowledgments 173
List of Abbreviations 177
Notes 179   Index 229

INTRODUCTION

Mary Rosemond's Rosemont

The age of the American expressway ended in the same place it began: Mary Rosemond's backyard.

In 1926, the year Mary Morgan was born in Jacksonville, Florida, her parents bought a brand-new house for their growing family: a Sears foursquare with a wide front porch on Moncrief Road, not far from the city's downtown.[1] Moncrief was part of Sugar Hill, a booming streetcar suburb connected to downtown by the "Colored Man's Railroad," the Black-owned North Jacksonville Street Railway, Town and Improvement Company.[2] People called Sugar Hill the "Harlem of the South," and through a child's eyes especially it could have seemed like paradise.[3] Five-and-dimes, bakeries, and confectioners lined Davis and Ashley Streets. Fancy dress and hat shops flaunted furs and feathers behind enormous plate-glass windows. Bluesmen and jazz singers browsed the Hollywood Music Store, and stars from the nearby Norman Film Studios posed and peacocked in hotel lobbies.[4] At night neon signs winked in the muggy darkness.

In the public realm, too, Sugar Hill was someplace special. In 1927, the city opened the Wilder Park Library, the Jacksonville Public Library's busiest branch, not far from the Morgans' house.[5] The thirty acres of green space surrounding the library became Wilder Park, Jacksonville's largest "colored" park. It had a track, a baseball diamond, a football stadium, and a sleek community center whose Saturday-night dances would be legendary.[6]

In sum: Sugar Hill was a nice place to grow up, a nice place to live, and a nice place to be from. In fact, historian Ennis Davis writes, "perhaps Sugar Hill was a little too nice for Jim Crow era Jacksonville."[7] And so Jim Crow Jacksonville struck back.

It started with a map.

In 1936, when Mary Morgan was ten years old, the city mothballed the last of its streetcars, replacing them with buses. It was the first of Florida's big cities to do so, and it did because, at least according to the 1931 City Plan, "as the town grew, its colored areas grew likewise, adjacent to the white areas. As a result, the several separate and distinct colored areas came into being. But now with the advent of business and industry into some of those old areas, the residents there are being forced farther and farther from their places of labor." In other words, the city was growing, white residents were moving into new suburban neighborhoods, and now their nannies and housekeepers might (planners fretted) "consume 40–45 minutes in continuous riding time in going from her home to the site of her day's work." This was "not only unfair to the negro element but"—and here was the main point, as far as planners were concerned—"likewise unfair to those dependent upon them for domestic service."[8]

In theory, buses were the solution to this problem. Their routes could be tweaked as the city grew and the population shifted, so no matter where white families moved, the people who washed their clothes, cooked their meals, scrubbed their toilets, and tended their children would still be just a short ride away. But this was only true if they weren't stuck in traffic. So, planners argued that the only way to guarantee the buses wouldn't be delayed was to build a system of high-speed roads to sweep them around the city.

What seemed a simple solution to a straightforward problem soon twisted into a way to reimagine the city itself. In particular, as Ennis Davis writes, Jacksonville's roadbuilders and public officials quickly came to see "the new highways as a way to eliminate blighted neighborhoods and serve as barriers to stop the spread of blight"—and what they meant by "blight," typically, was "Black people."[9] Thus in the mid-1940s, when the Chamber of Commerce drew a map for a 22-mile snare of highways and connectors across Jacksonville, they shot one right through Sugar Hill.[10] That expressway, which is now part of I-95, suffocated the businesses on Davis Street, the Wilder Park Community Center, the park, the library, the hospital, the Y, and hundreds of homes under a heavy cover of concrete and asphalt.[11]

The highway builders "just broke up the neighborhood," Mary Morgan—by then Mary Rosemond—said later, "but my mama wouldn't sell."[12] The Morgans were unusually lucky, because they could make that choice and make it stick: The city of Jacksonville didn't yet have the tools it would have needed to take the house from them anyway. So the Morgan family home kept standing where it stands today, with two lanes of traffic shrieking past its garden at 50 miles per hour.

While the bulldozers chewed through her childhood neighborhood in Jacksonville, Mary Morgan—now newly married to her first husband, Sterling Graves—graduated from college and got a job as a schoolteacher in West Baltimore. In 1954, the pair bought a home of their own: a bright, stocky rowhouse at the corner of Presstman and Rosedale Streets on what had once been Baltimore's far-western edge. The house sat just two blocks from the shoulder of Gwynns Falls Park, a 1,200-acre forest "reservation" straddling an old millstream: "a picturesque and sylvan sort" of park, the Olmsted Brothers once wrote, "seldom possible to retain so near a great city."[13]

Around the time Mary and Sterling Graves moved there, the neighborhood got a name: Rosemont. It hadn't always had one, because the developers who built its houses in the 1920s and '30s did so patchwork-style, block by block, on scraps of land carved out of old horse farms and summer estates. They'd vied with one another to sell the most amenities, like all-electric kitchens, bright tiled bathrooms, and Eastlake woodwork, for the lowest price, and their ads appealed "to the family desiring the best in environment with close proximity to downtown." "Everything up to the minute," they promised. "Let your rent buy a beautiful new home."[14]

Those first ads were aimed at working-class white people: butchers and bookkeepers and salesclerks and police officers who had enough for the mortgage but not much more. Black people stayed away, not because they wanted to but because they had to. Like Jacksonville, Baltimore was a Jim Crow city, and its politics aimed to define and defend white people's property. In particular, in the older parts of the city and in newer "suburban" places like Rosemont, legally segregated schools blocked and steered Black migration and branded the neighborhoods over which the schools stood sentry. The result: no schools for Black pupils in Rosemont, nor anywhere near it. And since most people would not choose to live where their children could not go to school, through the 1940s you could count the Black residents in that part of West Baltimore on the fingers of one hand.[15]

In 1951, though, the city's school board had initiated a spasm of what bureaucrats called "school conversions," turning officially "white" schools between Fulton Avenue and the Gwynns Falls Park into schools for Black students. These conversions opened a pressure valve out of the older parts of West Baltimore for those who could afford to take advantage of it. By the time school started that fall, so many middle-class Black families had moved west into Rosemont and the surrounding neighborhoods that school officials called it "the most unprecedented, the most historic population movement in Baltimore."[16]

Rosemont

Young bicyclist on Bentalou Street (n.d.), *The Settler: A Chronicle of Home Ownership in Baltimore*, March 1975. Courtesy of University of Baltimore Special Collections and Archives.

"Professional Blacks were moving into peaceful, clean, safe, attractive areas," Mary Rosemond later wrote. "We were buying our homes! We were happy in our homes! We cared for our homes and our families!"[17] A new community was born. But as soon as Rosemont became a Black neighborhood, it also became a target. In 1957, policymakers aimed an expressway right at it.

How this happened, and what Baltimore lost when it did, is the subject of this book.

The Ruins of a Once-Great City

"Urban History," N. D. B. Connolly writes in his afterword to a recent reprinting of Arnold R. Hirsch's classic *Making the Second Ghetto: Race and Housing in Chicago, 1940–1960*, illustrates "how white terrorism gets both abstracted and focused through wrecking balls and bulldozer blades."[18] It also shows how white terrorism needs only the *idea* of those tools to do its job. Since Hirsch first published his book in 1983, historians have been working to explain the many ways cities' segregated "second ghettoes" were, as Hirsch put it, "continually . . . renewed, reinforced, and reshaped."[19] Some have explained how policymakers at every level redefined local housing markets and consecrated the connection between white Americans' ideas about race and the politics of property ownership.[20] Others have shown how these same toxic ideas built and buoyed entire economies of exploitation around Black property and its owners, and how they shaped the infrastructures that made that exploitation look natural, even inevitable.[21]

In the 2017 book *Cutting School: Privatization, Segregation, and the End of Public Education*, the scholar Noliwe Rooks coined the term "segrenomics," "the business of profiting specifically from high levels of racial and economic segregation."[22] Rooks focuses on the ways in which policy interventions ostensibly aimed at improving education for poor and minoritized children, like charter schools and vouchers, have become a source of private profit, "a prize of staggering economic value and social importance."[23] Consequently, Rooks writes, "business-proposed 'cures' for educational inequality" may do "much more harm than healing."[24] Harm—not healing—is where the money is, and that's as true in urban neighborhoods as it is in their schools.

This is one way to explain what scholars call "racial capitalism," the idea that expropriation and accumulation unfold unevenly along racial lines because it profits white people when they do.[25] For instance, when the school board branded Rosemont a Black neighborhood, it started a vicious "segrenomic" cycle that kept spinning for generations.

The amount of money at stake made good-faith city planning unimaginable. Public policy that treated Rosemont's Black homeowners as if they were white, that protected their property instead of sacking it, would not have so efficiently reproduced the political and material inequalities that made the city work, at least for the people it worked for. And as far as the City of Baltimore was concerned, those people were the only ones who mattered. Whatever powerful white Baltimoreans *said* they thought their city should be or serve or do, their ideology boiled down to this: everything you have belongs to us.

One of their weapons was a word: "blight." What it meant could be anybody's guess, and that was the point. Take the brain-twisting definition the Baltimore Urban Renewal and Housing Authority (BURHA) presented in a 1964 report. "There are probably almost as many definitions of blight as there are people knowledgeable in urban problems," BURHA said. "However, underlying all these different definitions is a common theme. This theme is that many attributes are associated with a blighted area that are not ordinarily found in unblighted areas."[26] But as they had been in Jacksonville, those many attributes were often just one: Did Black people call a place home, or didn't they?[27]

In fact, almost every policymaker in every city used this same formula to give ballast to their prejudices and explain the choices they made about where to feed and where to starve. "Blight" was a fiction that had the power, literally and figuratively, to condemn. In fact, the work the word did was eugenic. It argued for its own annihilation, for its own good and (more important) everyone else's. And although Rosemont would not fit into this way of thinking about what a Black neighborhood should look like—insofar as "blight" was an aesthetic, Rosemont was self-evidently its opposite—this fiction proved more powerful than any fact. Baltimore's planners saw a Black neighborhood, and they mapped an expressway to destroy it.

In the end, that expressway was never finished. It dead ends on Rosemont's eastern shoulder, which is how it got its nickname: the "road to nowhere." But as *Sun* reporter James Dilts wrote in 1968, "plans for highways, if they are around long enough, become self-fulfilling prophecies."[28] To scar a city, you don't need to build a thing. You need only make a map.

Years ago, I found Rosemont in a box of old photos in the stacks at the Baltimore City Archives. The ones that caught my attention came from an early 1970s campaign by the Baltimore City Department of Housing and Community Development to create what officials called a "sound, safe, decent, and sanitary . . . *normal* city residential environment" in the neighborhood—which, by then, seemed to be none of those things.[29] The empty houses in the photos were not even 50 years old, not very old at all in Baltimore terms, but they call to mind something H. L. Mencken once told his friend James Thurber: "Drop off in Baltimore one day," he said, "and let me show you the ruins of a once great medieval city."[30] In the photographs, awnings sway over broken windows. Railings sag. Roofs leak. Talking to a newspaper reporter about the neighborhood in 1974, one city official groused: "We have spent a lot of money on a lot of blocks that have turned out to be unsalvageable."[31]

But "turned out to be" is exactly the wrong way to explain what happened here. If Rosemont was unsalvageable, it was that way because Baltimore had made it so.

Three Swindles

In Baltimore, planners, policymakers, and businessmen acted in tandem to preserve and reproduce white supremacy in space, to buoy it by public subsidy and vindicate it by private profit.³² In Rosemont, that meant three separate but overlapping bonanzas, whose stories are the three parts of this book: first the birth of Black Rosemont, then its destruction, and finally its scavenging.

For the first half of the twentieth century, segregated schools were official Baltimore's most reliable tool for sorting and maintaining formally "white" neighborhoods. And from the 1920s until the 1950s, those schools established and held what sociologist Samuel Joseph Rice called a "border line and barrier, separating the Negro and white population" in West Baltimore along Fulton Avenue, a north–south arterial that was roughly contiguous with the city's earliest western border.³³ As a result, a 1935 National Urban League report calculated that Black Baltimoreans were about 20 percent of the city's population yet occupied just 2 percent of its housing.³⁴ Most of these homes were in "Old" West Baltimore between the city center and the Fulton Avenue color line, where most of the city's Black schools clustered, too.

In the early 1950s, Baltimore's Board of School Commissioners pushed the color line west by "converting" white schools beyond it into "colored" ones. When they did, they created Black Rosemont. They also created a captive market. "SELECT COLORED HOMES," ads in the "City" section of the real estate pages blared. "EASY TERMS. WILL HELP FINANCE. FIRST CLASS CONDITION." Real estate men known as blockbusters—who got their name, writes journalist Antero Pietila, from "the huge Allied bombs that rained ruin on German cities in World War II"—bought low from white sellers they urged to flee and sold high to determined Black buyers.³⁵ They made more money, ruinous money, by financing those costly purchases, too.

In Baltimore as in cities across the country, mid-century blockbusting made blockbusters rich because the federal government promised it would.³⁶ Thousands of pages have been written about the ways in which mortgage-lending rules kept Black people from getting cheap government-guaranteed bank loans and inflated prices for Black housing by rationing its supply. These processes tied segregation to property values and alchemized the fiction that (as sociologist Dalton Conley puts it) "white housing is worth more, precisely because it is not Black housing" into federal government policy.³⁷

In Rosemont, the result of this was Black buyers stuck paying more for less. City records that document blockbusting are hard to find, but where they exist they clearly show that real estate companies bought low from white sellers and sold high—*very* high—to Black families with many fewer options. The loans they and their financial partners provided were pricier and more exploitative than the ones any similarly situated white family would have received.

There's no doubt that these financial instruments and real estate practices, and the public policies that made them possible, were predatory. They made life harder, more expensive, and more unpleasant for Mary Rosemond and her neighbors in Rosemont. But they did not make it impossible. During the 1950s and '60s, the Black newcomers to the neighborhood built a community that was radiant with promise and full of joy.[38] Blockbusting had strained their pocketbooks, but later studies would show that Black Rosemonters were 50 percent more likely to own their homes than the average Baltimorean. They spent thousands of dollars every year on upkeep and renovations. And in spite of the exploitative home loans they'd been forced to take, many did end up owning their homes outright.[39] They worried about appearances, fussed with lawns and shrubs and paint and porch furniture, because they had to—and because they wanted to. In sum: Rosemont was a nice middle-class place occupied by nice middle-class families. It was everything mid-century America was supposed to be.

Except that Black people lived there. And that made it vulnerable.

The idea that expressways could solve the problems facing aging American cities came, in part, from the most celebrated exhibit at the 1939 World's Fair in Queens, New York: the Futurama, in the General Motors Pavilion. Futurama was a 35,000-square-foot animated model of GM's ideal city in 1960. It was filled with cars—tens of millions of them, according to the booming voiceover. But the defining feature of GM's utopia was the sublime flow of automobile traffic through and around it, via what the exhibit's mastermind, designer Norman Bel Geddes, called "Magic Motorways." "Magic Motorways" were sleek, wide superhighways soaring high above the city's surface streets, and to Bel Geddes and GM they were the warp and weft of the American city of the future.[40] "The people who conduct polls to find out why other people do things, and the editorial writers, newspapermen and columnists who report daily on the doings of the human race, all had their theory as to why the Futurama was the most popular show of any Fair in history," Bel Geddes wrote. "And most of them agreed that the explanation was really very simple: All of these thousands of people who stood in line ride in motor cars and therefore are harassed by the daily task of getting from one place to another, by the nuisances of intersectional jams, narrow, congested bottlenecks, dangerous night driving, annoying policemen's whistles, honking horns, blinking traffic lights, confusing highway signs, and irritating traffic regulations; they are appalled by the daily toll of highway accidents and deaths; and they are eager to find a sensible way out of this planless, suicidal mess."[41]

Many people, especially those who had the power to bend American cities to their will, shared the vision at the Futurama's core.[42] They too thought bulldozers and cement mixers were the keys to a thriving metropolis. But where were all those "magic motorways" supposed to go?

In 1944, Baltimore's planners had invited New York City Parks Commissioner and master builder Robert Moses to design a freeway system that would carry the nineteenth-century city into its future. Moses's *Baltimore Arterial Report* was published that October. In its wake, planners would map more than a dozen highway systems through and around Charm City over the next decades. One would have carved a ring around the central business district, with radial highways extending outward like spokes from the hub of a gigantic wheel. One kept the ring road and dumped the radials. One dumped the ring and added a disjointed north–south segment that flowed with the Jones Falls to the Inner Harbor.

The details of these plans bleed together now. They often bled together then, too. (In fact, that would become its own problem. Officials' disinclination to choose a plan and live with their choice became part of Baltimore's background noise, easy to turn down and tune out.) Of those thousands of blurry details, here are the key ones. First, from the *Baltimore Arterial Report* on, every expressway system planners proposed included some version of an "East–West Expressway" across the city's midsection. Second, before Rosemont became a Black neighborhood, every version of that East–West Expressway gave the place a wide berth. Third, after Rosemont became a Black neighborhood, every version of that East–West Expressway save one would have gutted the neighborhood from stem to stern. A 1969 article about the expressway in *Architectural Forum* summed it up: "Obviously, the highway would never have been routed through Rosemont if it had been a white neighborhood."[43]

In 1967, Baltimore's city council formally voted to condemn some nine hundred houses in Rosemont for the East–West Expressway, then also known as Interstate 170. Appraisers from the Maryland State Highway Administration's Interstate Division swarmed into the neighborhood to set prices for the condemned houses. Those prices were high enough to make the blockbusting lenders whole, and high enough to enable Rosemont's homeowners to make down payments on new houses to those same lenders, but no higher. In the taking zone and alongside it, Rosemont's homeowners lost virtually everything.

Still, they and their neighbors fought back; and on paper, they won their fight. In 1968, a multiracial, cross-class coalition of Baltimoreans against the expressway persuaded the roadbuilders to adopt a new route, one that dipped the highway underneath Rosemont and through mostly vacant industrial land and a cemetery that had been there all along.[44] But this display of community power and solidarity was no match for a city determined to flex its own. The city council refused to lift the condemnation lines through Rosemont, and state highway officials refused to sell the houses they no longer needed there back to their owners. Many of these owners were pushed out to Baltimore's western suburbs, where familiar blockbusting real estate firms started the familiar extractive cycle all over again.

Some Rosemonters who lived outside the condemnation corridor left, too. Others, like Mary (since remarried) Rosemond, stayed behind and tried to resuscitate the community they'd worked so hard to build. But despite the neighbors' efforts, "in Rosemont," activists wrote, "the state has created chaos." Highway or no, a "viable area" had become a "blighted scar."[45]

And so Rosemont became a target for exploitation once again. As part of the federal Housing and Urban Development Act of 1968, Congress had created a lending program known as Section 235 that used mortgage-backed securities (which the law had also created) to finance home loans for poor people. These loans were supposed to be different—fairer, more equitable, and less exploitative—from the ones the blockbusters had given to that first generation of Rosemonters. However, as the historian Keeanga-Yamahtta Taylor writes in *Race for Profit: How Banks and the Real Estate Industry Undermined Black Homeownership*, different did not mean better. The Section 235 program promised to repay lenders in full if a buyer defaulted, which meant that "real estate and mortgage bankers valued these [new borrowers] because of the *likelihood* they would fail to keep up their home payments and slip into foreclosure."[46] With each foreclosure, companies recovered the capital to offer another risky mortgage. The result was something Taylor calls "predatory inclusion," in which lenders once again had every incentive to make unconscionable loans and vulnerable buyers paid the price.

It didn't take long for the municipal Department of Housing and Community Development to announce a campaign to use this federal money to recreate that "*normal* city residential environment" Rosemont had been just a few years before.[47] The campaign promised to restore hundreds of city-owned houses for sale—not back to their previous owners, who were long gone by now, but to anybody with $200 for a down payment. Buyers paid for the rest using those predatory loans that came, this time, not from blockbusters but from ordinary mortgage banks. For those banks, the new market for "subprime" mortgages in formerly middle-class Rosemont was another gold mine. They got paid when a buyer initiated a loan. They got paid if that buyer defaulted. And they got paid when the next buyer started the whole process over from the beginning.

Ads for the Section 235 program in Rosemont promised that the "rehabilitated" houses in the highway corridor would be a good investment for their buyers, most of whom were young families and many of whom were moving to the neighborhood from the city's public housing projects. The city was selling the houses for six and eight times what it had paid for them, a price ostensibly justified by the "cellar to roof" renovations officials promised.[48] The problem was, the contractors who were supposed to be renovating the houses were not actually renovating much at all. In 1972, the *Afro-American* newspaper and West Baltimore Congressman Parren Mitchell launched "a good, critical look at houses being offered for sale in the Rosemont area"[49] and were horrified by the conditions their investigation revealed. Mitchell noted that the supposedly top-of-the-line appliances in the remodeled homes were "the cheapest models you can get," and a child could knock a hole in the flimsy walls "in no time." The newcomers were in real danger, he said, of buying "a home with a 30-year mortgage only to have it fall apart in 10."[50]

When officials in the mid-1970s looked around Rosemont, they saw what they called "deteriorated, neglected properties" and a "lack of interest or pride in the home and community."[51] In other words, they saw the "blight" they'd always expected to see. What they did not see were the consequences of their own actions. In the official version of events, policymakers had tried their best to "renew" Rosemont, but Rosemont would not be renewed. Thus: "We have spent a lot of money on a lot of blocks that have turned out to be unsalvageable."[52]

Yet the new Rosemont homeowners, saddled now with houses they couldn't afford, couldn't sell, and could barely live in, did all they could to salvage them. Though they were stretched too thin to begin with, city mortgage records show they would spend years and decades digging deeper into debt to keep their homes and make them livable: subprime second mortgages, subprime home-improvement loans, sketchy loans from roofing companies, plumbing companies, and construction companies. Those mortgage records also show that long before the subprime crisis made headlines in the 2000s, many people in the neighborhood had lost their homes to one lender or another. "It seems," Mary Rosemond told a reporter in 2004, "as though we are seeing ourselves deteriorate."[53]

That the expressway did not go through Rosemont mattered far less, in the end, than the maps that put it there in the first place. Every map is a projection; and in Rosemont, the projection the roadbuilders' maps made didn't need to be made concrete to be made concrete.

"If there is a neighborhood success story connected to the bitter history of Baltimore's expressways, it is Rosemont," James Dilts wrote in the *Sun* in March 1976. "Rosemont is a success because the expressway did not go through it."[54] On the other hand: "That highway wreaked havoc in the neighborhood," neighborhood activist (and future city councilmember) Agnes Welch told the paper a few years later. "We had neighborhood bars that were quiet—no loitering. We had pastry shops, and drugstores with luncheonette counters, and corner grocery stores. We had doctors and dentists who lived and kept their offices here . . . it was almost suburban." "None of this was due to civil disturbance," she said, throwing her arms wide. "It was all the highway."[55] Further investigation revealed more of the same. "One young man who has lived in Rosemont all his life said it is a 'rough' area that he will move from as soon as he can," the reporter wrote. "I heard it was real nice once," the young man said, "but I think they were supposed to put a subway through or something."[56]

PART I

The Neighborhood

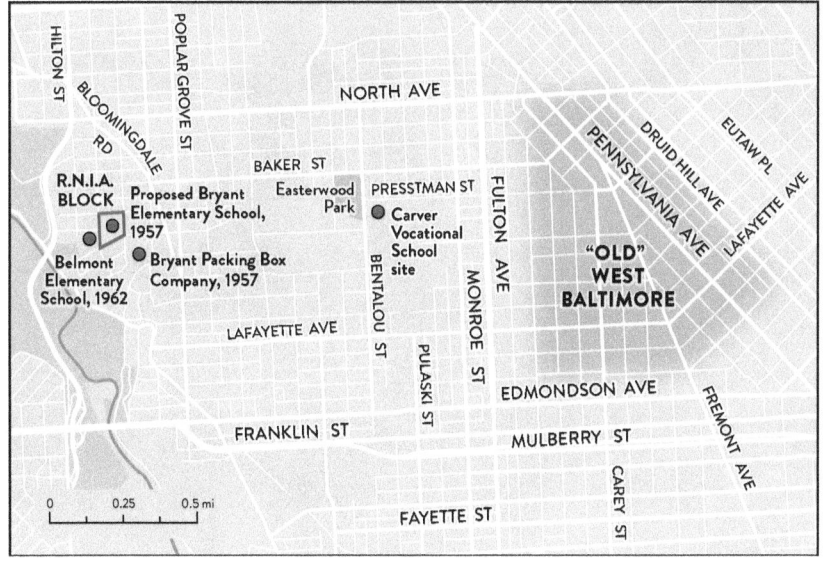

1

"Gone White to Negro": How Jim Crow Made Rosemont (1910–1952)

"Population Move Stumps School Board." That was *The Baltimore Sun* headline schoolteacher Gertrude Corbett would have seen one Friday in September 1952, if she'd had enough time before the morning bell to make it to page 36 of the paper. When she did, Corbett would have read that up and down the eastern edge of Gwynns Falls Park in West Baltimore, "entire city blocks were vacated during the three months of summer by white persons and supplanted by Negroes." School officials called it "the most unprecedented, the most historic population movement in Baltimore." After the jump there was a different headline: "Blocks Gone White to Negro."[1]

But Gertrude Corbett didn't need to read about all this. She was living it. Mrs. Corbett and her husband Thomas, a mechanic, had just moved into a red brick rowhouse with a Spanish tile roof on Belmont Avenue, a block away from Gwynns Falls Park. Both came from rural South Carolina—"Someplace, South Carolina," the census-taker scrawled in 1940—but had been in the city for more than a decade.[2] All that time, they'd lived on the ever-shifting northwestern edge of Black Baltimore. Now they were among the first Black families to buy on their new block, the bucolic trapezoid formed by Presstman, Rosedale, Belmont, and Ellamont Streets.

Only a few months before, the people who lived on the Corbetts' block were all white. Now, just like the newspaper said, many of those white people were selling and moving: to Gwynn Oak, to Halethorpe, to Catonsville, or just over the old Edmondson Avenue Bridge to the other side of the park. Their impending departure made them better neighbors than they might otherwise have been. "Everyone was very nice to me," Gertrude Corbett would later tell the *Evening Sun*, "because they wanted me to find someone to buy their house."[3]

According to that 1952 article, the school commissioners were "baffled" by "the ingress of Negro home owners and dwellers in hitherto white neighborhoods."[4] But as Gertrude Corbett likely knew, this bafflement was itself a little baffling. Those commissioners were as responsible as anybody was for greasing Black migration into white West Baltimore.[5]

For as long as there have been cities in the United States, white property owners and the policymakers who serve their interests have been pioneering ways to make and keep them segregated. But Jim Crow urbanism, a synoptic and enduring way of thinking about what the city is and who it's for, was born in Progressive-era Baltimore, a city that's always been Northern and Southern, Black and white.[6]

According to journalist Joel Garreau's 1981 bestseller *The Nine Nations of North America*, Maryland straddles the "Foundry–Dixie line" separating the Rust Belt's industrial cities, ports, and hinterlands from the Old South.[7] This separation stretches back generations. As early as 1850, historian Barbara Fields explains, there were "two Marylands": one that relied on the labor of enslaved people to plant and harvest its tobacco, and another much larger one "to which slavery was at most tangential."[8] Baltimore was the capital of the latter. Before the Civil War, there were about 28,000 Black people in the city, and barely 2,000 of them were enslaved.[9]

Nineteenth-century Baltimore was a commercial city whose elites were merchants and manufacturers, not planters. Its hinterland stretched westward. First the Cumberland Road and later the Baltimore & Ohio Railroad connected the city's mills to the grain- and coal-producing regions of the Pennsylvania piedmont and the Ohio Valley. In turn, clippers filled with flour and outfitted with sails made from Baltimore's own cotton duck exchanged the city's manufactured goods for more raw materials—like Peruvian guano, of which Baltimore was the country's leading importer—for the city's countless small factories.[10]

After the Civil War, jobs in textile manufacturing, sawmills, oystering, shipping, canning, and construction made Baltimore an attractive destination for migrants from rural Maryland, Virginia, and North Carolina.[11] Many of them were Black. Between 1870 and 1900, when Baltimore was among the largest cities in the United States, Black people were about 20 percent of its population.[12] Compared with other Southern cities, this was not an especially substantial fraction: In 1900, the average city in the former Confederacy was about one-third Black. But it made Baltimore unique among Northern industrial cities whose working class was typically made up of immigrants from places like Ireland, Italy, and Eastern Europe.[13]

Baltimore *had* once had a sizable immigrant community. In 1860, more than 50,000 Baltimoreans, or one-quarter of the population, had been born in Europe. But immigration to the city paused during the Civil War and never quite resumed, at least not at anything close to its earlier pace. After 1880, historian Matthew A. Crenson writes, "Baltimore's African American population equaled or exceeded its foreign-born population. Baltimore had a larger black population than any big city save the District of Columbia and a smaller percentage of foreign-born residents than any of the 10 largest cities in the country."[14]

Then came Jim Crow, but first came what historian Crenson calls "Jim Crow Lite." Postbellum Baltimore, he writes, "followed many southern communities in its imposition of Jim Crow restrictions, but with less consistency and vigor. The city's hotels and schools were rigidly segregated. Public transportation was supposed to be, too, but white riders were not sufficiently patient to wait for whites-only trolleys to maintain racial separation. Public parks, concert halls, and lecture rooms were open to the city's black residents without any discernible protest."[15] And Baltimore's working people—native-born whites, immigrants, and Black people—lived all throughout the city. Well-to-do merchants and manufacturers typically lived in grand rowhouses on the main streets and avenues, with skilled laborers and craftsmen cross-hatched on the side streets and poor and working-class people in little "alley houses" behind each block.[16] This relatively integrated pattern repeated almost everywhere inside the Baltimore city lines. Anthropologist Karen Olson did the math and found that in 1880, Black people were 10 percent or more of the total population in three-quarters of the city's twenty wards, but no single ward was more than one-third Black.[17]

In Maryland, Black men were free to vote, and as one result Maryland (and Baltimore) maintained a real two-party political system.[18] When Maryland's Republican Party had been founded in 1867, historian Margaret Law Callcott explains, "they saw one possible route to power and began to build their party accordingly: enfranchisement of the nearly 40,000 Negro freedmen in Maryland of voting age."[19] But Baltimore was predominantly Democratic, ruled by party boss Isaac Freeman Rasin and his gang of enforcers.[20] Black voters' Republican loyalty offered limited reward to the Democrats in charge, and starting with the election of 1871 the Rasin Ring suppressed their ballots by paying them to stay away from the polls and (Crenson writes) otherwise "arranging grand picnics or Chesapeake Bay excursions on election day."[21]

So, in the decades after the Civil War, the Maryland Republican Party's primary job was to temper Democratic enthusiasms and check its excesses, not threaten its power. But in 1895, disputes over taxes split the states'

Democrats into a farmer's faction and a businessmen's faction.[22] Without any other platform to speak of, the party followed its Southern brethren toward lurid appeals to white supremacy. For instance, per Callcott, "the Democrats' final campaign rally in Baltimore featured a huge night-time parade in which torch-lit transparencies decried mixed schools, a float depicted a mixed school presided over by a colored school teacher who flogged white children, and at the end of the parade a small boy carried a banner that asked: 'Papa, would you vote to put a negro alongside your little boy in school?'"[23] Yet the Republican candidate for governor (who didn't want to "put a negro alongside your little boy in school" either) carried almost every part of the state that year, teaching the Democrats that their hegemony in Maryland was not guaranteed. Thus, according to the historian Michael Perman, Jim Crow—*real* Jim Crow, not "Jim Crow lite"—became "a vital ingredient in the massive campaign launched by the Democrats in Maryland to gain a permanent majority in the state by eliminating the Republicans' black voters as well as stigmatizing them as social pariahs."[24]

As far as voting rights went, Jim Crow was a flop: Between 1903 and 1911, Democrats tried and failed three times to amend Maryland's constitution to outlaw Black suffrage. It was obvious to virtually everyone in Maryland that the point of all these suffrage restrictions was to grease Democratic votes and stall Republican ones, and they really weren't necessary for that. But the policies that aimed to reinforce white people's power on (and over) the ground by turning their Black neighbors into pariahs ran along a parallel track—and because they *did* seem necessary, at least to the people whose interests they served, they were considerably more successful. This kind of Jim Crow, and the way of thinking about and living in the city that it enabled, is what made modern Baltimore.

Jim Crow Schools

In Baltimore, segregated schools became the first tools white people used to define and police the physical and metaphysical boundaries of the neighborhoods they thought were theirs. As it turned out, they would also be the most durable. Segregated schools created segregated neighborhoods. Segregated neighborhoods, in turn, created the city.[25]

Ever since 1867, when Baltimore's Board of School Commissioners assumed responsibility for the city's Freedmen's Bureau schools, the board had assigned white children to "white" schools and Black children to "colored" ones.[26] The *Sun* newspaper later explained how this worked in practice: by placing white children in new schools and Black children in hand-me-downs converted "when the neighborhoods in which such schools were situated became colored neighborhoods."[27]

Except—what was a "colored" neighborhood, and what did it mean to "become" one? In Progressive-era Baltimore, like most every other Southern city, Black people and white people were still each other's neighbors.[28] As the city's Black population grew, it *had* become more concentrated. By the turn of the twentieth century, as anthropologist Olson noted, half of the Black people in Baltimore lived in the wedge-shaped area just west of downtown (between Druid Hill Avenue, Dolphin Street, Gilmor Street, and North Avenue) known as "Old" West Baltimore.[29] Yet by then, Black people were just about 15 percent of the city's population. Half of 15 percent was just not enough to fill the thousands of homes on the hundreds of blocks in that part of the city.[30]

In 1888, the residents of 7.5 square miles of what was then Baltimore County to the north and west voted to join the city proper, pulling Baltimore's western boundary from (roughly) Pulaski Street out past the Gwynns Falls and its northern boundary from North Avenue to Cold Spring Lane.[31] The toffs of Old West Baltimore headed to the fashionable new suburbs, like Roland Park, developers were building there. (These places *were* segregated by rule and covenant, historian Paige Glotzer explains, "as a tactic to attract residents and augment sales.")[32] Their exodus left "great blocks of handsome houses" in and around Old West Baltimore, local lawyer W. Ashbie Hawkins wrote in the NAACP journal *The Crisis*, which "had to be disposed of to anybody, and often on any terms."[33]

"Anybody" really meant anybody, at least according to the 1900 census. It counted native-born and immigrant white people—tailors, plumbers, wallpaper hangers—who could never afford to live in a place like Roland Park and would never have been welcome there anyway, along with Black people up and down the social ladder.[34] White newcomers to Old West Baltimore included people like Lewis Hirshberg, who sold insurance; Hirshberg's neighbors on Druid Hill Avenue were all white, too. Over on Pennsylvania, a paper-hanger named Frank Bartholomee lived in a row with a housepainter, a carpenter, two locksmiths, a shoemaker, two dressmakers, and one milliner—also all white. John Russell, a merchant sailor, and his wife and children were the only Black family on the block. Around the corner on Mosher, though, things were less homogeneous. At 551, grocer John Treffinger and his family were white; next door, at 549, waiter William Gassaway and his family were Black. Down the block, an Irish marble polisher lived between a white butter dealer and a Black musician.[35]

Up and down Old West Baltimore's rows, this pattern repeated itself. Some blocks were all white; some blocks were almost all white; and some more closely resembled what historian Thomas Hanchett calls "salt and pepper."³⁶ But the Board of School Commissioners' taxonomy said a place was "white" or it was "colored," with no in-between. If it was Frank Bartholomee's neighborhood, it couldn't have been John Russell's.

Jim Crow schools, then, were charged with naming "colored" neighborhoods where none existed. For instance, in 1901, the Board of School Commissioners proposed closing the English-German School at the corner of Pennsylvania Avenue and Dolphin Street and opening in its place a Colored High School and Polytechnic Institute. Why that school in that spot? The English-German School was one of a handful of bilingual public primary schools established in the city after the Civil War, but few German speakers still lived nearby, and half the desks in the school sat empty. Meanwhile, there were more than a dozen "white" schools within walking distance and just one for Black pupils.³⁷

To school officials, it was an easy decision. Why should John Russell's girls have to walk halfway to South Baltimore to go to school just so Frank Bartholomee could keep on pretending they weren't his neighbors? But to the Frank Bartholomees of white West Baltimore, most of whom did not speak German and many of whom did not even have school-aged children, the school board's plan was a catastrophe. Why? "We are not actuated by race prejudice," Lewis Hirshberg explained, "but we desire to preserve the value of our property, which has taken some of us a lifetime of hard work to accumulate."³⁸

"We desire to preserve the value of our property." Here was the nut of the issue. People like Lewis Hirshberg would live down the block from Black people, but a "colored" school was a different issue. The problem was the brand: "colored." This was what white people believed would make preserving "the value of our property" impossible.³⁹

Jim Crow Neighborhoods

They were wrong. Yet as many writers have noted, it was a profitable fiction, and the mythology of a market preference for segregation has been one of the most powerful forces shaping the twentieth-century American city.

As the battle for West Baltimore's schools dragged on—at Lanvale and Division; Mount and Saratoga; Fulton and Pennsylvania; Pennsylvania and Robert—all-white "protective associations" began to cast about for a more reliable solution to the neighborhood-branding problem they thought they saw.⁴⁰ In 1907, they came up with one: a "legislative enactment to prevent the encroachment of negroes in the white residential sections," which "provided that no negro be allowed to occupy a house in a block occupied entirely by white people without the consent of a majority of the residents."[41] In other words, the law would make it illegal for Black people and white people to be one another's neighbors, and a "white residential section" would remain so, officially, for all time.

The idea of a residential segregation law kept percolating through West Baltimore until June 1910, when a Black lawyer named George McMechen and his family moved into a house on McCulloh Street, the "Champs Élysées of Baltimore."[42] McMechen's new neighbors reacted to the prospect that theirs might one day be an officially "colored" neighborhood by forming a new neighborhood improvement association committed to the passage of an "ordinance ... for the prevention of further invasion." It would "permanently fix the value of real estate," they said, and "remove a large percentage of the risk now involved in investing in Baltimore property."[43]

City Councilman Samuel West, an enthusiastic racist, spent the month of August 1910 drafting the ordinance with the help of a local attorney named Milton Dashiell. What they came up with was as much a Baltimore innovation as the bottle cap, the "Star-Spangled Banner," or Old Bay seasoning: the nation's first residential segregation law.

Its first iteration was a quarantine. "In the territory bounded by North avenue, Charles street, Baltimore street and Fulton avenue," the law said, "no negroes shall move into houses on streets on which a majority of whites live."[44] It sounded simple enough. But the problem, per the *Sun*, was that "residents of sections contiguous to the segregation area feared that other parts of Baltimore would have to take care of a possible exodus of colored residents."[45] In other words, the paper implied, some white people would have to suffer more Black neighbors because other white people wanted none. According to this line of reasoning, the city's segregation ordinance would have to be an all-or-nothing enterprise. Dashiell and West quickly rewrote it to say that no Black person could move onto a majority-white block, or vice versa, anywhere in Baltimore.[46] From city line to city line, Baltimore would be a Jim Crow town.[47]

On December 19, Mayor J. Barry Mahool signed the revised ordinance into law. But not even a month later the city council amended it once again to add a third category: "mixed" blocks, or blocks that were neither "colored" nor "white." The *Sun* explained. "The amendment will provide that [mixed] blocks be allowed to remain so until such a time when it shall be wholly inhabited by either whites or negroes. When that becomes the case the block shall come under the provisions of the ordinance."[48]

The original ordinance protected all "white"-branded blocks equally.[49] This approach was consistent with the mythology of segregation economics that justified it: It preserved property values, in theory, by branding "white" blocks in permanent ink. But though the fiction implicit in the first version of the law collided with the reality of Baltimore, the amended version—which recognized the fundamental instability of the situation the law was trying to stabilize—introduced a new problem. "A mixed block, as it now is, may be bad enough," Dashiell explained, "but if a negro secures a foothold in a block and by the removal of other tenants other negroes come in, it can be seen that in a very short time the entire block would be peopled by negroes."[50]

The process Dashiell was describing would later become known as blockbusting, and it would be a gold mine—for some.[51] But under the new version of the segregation law, white homeowners on "mixed" blocks who wanted to sell to white buyers found they could not sell at all. If they were lucky enough to live in a corner rowhouse adjacent to a "white" block, they could build a new front door on that side, changing their address while keeping all the same neighbors. (Scars of these renovations are still visible on some houses today.) Otherwise, as W. Ashbie Hawkins pointed out in *The Crisis*, their houses would stand empty, "eating up their values in taxes, ground rent, insurance, etc., waiting for white tenants who won't come."[52] That's when the "pirates" descended, buying houses cheaply from whites and then selling them, at a preposterous markup, to Black families.

To white people, this process seemed to confirm what they already assumed: that Black neighbors lowered property values. But to Black people, property values were not declining at all. Though "there are many houses for sale to colored people in the more favored sections," a front-page article in the *Afro-American* newspaper explained in 1915, "they are offered at prices in excess of those expected from whites." "The segregation law practically confines the colored people to territory occupied by them at the time of the passage of the law," said the article, headlined "Segregation A Boon to Real-Estate Sharps." "This restricted area has to serve the race and those who want good homes have to pay dearly for the same."[53]

Nobody felt safe, and everybody felt exploited. As far as Old West Baltimore's white homeowners were concerned, public policy was supposed to protect *their* interests—not the interests of Black Baltimoreans, and not the interests of the "real estate sharps" whose actions seemed to threaten the value of their most significant asset. In the breach, many turned violent. "Feeling that there is no law under which they can prevent further inroads," the *Sun* reported in 1913, "the white people [of West Baltimore] have openly declared that they will use their own methods," restoring white-branded blocks by "disposing of the unwelcome neighbors."[54] Mobs paid by local "improvement" and protective associations catapulted rocks, bricks, marbles, and rotten vegetables through the windows of Black-owned houses. They dumped old garbage on stoops and splashed paint on doors and windows. They sawed off someone's front porch and tipped it into the street.[55] Everywhere in West Baltimore, houses burned—even houses on legally "colored" blocks, even houses on "mixed" blocks that had been Black-owned for years.[56] On Mosher Street that September, one Black woman was shot in her house while her neighbor was stabbed in the street.

Despite their apparent limitations, each version of Baltimore's residential segregation ordinance had stamped a template for similar laws in other cities. Because of those limitations, they were all short-lived. In 1914, the Louisville City Council had passed an ordinance making it illegal for its Black citizens to live on majority-white blocks and vice versa.[57] Louisville's law effectively made blockbusting illegal, which undermined the interests of realtors as well as Black people, so the local branch of the NAACP and the city's all-white Real Estate Exchange sued together to stop it.[58] The case, which came to be known as *Buchanan v. Warley*, was resolved by the US Supreme Court, which overturned Louisville's segregation law in 1917 on the grounds that it undermined property owners' right to sell what they owned to anyone they liked.[59] By extension, it also invalidated Baltimore's law. As one Black West Baltimorean told the *Sun*, "We all have to bow to the Supreme Court."[60]

Buchanan put Baltimore's aspiring segregationists back where they'd started: casting about for a permissible way to use public policy to map separate neighborhoods for Black and white people, branding "white" property and buoying its value. They still had plenty of options. *Buchanan* did not prohibit private parties like homeowners or developers from maintaining residential segregation agreements, such as deed restrictions or covenants preventing white buyers from selling or renting to Black people, that the courts could enforce. Wealthier neighborhoods, like Roland Park, had used restrictive covenants from their beginning.[61] Now less exclusive suburbs were starting to do it too. For instance, in 1915, ads for Edmondson Terraces—1,700 wider "daylight" rowhouses developers were building across the bottom of Greater Rosemont—boasted that the place was Baltimore's "only restricted Semi-Suburban development."[62] Likewise, zoning laws that regulated building size or lot size or land use became a powerful tool for keeping what planners still call "incompatible" uses, and users, in their place.[63] There were the courts, too. For instance, the white residents of Lauraville and other leafy Northeast Baltimore neighborhoods sued in 1917 to keep Morgan College, then operated by the Baltimore Conference of the Methodist Episcopal Church, from building its campus there on the grounds that the college was a "public nuisance" that would cause "irreparable injury" to property owners.[64]

(The neighbors lost, and the college was built.) And in 1918, the year after the *Buchanan* decision, Baltimore tripled its size by annexing 65 square miles of the surrounding counties. This "annex" was mostly empty land whose developers and property owners would be free to decide who to welcome and who to exclude.[65]

But the success of all these developments was pegged to the continued promise of white-branded schools. In West Baltimore, they mapped a whole new city. Over the years, "colored" schools made "colored" neighborhoods, and "white" schools made "white" ones.

School officials had paused conversions in West Baltimore for most of the 1910s, as the segregation ordinances took over their work. After *Buchanan*, they started again in earnest. By 1926, there were twelve public schools for white students and ten for Black students in Old West Baltimore. A decade later, the same area held twenty-five "colored" schools and eight white ones. By the end of World War II, there were no white schools left there at all. Conversely, during the 1920s and '30s, the frenzy of residential development in suburban West Baltimore was accompanied by an equivalent frenzy of school-building—but officials did not build a single school for Black children west of Fulton.[66] As one result, the sociologist Samuel Joseph Rice wrote in 1947, the avenue became "the border line and barrier separating the Negro and white population."[67]

The white people who lived beyond West Baltimore's color line expected "white" and "colored" schools to hold that line forever. Of course it was never totally impermeable. Individual Black families occasionally crossed it in search of better housing, as Rice and others chronicled.[68] But the idea was that Jim Crow schools would keep trickles of Black migration around the edges from turning into a flood, and the official brand they conferred would give the value of white-owned property a boost. And for a generation, they did. Then, virtually overnight, they did the opposite.

This is the process that made Gertrude Corbett's Rosemont.

The Birth of Rosemont

What we now call Rosemont and its surroundings were part of that 7.5-mile belt of Baltimore County the city annexed in 1888.[69] A topographical map the city published in 1894 shows the land that would be Gertrude Corbett's block straddling the Three Mile Race, a mill stream that formed the undulating northern and eastern boundary of Mrs. E. B. Tyler's "Rosedale" estate.[70] To Rosedale's west, on the land that would become the Gwynns Falls Park, flour mills churned.[71] To its east lay more grand estates: Mrs. I. B. Purnell's

Mothers walking with their children, Poplar Grove and Franklin Streets, September 1950. Courtesy of Jacques Kelly.

"Woodland," Mrs. S. B. Morgan's "Poplar Grove," the Berry family's enormous "Dukeland," *Sun* publisher Arunah Abell's summer retreat.

Over the course of the 1910s and 1920s, developers and streetcar operators would turn these sprawling horse farms, summer houses, and "county seats" into affordable suburbs for white working people. Tractors, pavers, and planers from the Department of Public Works unrolled the new street grids: first along the spines of the avenues where the electric trolleys ran, then filling in the gaps.[72] Some of the first developments to be built across Fulton Avenue, like Edmondson Terraces along Edmondson Avenue, were segregated—"refined and restricted," ads emphasized—by covenant.[73] "No stores, no saloons, and no colored people are allowed," promised the developers of Dukeland Park, off Bloomingdale Avenue. "Restrictions to ensure pretty homes and desirable tenants."[74] All were segregated by their schools. As the white population of these "semi-suburbs" between Fulton Avenue and the Gwynns Falls grew, the Board of School Commissioners built new schools to accommodate it—and only it.[75] World War II came and went, and nothing changed in this corner of Baltimore. One hundred percent of the schools in that 1.5 square-mile area served white students.[76] The 1940 and 1950 censuses found just a handful of "nonwhite" residents, and almost no "nonwhite" children, in that part of town.[77]

But the Great Migration of Black Americans from the rural South to the urban North had increased Baltimore's Black population considerably after 1910, from not quite 18 percent of the city's total in 1930 to 24 percent, or 225,000 people, in 1950.[78] Yet in 1944, the Urban League reported that Black

Baltimoreans, who then constituted one-fifth of the city's population, occupied barely 2 percent of its residential land (about as much as a few good-sized golf courses).[79] One result of this overcrowding was what the writer Fanny McConnell Buford, citing Nathaniel Hawthorne, called "the melancholy prophecy of decay."[80] As long as Black people had no choice about where they lived, Buford explained, the landlords who owned their housing would have no incentive to improve it, and so it would not be improved.

Segregation had produced bad housing, and the school buildings it produced were just as bad. Some problems were cosmetic. For instance, according to one 1930 *Afro-American* report on conditions in West Baltimore's Black schools, a soap and paint shortage meant "millions of little hands have left their smudges upon the once whitened walls, which soon become gray, then nearly black."[81] Others were worse. A 1939 survey found that some schools for Black pupils did not have indoor toilets and most still had old hand-pumped sinks. In one building, a reporter visiting in midwinter found 285 missing and broken windows.[82] And some schools did not have buildings at all. Black students were disproportionately assigned to temporary "portables," jerry-built structures with papery walls. They sweltered in the fall and spring, and in the winter they filled with greasy, toxic smoke and soot from the coal stoves that were their only sources of heat.[83]

The NAACP and the *Afro-American* had spent decades pushing city and school officials to improve these conditions. By the mid-1940s, finally, they were getting somewhere. However, this was not because school officials were feeling generous. The NAACP's Legal Defense Fund, now directed by Baltimore's own Thurgood Marshall, had begun to chip away at school segregation by exposing the fiction that was "separate but equal," and officials worried that bigger changes loomed if they failed to quiet protest.[84] In 1946, a handful of Black students petitioned to enroll in the all-white Mergenthaler Vocational High School on the grounds that its mechanics programs were not duplicated at the "colored" George Washington Carver Vocational High.[85] The Board of School Commissioners blocked the move but offered something in return: a new vocational school for Black students that would have all the same amenities as the whites-only Mergenthaler school. "With such bad conditions," school board president Thomsen told the *Sun*, "segregation cannot be defended much longer unless equal opportunities are afforded Negro high school students."[86]

School officials imagined they would build the new Carver school in segregated Old West Baltimore, where its prospective students lived, but this proved impossible. That part of the city was just too crowded to squeeze in a big high school, much less one with carpentry, metalworking, and other workshops equivalent to the ones at Mergenthaler. And so, in 1949, officials announced a new plan to build the Carver school on the empty lot at the top of the trainyard where the Maryland and Pennsylvania railroads met, about a half-mile across the Fulton Avenue color line. Then they suspended those plans, "pending the outcome" (the *Sun* reported) "of a dispute over whether the proposed site is in a white residential district."[87]

"Dispute" is putting it mildly. Thousands of white West Baltimoreans mobilized to demand that officials move the Carver school to some other, more definitively "colored" neighborhood. Some of their arguments were new. For instance, the president of the all-white Walbrook Improvement Association complained that the school board's plan was "pro-Russian," and the neighborhood's city council representative agreed: to be in favor of the Carver site, he told the *Sun*, was to be a "fellow traveler."[88] Most arguments, though, were familiar, inherited intact from an earlier time and place. "I just fixed up my home nicely," the vice president of another all-white neighborhood association said. "I don't want to spoil it."[89]

Despite the delay, the brand—"Colored"—stuck. Rumors of school conversions followed it.[90] The conversions themselves came next, tumbling west from Fulton Avenue toward Gwynns Falls Park. In the spring of 1951, school officials changed the designation of the Easterwood Park playground across from the proposed Carver School site from "White" to "Colored."[91] That June, they converted the all-white School No. 62, to the north of the Carver site at Smallwood and Walbrook, to School No. 142 for Black students.[92] (In Baltimore's school nomenclature, white-branded schools typically bore numbers between 1–99 [for elementary schools] and 200–399 [for junior high and high schools]. "Colored" schools were usually numbered in the 100s and 400s.)[93] The next fall, when the *Sun* sent its reporters out past the Carver School site to the place we now call "Greater Rosemont," the neighborhood was undergoing what one federal report called "one of the most rapid and extensive shifts in racial occupancy that has occurred in any city."[94]

Those shifts continued, rapidly and extensively. In June 1953, the *Sun* reported, "a hearing was held . . . on a protest against making elementary school No. 63, Rosedale street and Westwood avenue, a Negro school next September."[95] "The areas involved have become predominantly colored during recent years," the paper said. "School No. 63, according to public school statistics, is on the white-Negro boundary line. [School Board President] Thomsen said that the population around No. 63 is now two to one Negro and in September it, in all likelihood, will be three to one. . . . [The] superintendent of public instruction, explained that No. 63 was needed for colored children because other Negro schools in the area are overcrowded and the Negro population is only one block from No. 63."[96] In the fall, School No. 63's white pupils moved into a nearby church while they waited for a new school to be built for them near Lake Ashburton to the north, and School No. 63 became School No. 148. On the first day of school there, according to the *Sun*, "1,200 Negro students were registered—and between 700 and 900 had been expected. Classroom populations ranged up to 50."[97]

Likewise, that same fall, the James Mosher School (No. 89) on the old circus ground south of St. Peter's Cemetery became the James Mosher School (No. 144).[98] Mosher had been built in 1933 to accommodate 400 students but enrolled 900 on the first day of school in 1953.[99] In fact, the building was so crowded that at the last minute, the school district had to open a makeshift school for its new fifth and sixth graders at Bentalou and Saratoga—south of the busy Franklin-Mulberry corridor, which students had to cross on foot. The switch was so last-minute that nobody told the parents of its new pupils it was happening, spiking the first few days of the school year with moments of panic when children sent to one school in the morning were gone to another by afternoon.[100]

By the time *Brown v. Board of Education* ostensibly desegregated the city's schools in May 1954, there was just one school for white children remaining in the "new" West Baltimore rectangle between North Avenue and the Franklin-Mulberry corridor to the north and south and Fulton Avenue and Gwynns Falls Park to the east and west: the Alexander Hamilton School (No. 65) at Poplar Grove and Franklintown Road. By 1956, two years after *Brown* officially desegregated Baltimore's schools and the year construction finally began on Carver Vocational, Alexander Hamilton's number too had changed to 145.[101] By that June, there were not even 20 white families remaining on Gertrude Corbett's block. By December, Rosemont had become Rosemont.

Unlike tools like redlining and restrictive covenants and racist violence—all of which had their role to play in Baltimore, to be sure—segregated schools still seem perfectly normal and natural to many people, and when something is normal we look right past it. But in fact, schools make cities. They reflect its racial patterns. More than that, they create them. Rosemont came to be as we know it because of the choices city officials made about where Jim Crow schools would be.

And when they made those choices, they created a market.

2

"The Gigantic Conspiracy":
How Rosemont Made Blockbusters Rich (1950s)

In July 1952, a West Baltimore homemaker named Helen Murphy Bowers died, unexpectedly, of a heart attack.[1] Helen and her husband, Herbert, had bought their little rowhouse on Ellamont Street near Gwynns Falls Park in 1931, when the neighborhood was brand new, and they'd kept it spick-and-span for all the years since: They were a military family, and they lived like it. Herbert had been gassed—and contracted influenza, and sprained his ankle—at Verdun, then worked his way up to state commander at the Veterans of Foreign Wars.[2] Helen ran the ladies' auxiliary.[3] Son Gordon, who lived with his own young family in suburban Northeast Baltimore, was a senior commander in the Drum and Bugle Corps.[4] (Second son Charles had disappeared in a bombing raid over Europe in 1943.)[5]

But now Herbert was the only Bowers left in the house on Ellamont Street, and anyway the neighborhood around it was, so the story went, "changing." "ATTENTION COLORED," one real estate ad read. "Immediate possession. Will finance."[6] "DELUXE COLORED BEAUTIES," read another. "PRICED FOR QUICK SALE."[7] "Colored—beautiful—must sell."[8] "Colored: Buy it like rent."[9] "Colored: We finance."[10] "COLORED HOME BUYER: DON'T BE SORRY. SEE— BUY—NOW."[11] So the widower Herbert Bowers, who also happened to be the Federal-Aid Coordinator for the Maryland State Roads Commission, decided to sell.[12]

It took less than a month to find a buyer, and in August, another military family moved into the house on Ellamont Street. Joseph Wiles, the child of immigrants from Barbados, was born in Brooklyn and moved to Atlanta in 1941 to study biology at Morris Brown College. After serving as an army medic during the war, he married Esther Ogburn, a teacher from Youngstown, Ohio, and the couple moved to Baltimore so Wiles could begin his career in the medical-research laboratory at Edgewood Arsenal.[13] The Wileses had two daughters, Carmen and Carole, and in a few years they'd add a new member to their household, a fluffy, genial German shepherd named the Dutchess of Ellamont.[14] Joseph Wiles liked his new house, liked his new neighborhood, and was the type to get involved. Before the year was out, neighbors elected him the first president of the new Rosemont Home Improvement Association (R.H.I.A.).[15]

In the spring of 1953, newlyweds Dallas and Marian Barclift bought the house next door to the Wileses. They, too, joined the R.H.I.A. right away. Marian Barclift had grown up on Druid Hill Avenue in Baltimore, the daughter of a teacher and a mailman.[16] Like many of her new neighbors, she had graduated from Frederick Douglass High, about a third of a mile east of the old Fulton Avenue color line. She'd met her future husband, a navy veteran from Elizabeth City, North Carolina, in college at Morgan State.[17] When the two bought their rowhouse on Ellamont Street from the Van Horns, who moved to a new place just over the Edmondson Avenue Bridge, Marian Barclift had just joined the faculty at the "colored" Dunbar Junior High School in East Baltimore.[18] Dallas Barclift worked as a claims adjuster for the Social Security Administration in the iconic waterfront Candler Building.[19]

The block filled, and so did the R.H.I.A.'s roster: the Pinns and the Doughertys and the newlywed Gallops on the Rosedale side; the Bests and the Russells across from the Corbetts on Belmont; the Whitakers and the Armstrongs down the street and the Thomases on Presstman. Early in 1954, another pair of newlyweds moved to North Rosedale. Sterling Graves, the child of sharecroppers from Roxboro, North Carolina, and the former Mary Morgan of Jacksonville, Florida, had met in college at the Hampton Institute in Virginia and were married there, in the chaplain's house, in 1951.[20] Now Mr. Graves worked as an electrician at the Eastern Rolling Mill near Sparrows Point. His wife, who would eventually remarry and change her name to Mary Rosemond, was an elementary school teacher.

Rosemont was unusual, but it wasn't unique. According to the 1955 Maryland Commission on Interracial Problems and Relations study, about 15,000 houses in Baltimore (out of some 278,000 total) had "shifted to non-white use" since 1950.[21] Almost all of those, the MCIPR said, had been purchased by Black families to live in. By this math, people a lot like the new Rosemonters would soon occupy around 5 percent of the houses in Baltimore. Some Black families, like the people moving to the arcadian suburban boulevards of Northeast Baltimore near Morgan State College, may have been a little more genteel—upper-middle, not middle-middle or lower-middle.[22] Some, like those moving to the houses in the old Edmondson Terraces, may have had a little less. (Meanwhile, of course, the most common Black experience in Baltimore was poverty. In the early 1950s, historian Jane Berger calculates, more than half of all Black Baltimoreans were poor.[23] Plus, the exorbitant rents they had to pay made them disproportionately poorer than white households, and the bad housing conditions that resulted contributed to the general sense among wealthier people of all races that poor Black people were "trash," "riff-raff," problems to be solved.)[24] But the Black families who were moving into the 100-ish houses around the R.H.I.A.'s block shared some version of their day-to-day experience with thousands of others.

In the beginning, Mary Rosemond later wrote, the R.H.I.A. was mostly a "social club" whose regular meetings rotated "from house to house allowing the new black families of this changing neighborhood to get to know each other."[25] In that regard, it may not have been necessary. The society pages of the *Afro-American* newspaper carried daily dispatches from Rosemont and other parts of the new Black West Baltimore: notes on garden clubs, anniversary parties with punch served in silver bowls and cakes decorated with fresh roses, community meetings and lodge meetings and weddings and balls. Almost every organization in the Urban League's Directory of Organizations had recently established headquarters nearby: the Baltimore Business Council; the Baltimore Cossocks, dedicated to "wholesome fun and recreation"; the Bay Haven Rod & Gun Club; the Baltimore chapter of the Howard University Alumni Association; the Baltimore chapter of Jack and Jill of America; the Cardigans, Inc.; the Baltimore alumni chapter of Kappa Alpha Psi fraternity; the Kappa Silhouettes; Tots and Teens; the Tulip Club; We Moms.[26]

Rosemont's parents signed their sons up for the Kadets of America marching troop, then turned up the radio to drown out the racket they made practicing in Elbert Armstrong's Belmont Avenue garage.[27] They sent their daughters to learn ballet, jazz, and folk dancing at Francine's School of Dance on Bentalou Street. They went there themselves to practice the rhumba and the cha-cha when the Arthur Murray dance studio on North Charles turned them away because they were Black.[28] After 1955, when professional bowler Fern Scotland and her partner Estella "Peanuts" Finks bought the New Walbrook Bowling Center and turned it into one of the only alleys in Baltimore that welcomed Black players on its lanes and in its restrooms, they joined bowling leagues.[29] They saw movies at the theaters on North Avenue, which were no longer whites-only, and they whiled away hot summer afternoons at the brand-new, air-conditioned, integrated Walbrook branch of the Enoch Pratt Free Library.[30]

Rosemont's husbands, organized as the We Workers Social and Civic Club, pooled their funds and bought a lawnmower for anyone to use. "Working

We Workers and We Wives, Rosemont Neighborhood Improvement Association, 1950. Courtesy of University of Baltimore Special Collections and Archives.

together," Mary Rosemond remembered, the men "cut lawns, trimmed shrubbery, painted homes, and made minor plumbing and electrical repairs" for anyone who needed them.[31] They also cleared, mowed, and planted the city-owned lot at the center of the block, whitewashing tree trunks, building flowerboxes, arranging picnic tables.[32] "After work was over," Rosemond wrote, "the wives provided refreshment for their industrious husbands."[33]

All of which is to say: everyday life in Rosemont was just that. "Homeowners paint and plant," Mary Rosemond wrote. "Children form friendships. Community life is enjoyed."[34]

Once Baltimore's public schools broke the color line, Black families rushed into Rosemont to build lives that looked very much like the lives of the white families who had preceded them. But this good life cost them dearly. And the inexorable logic of white Baltimore would keep on charging.

The Segregated Mortgage Market

Segregated schools were good for business. Real estate men used the promise of white-branded schools in white-branded neighborhoods to lure families like the Van Horns out of the new Rosemont, and they used the promise of new Black schools there to secure another captive market: Black families who would pay almost any price for, as Mary Rosemond would later write, "better housing, street maintenance, better equipped schools . . . and open spaces where we could breathe cleaner air and enjoy the blessings of nature."[35]

And they did pay. "The Negro population needs more housing," the *Sun* explained in 1955. "It wants better housing. It intends to have it and can pay for it. But little or no new housing is built specifically for Negro ownership or Negro tenancy. Where else does the Negro turn, with money in his pocket . . . but to houses now occupied by whites, to the better hand-me-downs? That is the state of affairs that makes block-busting, with its admitted evils, a lucrative business."[36] Blockbusters bought low from fleeing white sellers and sold high to determined Black buyers, and made more money by financing those costly purchases, too.[37]

In Baltimore as in cities across the country, blockbusting worked—which is to say, it made blockbusters rich—because the federal government promised it would. Mortgage-lending rules made sure Black people couldn't get cheap government-guaranteed bank loans. They also tied segregation to property values even as they inflated prices for Black housing by rationing its supply.[38] The upshot was that Joseph Wiles and Gertrude Corbett and all their neighbors were stuck paying more for less.

It all started during the New Deal, when an alphabet soup of federal agencies designed to boost the flow of capital into and through the mortgage-lending system started a process that would permanently change just about everything about life in the American metropolis.[39] The 1920s had seen a great expansion of mortgage credit, but these were not the kind of mortgages—20 percent down payment, thirty-year, fixed-rate—most of us are familiar with today.[40] Their terms were short (3–5 years). They demanded high down payments (up to 80 percent of a home's appraised value) and charged high interest (up to 9 percent). And when the loan's term was up, principal and interest often were not paid in full. This, in turn, usually meant that every few years homeowners had to roll their old loan into a new one and start the process all over again.[41] But banks could also stop renewing mortgages when the loans came due—which they did, in chorus, when the markets crashed in 1929. Suddenly, unexpectedly, hundreds of thousands of homeowners found themselves on the hook for the entire amount that they owed.[42]

As a result, half of all home mortgages in the United States were in default in the spring of 1933, and banks were foreclosing on a thousand mortgages every day.[43] To stop this catastrophe, and to put money back into the pockets of (said one Treasury official) "everyone, from the manufacturer of lace curtains to the manufacturers of lumber, bricks, cement, and electrical appliances," Congress created the Home Owners' Loan Corporation (HOLC) to refinance mortgages in default.[44] The HOLC produced a series of "Residential Security Maps" designed to tell lenders at a glance whether a property was located in a place that was a good risk for investment, colored green or blue on the maps, or a "hazardous" one, colored red. (The word "redlining" comes from those red lines on HOLC's maps.) Green-colored neighborhoods were filled with newer single-family houses, and they excluded industry, commerce, poor people, and most anyone who was not considered white (except live-in domestic workers). Yellow and red neighborhoods featured "special hazards" such as older houses, apartment houses, stores, busy streets, Black people, brown people, white immigrants, mixed-income neighborhoods, and other typically urban characteristics.[45]

Today, we can look at these maps and see how accurately they seem to have predicted, or prescribed, disinvestment in urban neighborhoods across the country. However, scholars point out that HOLC itself did less to shape and steer investment patterns than we might think, in part because the scope of its work was so limited.[46] The National Housing Act of 1934 was more important in this regard. It established the new Federal Housing Administration (FHA), a public agency designed to lure private capital back into the mortgage market by insuring the loans that banks and other financial institutions made.

FHA insurance made mortgage lending a risk-free venture for lenders, because it guaranteed they would get their money back from the federal government even if borrowers stopped paying their bills. It also created an entirely new kind of home loan: long-term (20 years at first, later extended to 30), low-interest (around 5 percent), fixed-rate, self-amortizing, and requiring only 20 percent down.[47] After World War II, the GI Bill of Rights guaranteed some veterans' access to FHA-style mortgages that required no down payment.[48] Together, the FHA and the Veterans Administration (VA) standardized mortgage lending and flooded the postwar residential real estate market with capital, making it possible for millions of Americans to own homes who would not otherwise have been able to afford them. In 1940, some 44 percent of Americans owned their own homes. By 1960, 62 percent did.[49]

An FHA-guaranteed mortgage, for the people who could get one, could make buying cheaper than renting. It also kept buyers from getting scammed. As one congressional report explained later, "an FHA house must be sold at the appraised fair market value, and the house must be in good condition."[50] And of course, when you bought a house using this kind of bank mortgage, you built equity—wealth—with each monthly payment. Every mortgage check you wrote was an investment in something that belongs to you, not somebody else, and if luck held, your investment increased in value. Your house was your home, but it could also be your children's inheritance or college tuition. It could be your retirement savings. It wasn't a guarantee against financial disaster, but it could be a cushion when you desperately needed one.

For all these reasons, it is impossible to overstate how big a gift this new mortgage-credit system was to the people who benefited from it. In fact, after World War II, government credit built the white middle class—full stop. But Black people paid for it.

The FHA drew capital into the housing market by encouraging banks to lend to buyers, and by making it possible for the new Federal National Mortgage Association, or Fannie Mae, to turn insured mortgages into commodities. This meant buying them from local lenders and selling them to big national and institutional investors, giving lenders the capital they needed to make more loans. The most important tools for *this* work were not the HOLC maps but the FHA's guidelines telling lenders where they could and could not invest. The agency's *Underwriting Manual* covered physical standards for a home's construction, floor plan, and condition. It also covered standards for a home's neighborhood and neighbors—which, said housing reformer Charles Abrams in 1955, "could well have been culled from the Nuremberg laws."[51] To receive an "A" (green) rating from the FHA, the manual said, a property should be in a neighborhood free from "lower class occupancy" or "the infiltration of . . . inharmonious racial and nationality groups," and its schools should not have "a goodly number of the pupils represent a far lower level of society or an incompatible racial element."[52] As a general matter, the enormous majority of loans the FHA insured in cities across the country were to "A" (green) or "B" (blue) neighborhoods. In Baltimore in 1940, scholars have calculated that some 13 percent of FHA-insured loans went to "A" neighborhoods, 54.5 percent to

"B" neighborhoods, 24 percent to "C" (yellow) neighborhoods, and less than 2 percent to "D" (red) neighborhoods.[53] On Baltimore's residential security map, "D" neighborhoods appear to constitute about a quarter of the city.[54]

In other words, the standards the federal government invented to determine which properties were creditworthy and which were not excluded Black people from the mortgage-credit system that built postwar American prosperity.[55] As historian David M. P. Freund writes in his book *Colored Property: State Policy and Racial Politics in Suburban America*, with the FHA the federal government built "a stimulus program that defined minority occupancy as a threat to property values."[56] "By accepting the myth that the market for housing demanded segregation," Freund continues, "the government in turn forged a new market for housing that demanded it."[57]

A conventional mortgage loan to a Black buyer created what the scholar Mehrsa Baradaran calls "severe balance sheet problems" for the bank that issued it. "Blacks paid much more for properties, which came to be worth much less the second they were purchased by Blacks," she explains, and so "loans went 'underwater' as soon as they were issued."[58] This was especially true now that a property's value derived by federal government policy from the whiteness of its owner. Consequently, white banks mostly did not make these loans. (Black banks would make them when they could, but as Baradaran points out, they were trapped in the same negative feedback loop as Black homebuyers: they could not lend at a profit because all their assets were upside down.) The FHA sometimes loosened its official commitment to segregation—by refusing to guarantee mortgages made to properties covered by racist restrictive covenants, for instance, as it did two years after the Supreme Court's 1948 *Shelley v. Kraemer* decision rendered those covenants unenforceable, or by offering to back mortgages in brand-new Black subdivisions.[59] Even so, Black buyers still struggled to obtain FHA or conventional bank mortgages.

What made FHA-insured mortgages so appealing to lenders was that those mortgages could be packaged and resold, via Fannie Mae, on the secondary mortgage market, giving those lenders the capital they needed to make more loans, sell them on the secondary market, and round and round again. For this scheme to work, investors (insurance companies, for instance) needed to see value in the mortgages and want to buy them. There simply weren't enough willing investors to support mortgage lending to "D"-rated properties on the scale that aspiring Black homeowners required.[60]

Meanwhile, a 1956 report by the federal Voluntary Home Mortgage Credit Program found that "the scarcity of minority housing" segregation created "tends to drive the price of available properties [up] to a point where FHA and VA financing ... cannot be used."[61] In other words, the inflated prices Black people had to pay for housing were so expensive that they blew through the FHA's cap on the loans it would insure. As a result, between 1934 and 1968, fully 98 percent of FHA-guaranteed loans went to white people.[62] And when Black buyers did manage to get a conventional non-FHA bank loan, they paid higher interest rates than their white counterparts because they were "riskier" customers. This meant that they could borrow less for the same money even as their dollar, because of the inflated cost of the segregated housing available to them, did not stretch nearly as far.[63]

How, then, did Black homeownership rates soar alongside—and sometimes even faster than—white ones in the 1950s and '60s?[64] For instance, reporter Antero Pietila calculates that in Baltimore, Black homeownership rates shot up by nearly 200 percent between 1940 and 1950, compared to a 60 percent increase among whites.[65] The surge continued in the next decade: the 1950 census showed that 24 percent of Black householders in Baltimore owned their homes, a number that increased to 38 percent just five years later.[66] In Baltimore as elsewhere, the great majority of Black home buyers were like everyone else in the American middle class. Most didn't have the ready cash to simply buy a house out of pocket, without a loan. But as far as lenders were concerned, they were *not* like everybody else, and therefore they were not eligible for the easy, cheap mortgages that were reshaping the housing market for white people across the country. Black people who wanted to buy a house would have to get their credit some other way.

The Blockbusters' Trap

Enter the blockbusters.

In a 1962 *Saturday Evening Post* article called "Confessions of a Block-Buster," a pseudonymous real estate operative from Chicago summarized the process, which in theory is pretty straightforward. "I make my money—quite a lot of it, incidentally—in three ways," he wrote:

(1) By beating down the prices I pay the white owners by stimulating their fear of what is to come;
(2) by selling to the eager Negroes at inflated prices; and
(3) by financing these purchases at what amounts to a very high rate of interest.[67]

In Baltimore (and elsewhere), the practice worked similarly. We know this, at least in Baltimore, because the swindled buyers eventually told us so. A series of reports published by the housing-justice outfit Activists, Inc. in 1971 and a

1972 civil rights and antitrust lawsuit charged that a tangled web of blockbusting real estate firms operated by Morris Goldseker and his nephew Sheldon had taken (the *Sun* reported) "'full advantage' of Baltimore's segregated housing patterns to reap unreasonable profits from black citizens unable to deal in the open market available to whites," buying homes cheaply from "panic selling" white people and selling them for thousands of dollars above "fair market value" to Black buyers with few alternatives.[68] "Maybe Goldseker did charge a little too much," Sheldon Goldseker told the paper in 1971, but "we were performing a service."[69] (The Goldsekers weren't Baltimore's only blockbusters—not by a long shot—but they were its most shameless ones, so they got most of the attention.) Besides, he said, "there's more than one fair-market value, depending on which market you're in."[70]

Historian Edward Orser's 1994 book *Blockbusting in Baltimore: The Edmondson Village Story* uses the Activists' data and oral-history interviews to tell a comprehensive story of how the process worked in Edmondson Village, the neighborhood just west of Rosemont, in the 1960s.[71] As a general matter, however, blockbusting in Baltimore is easier to explain than to prove. One problem is that it's not easy to find out exactly what someone has paid for a house. In Maryland, land records are filed with the state, so you can search backward to learn when a house or property stopped belonging to one person and started belonging to another, but home prices do not appear on deeds. The state's database *does* attach mortgage records to those public documents, which means that if someone used a mortgage loan to pay for all or some of their purchase we can usually see the amount and terms of that loan. But if a buyer paid cash for all or some of the purchase, or got a different kind of loan (like an unrecorded land-installment contract, a lease-option contract, or a second mortgage later on), that information is often either unrecorded or can't be searched in any kind of systematic way.

So, to understand the economics associated with the birth of Black Rosemont—how, in other words, the new Rosemonters and their neighbors financed the purchase of their new homes—we have to make some educated extrapolations. To start, we'll turn our attention east and south, to the 2400 block of Lauretta Avenue in the old "restricted" Edmondson Terraces development, about a mile closer to the Fulton Avenue color line than the block where the R.H.I.A. created Rosemont.

During the early 1950s, the people we've been talking about so far—the Corbetts and the Wilses, the Barclifts and the Pinns—did not really consider the people who lived on the Edmondson Terraces blocks along Lauretta and Arunah and Harlem Avenues to be part of *their* neighborhood. (They were not, for example, eligible to be part of its improvement association.) The

Looking east down 2400 block of Lauretta Avenue, Baltimore, ca. 1918. Courtesy of Maryland Center for History and Culture, MC7262.

Edmondson Terraces houses were a little older, a little less expensive, closer to busy commercial streets and further from the park. There were more renters down there, and more people with blue-collar jobs. As the Rosemonters themselves might have put it, the R.H.I.A.'s block was "*middle*-middle class," and Edmondson Terraces was not—not quite.[72] The city's plans for the expressway would soon blur these distinctions, though. And because the Edmondson Terraces houses were eventually condemned for the expressway and the R.H.I.A.'s block was not, we have a little more information on their sales history, which will be important later. So, we'll use that block as our example now.

State land records tell us that in February 1954, when Frank and Frances Clements took title to the little two-bedroom rowhouse at 2406 Lauretta from real estate man LeRoy Kappelman, they paid for it with a $6,630 loan from New Michaels Permanent Savings and Loan.[73] (Each week, they paid $10.20 in "dues," $7.65 "interest and premium," and $4.75 for ground rent, taxes, water and sewer, and "fines.")[74] We can see, too, that LeRoy Kappelman had bought that same house the previous September, and we can see that when he did, New Michaels Permanent Savings & Loan issued *him* a mortgage for $4,940—which suggests that he made a profit of at least 35 percent in less than six months.[75] Down the block, we can see that Thomas and Amelia Imes bought their house at 2416 from the Bedford Holding Company in 1955, and we can see that they paid for it with a $7,450 loan at 4.5 percent interest (a reasonable rate, pegged to the cap for FHA-insured mortgages) from Baltimore Federal Savings and Loan.[76] We can also see that Topaz Realty bought the house the same month from Wilbur and Jessie Leitch, who had lived there since 1935, and transferred it to Bedford Holding. We cannot, however, see what they paid the Leitches for the property, since they did not use a mortgage loan to do it. As a result, we can't calculate their markup or their profit.[77] This pattern, complete with its blank spaces and unknowns, is typical.

What we *do* know is that almost all the Black families on the 2400 block of Lauretta bought their houses at around that same time from either the Kappelmans or Bedford Holding, and almost every buyer got a mortgage loan from New Michaels Permanent Savings and Loan or Baltimore Federal Savings and Loan. New Michaels and Baltimore Federal were savings and loan associations, not banks—and in Maryland, savings and loans were largely unregulated. Anyone could start one. Anyone could operate one. They could make virtually any kind of loan to anyone, on any terms.[78] They had nothing to do with the FHA. In theory, the purpose of a savings or building and loan association was to promote home ownership among working people.[79] But according to the 1971 Activists, Inc. report, "the enticements involved in perverting a savings and loan into the mistress of the exploiter and the landlord [were] greater" than these lofty ideals.[80]

By the mid-1950s, many of Baltimore's savings and loan associations made their loans to investors or families buying from investors in Black neighborhoods. What's more, their boards of directors were packed with those very same investors, who profited from every commission and fee associated with the loan. For instance, the same family that owned Topaz Realty and Bedford Holding Company, the Goldsekers, controlled the Baltimore Federal Savings and Loan and dozens of other real estate companies and lenders. The Kappelmans helped run New Michaels.[81]

Baltimore's blockbusters were joined on the savings and loan boards by bankers, lawyers, developers, and insurance men from Baltimore's blue-chip families and firms—the kind of people who would never be caught trafficking in real estate in "changing" neighborhoods. Yet still they profited from it. For one thing, they were often financing the speculators themselves. For example, Morris Goldseker received millions of dollars from major banks like Equitable Trust and Maryland National to buy hundreds of houses in neighborhoods like Rosemont.[82] "Certain loans we agreed to make him took some imagination," the director of the Equitable Trust Company told the *Sun* after Goldseker died. "They were not the conventional loans you'd make to General Motors. [But] he said, 'Don't worry, they'll always be paid back as agreed.' And they were."[83] Of course they were. The blockbuster made a fortune by turning around and reselling the properties bought with borrowed money at a towering markup to people who had no choice but to pay it.

The limits of the Maryland land records mean that we can only sometimes calculate that markup on the homes the first Black Rosemonters bought in the 1950s. However, for their counterparts in the 1960s at least, the Activists, Inc. *could* calculate it. In 1971, 200 volunteers spent thousands of hours sifting through the Lusk Reports of real estate transactions to find key data—sale price, purchase price, mortgage, and interest rate—on 60,000 Baltimore home sales between 1960 and 1970. Using key-punch cards, analysts at the Rouse Company processed all that data, building a computerized record of the speculators' exploitation.[84] Their math showed that during the 1960s anyway, the average markup for a Goldseker property was about 85 percent. Other firms were more circumspect, but not much: their profits ranged from 54 percent to 84 percent.[85] Unfortunately, the Lusk Reports from the 1950s appear to be lost to time, so we'll have to use what the Activists learned in the next decade to infer what we can.

We see the same patterns on the R.H.I.A.'s block, just with higher numbers attached to them. At 3130 Belmont, William and Estelle Stanley bought from Post Realty using a $9,150 loan from Baltimore Federal Savings and Loan in 1958.[86] Around the corner, Straw Man, Inc.—yes, that's really what it was called—sold to Alexander and Doris Odum, who borrowed at least $6,000 from Baltimore Federal.[87] (That comparatively low amount suggests a second, overlapping mortgage, but it's not attached to the deed.) At 3118 Presstman, Elzie and Maccabee Johnson bought from Bedford Holding using an $8,000 mortgage from Baltimore Federal.[88]

Often, blockbusters left the savings and loan associations out of it entirely and financed land-installment contracts themselves. According to a 1955 survey compiled by the Maryland Commission on Interracial Problems and Relations, 53 percent of Baltimore's Black homeowners had made their purchases via these contract sales.[89] For instance, in June 1953, the John P. Rafferty Realty Company sold the house at 2410 Lauretta to Johnnie and Larene Simmons for $7,950 ($300 down plus $22 a month) via a self-funded land-installment contract that was never recorded in the state's land records. The only way we know the Simmonses were there at all is that, when the house was eventually sold for the expressway, highway officials recorded the Simmonses as the sellers, tracked down a copy of their contract, and filed it with the other land-acquisition files in the city archive. As far as every other city and state agency was concerned, Rafferty Realty had owned the property all along.[90]

To varying degrees, all these loans offered what one recent report from the Samuel DuBois Cook Center on Social Equity at Duke University called "the illusion of a mortgage without the protection of a mortgage."[91] In a land-installment sale, for instance, there was no inspection, no appraisal, no closing. No deed changed hands, or it changed hands only belatedly. The buyer made weekly payments to the speculator, but her payments did not build any equity. "Maryland law restricted the interest rate on land-installment contracts to 6 percent," Antero Pietila writes, "but 6 percent of what? The law did not specify. By flipping properties and offering them at inflated prices, speculators could achieve a high interest rate that rendered the legally sanctioned maximum meaningless."[92] And until the buyer paid off the principal and the interest she owed in full, 20 or 40 or 75 years down the line, the speculator kept title to (and could keep on borrowing against) the property. Meanwhile, if the buyer missed even one payment, she could be tossed out with nothing to show for whatever money she'd put into the property so far. Compare this with what happens when an owner defaults on a bank mortgage. It's no picnic, certainly, but they have rights and protections as they move through the steps of a well-defined process, and they get credit for the equity they've built along the way.

According to the terms of these deals, the contract buyer didn't really own her house, but when the roof leaked or the furnace broke, she was responsible for repairs. But when she installed a new furnace and then missed a "mortgage" payment and lost her home, her costly improvement belonged to the speculator, who would turn around and sell the house to someone else—probably using the new furnace as a selling point. Likewise, when the city's code-enforcement teams came around, the homeowner, not the blockbuster, was on the hook for any violations they happened to find.[93] Even when everything went as well as could be, buyers often had very little money left over, for maintenance or for anything else. It also meant that those buyers would eventually find that what they owned was worth very little: "far less," said the Duke report, "than what they had paid over the term of the contract."[94]

Most Black buyers who defaulted on their mortgage loans never saw their money again. But most Rosemonters and their neighbors did not default. They kept up their payments, sky-high as they were, in what one speculator said was "the hottest real estate market I have ever seen."[95] The result? In 1975, Black West Baltimore's congressional representative Parren Mitchell testified: "Money was literally carted out of [neighborhoods like Rosemont] for redistribution in the more affluent areas of the city and the suburbs."[96] It was, the Activists wrote, a "gigantic conspiracy."[97]

To be clear, the Black people who moved out past the Fulton Avenue color line in the 1950s weren't duped. They knew what they were doing when they bought their houses from Bedford Holding and the Kappelmans and the other speculators whose listings appeared in the "Colored" section of the real estate pages; and they knew, vaguely, what it would cost them in the end. But they lived in the world they lived in. The choices available to them were their choices. And so they made the best of it.

And for a while, the best was pretty good.

3

"Elected to Be the Sacrificers":
How Rosemont Saw Its Future (1957)

One Tuesday night in April 1957, more than five hundred Rosemont neighbors crowded the Whitestone Baptist Church on Baker Street. They were there to confront Harry J. McGuirk, a youngish white man wearing a lustrous suit, an equally lustrous hairdo, and (one observer said) "the look of a businessman who will outslick you at every turn."[1] He was a real estate dealer and big wheel at South Baltimore's Stonewall Democratic Club, which *The Washington Post* later explained was "one of the bastions of traditional city politics, going back to the days when patronage, arm-twisting and walk-around money were as much a part of the political process as voting booths."[2] At Stonewall, McGuirk had earned the nickname "Soft Shoes," because people said you'd never hear him coming for you.[3]

What was such a man doing in a Black Baptist church in almost-suburban West Baltimore? In addition to everything else on his résumé, Soft Shoes McGuirk was the vice president of his uncle Guy Bryant's South Baltimore-based box company.[4] And a few weeks earlier, the Bryant Packing Box Company had announced its plans to build a new factory for manufacturing wooden packing crates right here in residential Rosemont. The neighborhood's improvement association had called a meeting to protest the factory, and Uncle Guy had dispatched his nephew to defend it.

People settled in the pews and Dallas Barclift stood up. "Anyone can readily see that if this factory is allowed to be built it won't be long before this new residential area will be completely slum ridden," he said. "We'll fight for our community, no matter how big a man the builder may be."[5]

When Dallas Barclift and his neighbors moved onto their little block near the park in 1952 and 1953 and 1954 and created the Rosemont Home Improvement

Association there, they also created Rosemont itself. In the most mundane terms, the R.H.I.A. established boundaries for the neighborhood—Ellamont, Presstman, Rosedale, and Belmont—and those boundaries gave the place its name. Yet there was something exceptional, too, in the R.H.I.A.'s act of creation. Rosemont was an idea, a promise, a prayer for the possibility that Baltimore's future might be different from its past. And so in 1954, the Rosemont Home Improvement Association became the Rosemont Neighborhood Improvement Association (R.N.I.A.), the name it still has today. Home improvement was cutting the grass, painting the porch, storing the Radio Flyer in the basement instead of on the sidewalk. It was personal. *Neighborhood* improvement was political: it staked a claim on the city itself.[6]

"A 'block association' defines a material fact," the novelist Jonathan Lethem wrote, of Brooklyn, in *The New Yorker* in 2023. "If you live on the block, you may choose to ignore its activities, yet still live there." By contrast, "a 'neighborhood association' describes an assertion in free space—civic space, historical space, racial space."[7] We can see what Lethem is getting at in the Letter of Philosophy the new R.N.I.A. mailed out. "The citizens who would put this Association together did not come as blockbusters," it read. "We/ They came as citizens, voters, employed Americans in search of better housing, street maintenance, better equipped schools in terms of materials, and open spaces where we could breathe cleaner air and enjoy the blessings of nature in terms of greenery and trees." The letter continued:

> The central core of our philosophy has been and still is:
> - the creation of a neighborhood that for want of a better example: a Roland Park within the central city—for that this implies; beautification, police protection, adequate fire protection and all the amenities of suburban living afforded to voting, tax paying citizens.
> - the human spirit where people live without fear, cut their grass, mend their fences and respect the dignity of each person.
> - the participation in the body politics, for in America he or she who does not exercise his or her franchise is not a person in the classic sense of the word.[8]

The R.N.I.A. existed because its members had *earned* "better housing, street maintenance, better equipped schools" for themselves and their families, and they intended to seize them. This vision of community—the employed Americans, tax-paying citizens, voters, people "in the classic sense of the word"—embraced and excluded at the same time. The R.N.I.A. was about as different as it could be from the neighborhood improvement associations whose members had filed lawsuits and lobbed bombs and, in Roland Park's case, pioneered the use of deed covenants restricting "nuisances" like "any negro or person of negro extraction" except servants.[9] Its members knew better than anyone how quickly the ideology of homeownership, the one that says I have also purchased the right to say who my neighbors might be and what they might do, could curdle. Yet they believed in it, too.

What the R.N.I.A.'s members wanted was to be treated like anybody else in Baltimore who lived the same essentially middle-class lives they did. They understood that this was the only case they could make for keeping what they had. Yet in 1957, they started to see that it wouldn't be enough.

The Factory

Guy Bryant's plan to build a box factory on Rosedale Street was the first strike. Manufacturing wooden boxes wasn't as hazardous or disruptive as manufacturing benzene or rubber tires or steel, but it was still noisy and dirty. It would also, neighbors noted, draw daily swarms of trucks to idle in the street. In fact, for all these reasons, building a factory in a residential neighborhood would seem to be just what Baltimore's zoning ordinance, first passed in the 1920s, was intended to prevent.[10] But the Western Maryland Railway had already run its tracks along the Gwynns Falls by the time the city adopted exclusionary zoning. Officials zoned the rest of the land to suit the residential suburbs developers were in the process of building, but they declared the pinstripes of land on either side of the existing freight tracks a "Second Commercial Use District" that allowed "heavy manufacturing not of the nuisance type."[11] Yet all the time Herbert Bowers and his white neighbors called the blocks around it home, nobody put anything there.[12] That's probably because it was still owned by Ephraim Macht, the broker and developer who built the neighborhood and sold its houses, and it is likely how the "Second Commercial Use" designation survived through the 1948 revision of the zoning map even as the residential neighborhood swelled around it. Macht died in 1944, but it took more than a decade for his estate to drag through probate, during which time its trustees maintained the status quo.[13] It wasn't until 1956 that Macht's heirs could sell the land they'd inherited, which is how it wound up in Guy Bryant's hands in February 1957.[14]

Had they given the matter any thought, Rosemont's Black homeowners would not have shared their predecessors' arrogance about the social contract that kept the zoning issue settled. They would have known that the deference white real estate men showed to white property owners would not likely extend to them. But they probably didn't think about it much either, until they had to.

In the meantime, as Mary Rosemond wrote later, the wedge of land next to the tracks one block south of her house remained a "beautiful open green space," and by 1957 it had become one of the neighborhood's best-used, if unofficial, parks.[15] It was larger than the vacant lot behind the houses on Presstman Street, and better suited to games like stickball and capture the flag. It was flatter and more accessible than the Gwynns Falls Park, which was anyhow more of a wilderness than a recreational space.[16] Gwynns Falls did eventually get a swimming pool, but—and here was the most salient reason the new Rosemonters might have preferred the "open green space" on Normount Street to the city park next door—the pool, like the park that surrounded it, had only been open to white Baltimoreans until *Brown v. Board of Education* had formally desegregated Baltimore's parks along with its schools in May 1954.[17]

In 1946, the *Sun* had tallied all the park amenities that were available to white Baltimoreans and not Black ones: "boat house, boat lakes, bridle path, croquet fields, dance floors, dodge ball courts, floral gardens, golf courses, greenhouses, 'outdoor gymnasiums,' hockey fields, kickball fields, lacrosse fields, bandstands, picnic groves, quoit pits, roller rinks, running tracks, soccer fields, volleyball courts, wading pools."[18] The city's Park Board, established by Mayor Thomas D'Alesandro in 1947, refused to issue permits for interracial softball games, forbade "mixed play" on tennis courts, and implemented segregated tee times on the city's public courses.[19] In 1951, after Black golfers filed a lawsuit, the Park Board opened four golf courses, seven tennis courts, six softball fields, six playgrounds, and a cricket pitch to "interracial play" in 1951.[20] But nothing in Gwynns Falls Park was on this list.

So, even if it had been a good park for playing in, the Rosemonters' children wouldn't have gotten in the habit of doing so. Before 1954, they had no right to be there. After 1954, they weren't welcomed. (As for the pool, it wasn't even theoretically open to Black swimmers until 1956, and even then few felt safe using it.)[21] Meanwhile, the next nearest playground was in Easterwood Park across from the new Carver Vocational School, and officials had, the *Afro-American* newspaper reported, "turned [it] over exclusively to colored children" in 1951.[22] But it was about ten minutes away by bicycle or a half-hour walk, both of which modes involved crossing two sets of train tracks and a busy street. For these reasons, the R.N.I.A. had been trying to get the Bureau of Recreation to build a real playground on the lot behind the houses on their block for years, but they'd had no luck so far.[23]

The point is, Guy Bryant's lot on Rosedale Street was the nearest thing the Rosemonters and their children had to a playground. If the box-factory plan went through, Rosemonters would gain a factory *and* lose some of what had drawn them to the neighborhood in the first place: the "open spaces where we could breathe cleaner air and enjoy the blessings of nature in terms of greenery and trees," and "the amenities of suburban living afforded to voting, tax paying citizens."

As soon as word of Bryant's February 1957 land purchase got out, the R.N.I.A. had voted to expand its roster. Now anyone who lived on the thirty or so square blocks between Brighton Street and the railroad tracks to the north and south, and between Longwood Street and the park to the west and east, was welcome to join.[24] With so many more dues-paying members, the association could afford to buy the land, but Bryant refused to sell it. There seemed only one recourse: to go over his head to the city.

There was plenty of precedent in Baltimore for closing zoning loopholes that made life in residential neighborhoods unpleasant. "Large groups of residents appear at Council hearings protesting the use of land zoned for second commercial or industrial use," one industrialist complained in the *Sun* in 1949, "and councilmen are prone to yield to their constituents' view and enact ordinances rezoning such areas for residential use."[25] And as it happened, Mayor D'Alesandro had just established a new zoning commission that would have the power to overhaul land-use designations citywide.[26] Why not take this chance to delete the Second Commercial Use District from Rosemont's corner of the map altogether? But Soft Shoes McGuirk was a charter member of that commission, and he was not about to zone himself off his own land.[27] "We are doing what we can," one of the neighborhood's city council representatives said to the five dozen constituents who flooded city hall one day in April 1957, "but we can't rezone it."[28]

The only thing the neighbors could do, the *Sun* reported, was wait until the factory was built and "seek a court injunction against any nuisances, if they develop."[29] The deal was done. "The land was for sale and the company bought it," McGuirk told the assembled audience at Whitestone Baptist. "We are going ahead with the building of the factory."[30]

The School

The box-factory episode represented one kind of incursion. The land was for sale, as McGuirk said, and the company had bought it. A private business was doing what it wanted with property it owned. It was an attack, but not a betrayal. The second thing that happened to Rosemont in 1957 was different. This time the aggressor was the city government, not a private business, and the property at stake belonged, in theory, to everybody.

At first it seemed like good news: in May 1957, Baltimore's Board of School Commissioners announced plans to build a brand-new elementary school in

Rosemont. The recent influx of younger families into the neighborhood had pushed its two nearest elementary schools over their capacity by nearly fifteen hundred students, and without a new building, children were going to have to start attending classes in "portable" trailers or part-time—just the situation their parents had moved here to avoid.[31] Not for nothing, a new elementary school also meant a school's worth of jobs for the teachers who lived nearby, and a brand-new school instead of a hand-me-down would be a real coup.

Even if parents had wanted to transfer their children out of neighborhood schools and into ones nearby that were less crowded—such as, for instance, Schools No. 63 at Walbrook and Rosedale a few blocks to the north and No. 88 on the other side of the Edmondson Avenue Bridge, which had both been officially "white" schools until *Brown*—they couldn't.[32] Baltimore's schools had never been divided into geographic districts.[33] Before *Brown*, any white child could attend any "white" school in the city, and any Black child any "colored" school. However, school officials *did* have the power to declare a school "likely to be crowded beyond its reasonable capacity," in which case principals could limit attendance to the children who lived nearby, in whatever officials decided its "district" was.[34] After *Brown*, this extemporary "districting," though it was ostensibly color-blind, built moats around historically white schools in Baltimore that might have been vulnerable to integration by transfer, such as those adjacent to the actually overcrowded schools in Black neighborhoods.[35] Between 1954 and 1963, when the Board of School Commissioners abolished the policy, one-quarter of all elementary schools in Baltimore were districted to exclude transfer students—including No. 63 and No. 88.[36]

So: a new school it would have to be. As far as the R.N.I.A. was concerned, this was not the problem. The problem was where officials wanted to build it: on the vacant lot the city owned on Presstman Street, the one where We Workers whitewashed the trees and the R.N.I.A. wanted the Bureau of Recreation to build a playground. Even worse, that lot was plainly not large enough for a whole elementary school and its grounds. To get the space they needed, officials planned to seize more than two dozen nearby houses—more than a quarter of the homes on the Ellamont-Presstman-Rosedale-Belmont block—and bulldoze them to the ground.[37] Mary and Sterling Graves, Marian and Dallas Barclift, Joseph and Esther Wiles, the Doughertys and the Pinns and their neighbors were going to lose the homes they'd just bought.

Scholars trace the widespread use of eminent domain, the legal theory under which the government can take private property for public use, to another key case the Supreme Court decided in 1954: *Berman v. Parker*. Before *Berman*, legal precedent limited its use to cases in which officials could demonstrate how the takings they proposed would serve the public's interest.[38]

Berman took a much broader view. "When the legislature has spoken," the justices wrote, "the public interest has been declared."[39] What the government wanted, in other words, now the government could take.

Urban renewal's advocates typically used the phrase "slum clearance" to describe this process, and the justices adopted this way of thinking about eminent domain's benefits. "It is within the power of the legislature," they wrote, "to determine that the community should be beautiful as well as healthy, spacious as well as clean, well-balanced as well as carefully controlled"—which implied that what came before was not beautiful, not healthy, not clean, not carefully controlled.[40] But, crucially, this was only an implication. "Slum clearance" didn't require any slum. There didn't need to be anything wrong with eminent domain's "before" at all. As long as lawmakers said the public's interest would be better served by a different way of using the land, and as long as they paid "fair market value" for the properties they took, *Berman* gave officials free rein to do what they liked.[41] And according to this way of thinking, a person who lost her home or business to urban renewal could hardly complain; she was just serving the greater good, making (the historian Francesca Russello Ammon writes) "the sacrifices that postwar citizenship increasingly required."[42]

Nobody was arguing that Rosemont was a "slum" or a "blighted area"—not yet. But they didn't have to. School officials were simply saying that a school on the R.N.I.A.'s block would be a better use of the land than the houses that were currently standing there. Besides, officials claimed, the Rosemonters had brought the problem on themselves by having too many children. "The same thing will happen over and over again where Negroes move in with their higher population density," the assistant superintendent of school facilities explained. "When you take a builtup area and double and triple its child population, you have to build more schools."[43] "Either houses will have to be torn down to build a new school," another official said, "or the children will have to go to school part time."[44]

In fact, these were not the only available choices. There was, as it happened, a whole block with nothing on it directly across Ellamont Street from the homes the school board was trying to seize. The city didn't own it—speculators' realty companies did—but this should not have been an insurmountable obstacle.[45] In the years since the end of the war, the city had spent more than $7 million on site acquisitions for dozens of new schools in neighborhoods across the city.[46] Furthermore, the city didn't yet own all the land it needed for the Presstman Street site, either. Officials were going to have to spend money either way.

Why didn't they start with the option that wouldn't have required anyone to lose their home? It's hard to know for sure. Old maps show a millstream meandering across the empty Ellamont Street block, and its gully might be why nothing had ever been built there. On the other hand, that same stream looped up through the empty lot on Presstman, too, which may likewise explain why *it* was empty.[47] Also, over the years, the people who worked at the Rosedale estate had used the stream's bank as a makeshift cemetery.[48] When construction workers finally arrived to build the R.N.I.A.'s block in the late 1920s, old-timers reported, they found long-buried bones in the glop—which may be another reason the lots went undeveloped for so long.[49] But the most obvious explanation for officials' initial choice is the least sympathetic one: that they would rather tear down Black people's houses, and keep speculators in a position to profit.

(In her book *From Slave Cabins to the White House: Homemade Citizenship in African American Culture*, scholar Koritha Mitchell writes about a process she calls "know-your-place aggression," "a way of reminding everyone of the target's 'proper' place, a way of insisting that certain people should not feel secure in claiming space and resources." This kind of aggression can be physical or not, Mitchell writes, but either way it is "a performance of the denial of citizenship, an active rejection of the idea that one belongs," and it "become[s] most necessary when purportedly inferior people are proving their mettle."[50] Is this what school officials were doing? They didn't say so. But that doesn't mean it isn't.)

Yet at the time, this was not the argument the Rosemont neighbors made in defense of their homes. On the contrary, they appeared to accept the city's either/or. "[My] clients recognize the urgency of building schools and the necessity of purchasing privately owned property in most cases," Dallas Nicholas, the R.N.I.A.'s lawyer, assured the officials assembled at the Board of School Commissioners' meeting in May 1957, and they also appreciated "the difficulties which the School Board faces in trying to select school sites which will meet school needs and at the same time inconvenience the smallest number of property owners."[51] But his clients "have recently purchased their present homes," he said, "and in many cases had improved them at substantial expense."[52] Couldn't "some other site involving cheaper houses" be chosen for the school instead?[53]

In other words, the issue as the R.N.I.A. explained it was not that houses were being destroyed; it was that the houses being destroyed were theirs. They were thinking like property owners who were entitled to consideration: asking for a break from their peers, not questioning the logic of racial capitalism. Yet the city did not think of them that way, not really. "The members of the Board assured Mr. Nicholas and his clients that the board was aware of their situation," the meeting's minutes note, "and would not want to inconvenience

IN PLAN — "It has been approved to go into the master plan. The next move is up to the School Board." John Lang, secretary of the City Planning Commission, speaking at presstime, was referring to to the area bounded by Presstman Ellamont, Rosedale and Belmont, where the School Board hopes to erect a new elementary school, to ease overcrowded conditions in the Belmont area. These homes in the 1400 block Ellamont St., are among the 26 that must go for the new school, unless the City Council can be persuaded to pass an ordinance to save the properties.

1400 block of Ellamont Street, *Baltimore Afro-American*, May 28, 1957. Courtesy of the AFRO Archives.

them or any other property owners if school needs could be met without such inconvenience."[54] Unfortunately, apparently, they could not. "Sacrifices have to be made," school board member John R. Sherwood said to Nicholas and the Rosemont neighbors who filled the room at city hall. "You have been elected to be the sacrificers."[55]

As it happened, in this case, Sherwood was wrong. In Baltimore, land seizures like this one required the entire city council to pass a condemnation ordinance, and the neighborhood's councilmen, perhaps trying to make up for the box-factory episode, pledged they would not go along. "Before the School Board goes to the point of definitively determining it must have this land involving tearing down 26 perfectly good homes," one told the newspaper, "it should contemplate that it will have to have a condemnation ordinance"—and that he and his colleagues would not vote to condemn dozens of homes "in perfect condition" that represented "a recent investment by their owners of at least $300,000."[56] Thus the proposal died.[57] Still, it made its point.

There are two ways of interpreting this story. In one, it is an example of the city government doing its job, checks and balances working just as they should. In the other, it is an example of the city government doing a different job. To board member Sherwood's larger point—if sacrifices did not actually have to be made to get the school built, if the new school could go someplace else more or less as easily, then what were those sacrifices really for? Because in the end, even if the stream and gully made building on the vacant land across Ellamont Street difficult, they plainly did not make it impossible. In 1959 and 1960, school officials bought up the 3.6 acres of land they needed, hired an architect, and prepared to build the new Belmont Elementary there after all.⁵⁸

When the new school finally opened in 1962, Mary Rosemond wrote, it "was one of the highest rated schools in the city."⁵⁹ It could hold more than eight hundred pupils and had two kindergartens, an auditorium, a gym, an art room, a library, and a room for speech therapy.⁶⁰ A souvenir booklet published by the school's Parent-Teacher-Community Association—the first one in the state of Maryland and maybe the entire United States—underlines its ambitions. "A good program of education should increase the 'yearning power' of the learner," the foreword read. "The family-trips we plan, the adult education classes we conduct, the study groups we foster, the use of our building at all times, the increased services which are provided for our children, are all designed to help us 'want' and strive for the best. This spirit will pilot Belmont and its community to a worthy destiny."⁶¹

In other words, life went on in Rosemont. "Without a crisis around which to mobilize," Mary Rosemond wrote later, the R.N.I.A. went back to being "a social group."⁶² The association's files from the period bulge with photographs of We Wives' parties and We Workers' food drives and Kadets of America drills. There are no petitions or protest signs.

But although things ended all right this first time the Rosemonters would find themselves elected to be the sacrificers, it was only the first time. There would be plenty more to come.

PART II

The Highway

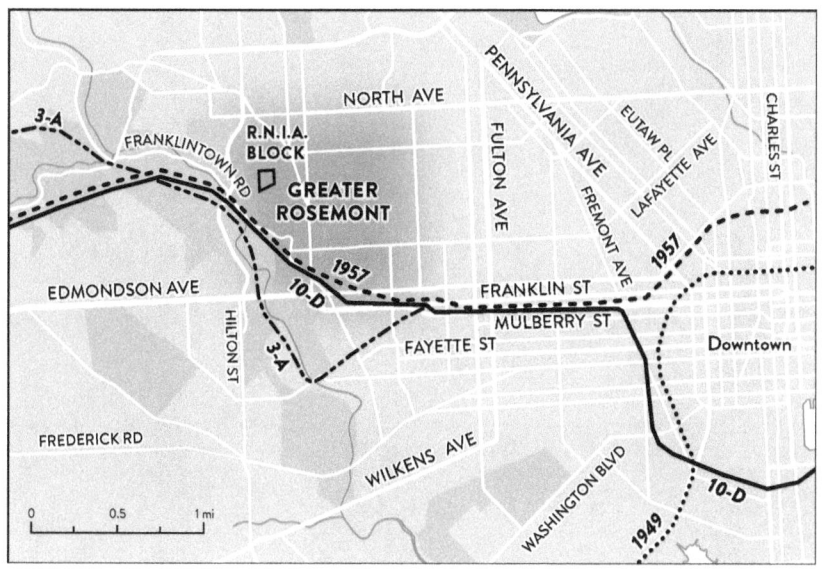

4

"As Bad to Us as a Bomb": How the Highway Got Its Map (1957)

In 1946, the artist Eddie Rosenfeld moved into an old rowhouse he'd restored on Tyson Street, just north of downtown Baltimore. Tyson was a little street lined with little houses, built a century before for the white working people the *Sun* would later call "arty Irish": rugmakers, carpenters, bootleggers, a manufacturer of artificial eyes.[1] The neighborhood surrounding Tyson Street, Mount Vernon, was much more storied and elegant, filled with grand mansions and monuments. It was also a part of Old West Baltimore, and by the time Eddie Rosenfeld got there most of the people who lived on his block and nearby were Black.[2]

This would not be true for long.

"A small avalanche of other artists, musicians, decorators and the like" followed Rosenfeld to Tyson Street, the *Sun* reported, all drawn to the old block's "new Greenwich Village touch."[3] The small avalanche soon became a large one, and a visitor the newspaper sent in 1948 found a "surrealistic" block "full of . . . new settlers who have interspersed the standard red housefronts with giddy color patterns combining mustard yellow, bottle green, eggplant purple."[4] These were the kinds of places, she wrote, that looked like they should have been filled with "Matisse and Picasso, kidney-shaped tables and low-slung chairs, fawn carpets and hurricane lamps."[5]

In 1949, *Baltimore Magazine* commissioned Eddie Rosenfeld's next-door neighbor to write a profile of the new Tyson Street it called "Slum Clearance à La Mode."[6] "This little street in downtown Baltimore and the group of people who have re-created it, have set an example for the city and the rest of the country for that matter in the campaign for better housing and slum clearance," the neighbor, a gallerist named Shelley Murphy, wrote. "Tyson Street was a slum area! [But] the character and spirit of early 19th century

"Picasso, Cats, and Gay Facades—That's Arty Tyson Street Now," *Baltimore Sun*, May 17, 1948. Courtesy of *The Baltimore Sun* and the Enoch Pratt Free Library Maryland Department Vertical Files (Tyson Street). Permission from Baltimore Sun Media. All rights reserved.

Baltimore was in these houses, and needed only a little lumber, a little paint, and a car-load of elbow grease to be brought to the surface."[7] It also needed a carload of money. In 1946, Eddie Rosenfeld had paid $1,800 for his house. Six months later, someone bought a house down the block for $3,000. By 1948, the *Sun*'s reporter wrote, "a half-improved place is up for $6,500," and neighbors reported spending more than $16,000 on renovations.[8] With all that investment, the quickly gentrifying "Pastel Block" became a celebrity. Profiles of its new residents and photographs of its rehabilitated houses often appeared in the pages of the *Sun, Baltimore, Living for Young Homemakers,* even the *Encyclopedia Britannica* (under "Baltimore landmarks: Private urban renewal").[9]

Yet in the summer of 1957, Shelley Murphy wrote, she was "lolling on a beach in New England" when the telephone rang: a long-distance call from Tyson Street. "Come home at once!" the neighbor wailed. "They're going to run the Jones Falls Expressway through your kitchen."[10]

"The Baltimore bottleneck is about to be broken," wrote Charles LeViness, director of public relations for the Maryland State Roads Commission, in July 1956.[11] Municipal maps from the 1930s and 40s show the bottleneck he meant. Wide, fast limited-access roads poured into town from almost every direction, then reticulated onto city streets "built" (one official said) "for the horse and buggy."[12] And as cars on the road multiplied—the number of vehicles registered in Maryland more than doubled between 1940 and 1960—the problem got worse and worse.[13]

The cars clogging Baltimore did not just come from Maryland, either, since as LeViness pointed out, the city was "a perfect roadblock," "directly in the natural path of traffic from New England to Washington and the South."[14] Thus the city's first real highway plan involved a 39-mile beltway that circled Baltimore like a collar, or a noose. As far as the roads commission was concerned, the beltway was a quick fix—there was plenty of unoccupied space out there in Baltimore County to build it in—but not an ideal one. "The shortest distance between two points is still the straight line," LeViness wrote, and the beltway would pull Philadelphia-to-Washington drivers "miles out of [their] true course." "The best by-pass of the Baltimore bottleneck is no by-pass at all," he concluded. It was "an expressway cut through the heart of the city."[15]

Curiously, the men who owned "the heart of the city" agreed with him. In July 1956, the year-old Greater Baltimore Committee (GBC), an organization of "outstanding local business and industrial executives," formed a highway subcommittee to "emphasize its conviction that a properly planned and coordinated highway program will be of immeasurable benefit to our city and its citizens."[16] Whose city, and which citizens? Besides being "outstanding local business and industrial executives," most of the highway subcommittee's members didn't live in Baltimore at all. The subcommittee's chairman was Leonard J. Novogrod, the general manager of the May Company department stores, who lived in a Tudor-style castle in Pikesville, just over the northwestern city line.[17] Albert D. Hutzler Jr., department-store president, also lived in Pikesville, and so did Hugo Dalsheimer, the president of the Lord Baltimore Press. Then there were Bill Rouse, a mortgage banker (Roland Park, the prototypical in-town suburb) and his neighbor C. Warren Black, the president and chairman of a sand-and-gravel–mining concern; the executive vice president of the Mercantile-Safe Deposit and Trust Company (Towson); and the vice president of the United States Fidelity and Guarantee Company (Towson again).[18]

These men were literally invested in downtown Baltimore. Their wealth, and their companies' wealth, depended on the value of the real estate they owned there. But they and the other people who owned Baltimore did not think of it as their home. They thought of it as their piggy bank. And that way of thinking made the prospect of bulldozing their investments and paving them over an unexpectedly compelling one.

Renewing Downtown Baltimore

What downtown's boosters were framing as a technical solution (highways) to a practical problem (traffic) was also an ideological gambit, an announcement of their intent to reshape the metropolitan landscape so that it served only the needs of people like themselves. The arcana of transportation policy, and the conversation about downtown redevelopment it accompanied, doubled as a discourse on what a city was and who it was for.

Yet the boosters weren't exactly wrong about the problem they thought they saw. Nobody *was* coming downtown anymore, especially not to go shopping. For fifty years, department stores had monopolized the city's commercial life, as renowned for their spectacle—their window displays, their Christmas parades—as for the volume and variety of the things they sold.[19] Most cities had stores like this, of course, but when it came to the industries that might define a place Baltimore had little else.[20] Akron had tires. Pittsburgh had steel. Grand Rapids had furniture. Baltimore, by contrast, was known as a branch-plant town. Plenty of big companies had outposts there, like American Can, Domino Sugar, Bethlehem Steel, and Standard Oil, but few had headquarters. As a result, Baltimore's downtown economy was unusually lopsided, skewed toward the old grandes dames like O'Neill's (opened in 1882), Gutman's (1886), Hutzler's (1888), Hecht's (1897), Hochschild, Kohn (1897), Stewart's (1902), and more.[21] According to one executive's calculations, Chicago, with three times as many people as Baltimore, had the same number of major stores, while Detroit, which was much closer in size, had just two.[22]

But as the suburbs grew after World War II, they pulled with them the functions of downtown. Downtown office vacancies rose and the condition of office buildings there deteriorated. Property-tax revenue fell. Between 1931 and 1945, the assessed value of Baltimore's central business district dropped by nearly one-quarter.[23]

Suburban shopping took downtown's place. In May 1947, the Edmondson

Village Shopping Center, built in the style of Colonial Williamsburg, opened just west of the neighborhood that would become Rosemont.[24] Behind an oversized parking lot, it featured Baltimore's first branch department store, a Hochschild, Kohn. In 1948, Hochschild, Kohn opened a second branch at the city's northern edge: 15,000 streamlined square feet designed by Raymond Loewy, about as far from "Colonial Williamsburg" as it was possible to get. Six years later, Hecht's opened "not a branch, but a complete department store" (160,000 square feet) in the northern suburbs.[25] In 1956, Hecht's joined Hochschild, Kohn on Edmondson: 150,000 square feet of retail space with parking for 1,300 cars. ("The women's fashion department," its designer said, "will have four chandeliers growing out of columns, which will offer a dream-forest appearance. The children's shoe department will have a circus motif, putting the child in the 'center of the ring.' The men's department will have walnut panels and brass fixtures, setting a mood out of Greek mythology. Housewares will be displayed against a wall of Italian marble."[26]) A 1956 telephone survey of white women shoppers in the Baltimore metro area showed that most did "a lot" or "nearly all" of their shopping in branch stores, since they were "convenient," "attractive," and—crucially—had "good parking facilities."[27]

This same thing was happening all over the country. Historian Alison Isenberg found a 1954 survey of American retailers showing that though consumer sales in forty-five metropolitan areas had increased by 32.3 percent since 1948, sales in the corresponding downtowns only increased by 1.6 percent.[28] But Baltimore had it worse than most. Between 1948 and 1954, retail trade in the Charles Street department-store corridor had declined by 12 percent, compared with a 25 percent increase across the whole metropolitan area, and the number of downtown *transactions* ("a better measure of retail activity," some proprietors argued, because it more accurately represented the number of shoppers in the stores and on the streets) had fallen even more precipitously.[29]

Why the difference? For one thing, by 1950, nearly 25 percent of the city's population was Black. But not one of the city's downtown department stores welcomed Black shoppers.[30]

This might not seem so unusual for the time, but it was. As historian Grace Elizabeth Hale writes, Black shoppers everywhere encountered a "tension between segregation's claims of absolute racial ordering and the . . . messiness of consumer culture in a place that depended upon both white and black customers."[31] In other words, sometimes they were welcome, and sometimes not. Yet Baltimore's department-store proprietors chose to resolve this tension with absolutes. In 1923, O'Neill's had become the first explicitly whites-only department store in the United States, and the others in town had quickly followed its lead.[32] "Nobody can understand women," the vice-president of

Stewart's told the *Afro-American* in 1929. "Many of them sleep in the same room as colored people, they eat out of the same dishes, stay in the house all day long with them, yet they object to buying at the same counter in a department store." It was "silly," he conceded, but his "main job" was "not to solve social problems, but to make money."[33]

In that case, he'd got it backward. Even in the much deeper South, the job of making money forced stores to sell to Black customers.[34] In "Atlanta, Memphis, Tennessee, etc. department stores waited on colored people with no holds barred," May Company executive Leonard Novogrod explained. "Colored people can trade in any department of the store on an equal basis . . . Baltimore is the only place where this is not true."[35] "No holds barred" was an overstatement, but as a general matter (Hale writes) "very few white southern businesses could afford to exclude a paying customer no matter their color, especially when the next store down the street would probably make the sale anyway."[36]

But Baltimore's big department stores stuck with Jim Crow.[37] Some employed "spotters" to catch any "light colored people" who tried to sneak in and spend money. ("You'd be surprised," one store manager told a "blue-eyed, brunette" reporter shopping undercover in 1947. "Sometimes these colored people are as light as you and I!")[38] Others got more flexible over time, only refusing to serve Black customers in certain departments—in beach wear, or millinery, or corsets; or in their beauty parlors; or in their coffee shops and tea rooms—or (the *Afro* reported) they "welcome colored shoppers provided they did not attempt to try on merchandise." Still others practiced segregation-on-the-spot, adjusting their policies depending on how many white patrons were in the store.[39]

Whatever form this racist exclusion took, it was counterproductive. As Novogrod explained, "colored people's money is just as green as other people's money."[40] But in Baltimore, where North and South collided, Jim Crow helped destroy downtown. As the *Afro* and others pointed out repeatedly, Baltimore had plenty of Black people with money, people like Gertrude Corbett and Mary Rosemond, who might have shopped in the big department stores had they been allowed to do so. (To wit: in the early 1960s, Hochschild's became the first big department store in Baltimore to serve Black customers equally—and, per the *Sun*, this progressive turn "boosted sales throughout the '60s.")[41] Had they got in the habit of shopping downtown, they might even have kept the place afloat—at least for a little while.

Of course desegregating Baltimore's department stores wouldn't have solved all the Greater Baltimore Committee's problems. Other cities' downtowns were, as one planner put it, "in a hollow now," too.[42] But the episode demonstrates the limits of the downtown boosters' good faith when it came to the way they diagnosed the ailments they thought they had—and the prescriptions they imagined would be the cure.

On the day after Christmas 1954, Jim Crow pioneer O'Neill's went out of business.[43] The next week, in a tizzy, downtown Baltimore's "outstanding local business and industrial executives" established the GBC.[44] They had already invested in downtown: their capital was the land and buildings there, and now (one mailer explained) "YOUR dollars" were "slipping through your fingers this very moment like a handful of sand."[45] "Time is running out," one GBC man told a reporter. "We'd better get started on an answer down here, or it's going to be impossible to keep up with the parade."[46]

The answer they identified was urban renewal. Pedantically, "urban renewal" refers to the residential clearance and redevelopment projects the federal government funded via the Housing Acts of 1949 and 1954 (which is to say, projects in which housing was either built or—and much more often—demolished). On the ground, it also includes the whole gamut of mid-century projects that claimed as their purpose the redevelopment—"reclamation," people sometimes said—of "slums" or "blighted areas" in cities nationwide.[47] In brief, and in general, urban renewal and urban-renewal–adjacent projects gave public subsidy to private developers to turn "obsolete" buildings, blocks, and neighborhoods into something new.[48]

"Should we try to attract people back into the core to support the retail businesses that have flourished in the past?" a Baltimore planner asked in a 1957 interview. "Or should we make of the core a kind of 'world's fair'—gay and charming, something aesthetically pleasing, a place where all would want to come and trade and work—a bazaar, a fair, an urban park?—that serves as the heart for the entire metropolitan area?"[49] The idea, as another planner put it, was to "raise the number and quality of the people that were downtown," and therefore raise downtown property values, by turning the place into a glass-and-steel spectacle for suburbanites.[50] To that end, downtown urban-renewal projects in cities nationwide typically included hospitals and health complexes, cultural centers and sports arenas, university labs and libraries, office buildings, parking lots, shopping malls. These were lures for people who did not live in cities anymore more than they were services for people who did.

But it wasn't just a matter of what planners and developers built. It was also a matter of what—and who—they chose to destroy to do it. Here was urban renewal's essential promise: "armies of bulldozers," as federal housing official Albert M. Cole put it, "smashing down acres of slums."[51]

"Slum clearance" was hardly a new concept, but the Supreme Court's 1954 ruling in *Berman v. Parker* stretched it far beyond its previous shape. *Berman* held that governments could seize private property for redevelopment projects so long as they said those projects would serve the public's interest by eliminating "not only slums, but also the blighted areas that tend to produce slums," and these could be anything at all.[52] If the government said a building was blighted, it was blighted. If a neighborhood could be cleared for profit, it was a slum.

Like a car full of Philadelphians wheeling around the beltway, we've taken a long ride, but we've reached our destination. The people who had the power in Baltimore and other cities were invested, literally and figuratively, in downtown. Those investments were losing value. To stop the loss, urban renewal and its counterparts aimed to rebuild the central business district, or CBD—planners' shorthand that made the place sound, Lewis Mumford said, "like an unmentionable disease"—to draw suburban commuters and shoppers downtown again.[53] (Thus Baltimore would get its Charles Center on the 22-acre downtown parcel that had once housed O'Neill's and its neighbors. Charles Center was not technically an urban-renewal project at first, because it didn't qualify as "residential redevelopment," but it was still funded by state and city grants and bonds along with seed investments from the GBC and the Committee for Downtown.)[54] "Imagine it!" the GBC gushed. "A Downtown with an all-new, greater meaning and purpose and productiveness than ever before! A Downtown with property values, and the return on them, at a healthily increased and stabilized level! . . . YOU will have a share in a downtown greater than your fondest dreams of the past."[55]

But those dreams could only come true if people could actually *get* downtown. Hence all the mewling about traffic jams and horse-and-buggy streets, and hence the boosters' belief that, as one suburban GBC man wrote another in the summer of 1956, "a modern highway system that will enable modern traffic to move freely and economically" was "one of the most important projects facing the Greater Baltimore Committee."[56] To the people who had the power in Baltimore, an "expressway cut through the heart of the city" seemed like the best way to save it.[57]

The 1957 Expressway Plan

Since 1942, Baltimore's planners had considered and rejected plans for more expressway systems than a person could count on two hands.[58] But each one was mostly theoretical, because before 1956 state and local governments interested in building big roads had to find a way—gasoline taxes, highway bonds, road tolls—to pay for them. Some federal aid to highways was available, but it was spread thin among urban, suburban, and rural farm-to-market roadbuilding projects.⁵⁹ Having to scramble for the money to build roads meant that planners had to be careful what they spent and where they spent it, giving the hustle a more figurative purpose: It made it hard to forget that roads had costs.

But then, in June 1956, President Eisenhower signed the $26 billion Federal-Aid Highway Act, which promised to pay 90 percent of the cost of building a 41,000-mile "National System of Interstate and Defense Highways": wide, high-speed, usually limited-access roads connecting cities from coast to coast.⁶⁰ The 1956 law inaugurated the biggest public works project the country had ever seen.⁶¹ "Each federal dollar," the writer Tom Lewis explains in his book *Divided Highways: Building the Interstate Highways, Transforming American Life*, "generated close to a half hour of employment, not only in construction but in steel mills, cement plants, and mines, and among various manufacturers."⁶² "Drivers . . . would have to purchase cars and trucks—and then gasoline, tires, and insurance—to ride on it. If that [highway] was in the Northeast, say New Hampshire or New York, road crews would have to spend many dollars to maintain it, including money for salt and sand and plows to keep it open in the winter. Police would have to patrol it night and day. If [a mile of highway] happened to be near an exit or entrance, businesses and small companies might locate there."⁶³ The interstate highway program, Lewis reports, was "a great tidal wave of federal money breaking over every sector of the American economy and influencing every aspect of American life."⁶⁴

With ten-cent dollars from the federal government, cities and states could afford to build the highways they wanted, and they could make money doing it. "It appears that between $350,000,000 and $400,000,000 will be spent <u>within</u> Baltimore City under this and related highway programs," the GBC highway subcommittee estimated in 1957.⁶⁵ "With such mouthwatering subsidies," Baltimore reporter Mark Reutter explained later, "it was hardly worth *not* building expressways."⁶⁶ Cities just needed to decide which ones.

The summer Eisenhower signed the Federal-Aid Highway Act, Baltimore pulled out its fifteen-year-old catalogue of notional expressways and started adjusting them to suit this new context. Among the federal Department of Transportation's rules about the kinds of roads it would pay for was one that said any urban interstate had to "pass through or connect" to others. That meant the early maps, with their parallel lines draped here to there, were out. Now an expressway system really had to be a *system*. Crucially, most planners and city officials interpreted this rule to mean that taking federal money for any one part was a pledge to build the whole thing.⁶⁷ If planners lost their nerve down the line and decided to leave the system unfinished—like, for instance, if they decided to build a north–south radial but not the East–West

Expressway—that would be just fine with the federal government, "provided" (activists said later) "the city gave the money back."[68] From the perspective of the federal roadbuilders it was the network that mattered, not the nodes.

With this guidance in mind, in 1957 the Baltimore Department of Planning worked out a plan for an elaborately interconnected expressway system. It looked like a jellyfish, with an "Inner Ring" and six sprawling, tangled tentacles, and for our purposes it had two key parts.[69] First, the old "east-west" route across the Franklin-Mulberry corridor now canted up through Rosemont for the first time. Second, the eleven o'clock portion of the Inner Ring traced the southeastern boundary of "Old" West Baltimore and—yes—threaded through Shelley Murphy's Tyson Street kitchen.

At the time, nobody noticed the first of these and everybody noticed the second. "There's No Joy In Tyson Street," lamented one headline.[70] "DEATH SENTENCE," blared another. "Some men drew some lines on some charts and Tyson Street was sentenced to execution."[71]

A street sentenced to execution is, of course, the inevitability of the urban highway. As Robert Moses had written in his 1944 *Baltimore Arterial Report*, this "solidly built town has no continuous opening through which to lay down an expressway," and as he told Congress a few years later, "when you're operating in an overbuilt metropolis you have to hack your way with a meat axe."[72] Faced with a meat axe, something had to yield. In this case, it was Tyson Street. But why?

The idea that highway construction could double as slum clearance had been around for as long as highways themselves. In Baltimore, for example, the parts of Franklin and Mulberry Streets that ran through the oldest part of the city had been crowded with shops and taverns and houses—and traffic, and complaints about traffic—forever, and planners had been volunteering them for "renewal" for almost as long. In 1891, plans for the city's first municipal rapid-transit system had drawn trolley tracks right down the middle of Franklin. When that didn't happen, in 1917 engineers proposed to dig a tunnel for an electric railway under the street.[73] Both plans threatened the homes that lay in their path, and both times property owners had scrambled to sell while they could. When the city dragged its heels, speculators and slumlords moved in.[74] Properties slated for demolition went unmaintained, and then their neighbors did, too. Under "Detrimental Influences," the cartographers who put together Baltimore's HOLC Residential Security Map in 1937 noted the "obsolescence" and "Negro concentration (80 percent)" they saw there, coloring it bright red between downtown and Fulton Avenue.[75]

Thus Robert Moses's 1944 plan had drawn its east–west expressway along Franklin Street. "The slum areas through which the Franklin Expressway passes are a disgrace to the community," Moses wrote in his *Baltimore Arterial Report*. "Merely as a matter of local pride . . . business leaders as well as citizens sensitive about the appearance and reputation of their city should be unwilling any longer to tolerate this close juxtaposition of civic center and slum. We do not propose to tear down familiar and cherished landmarks which cannot be replaced, nor will the Franklin Expressway make the town unrecognizable. Nothing which we propose to remove will constitute any loss to Baltimore."[76] The list of buildings to be demolished for the Franklin Expressway included two hundred blocks of shops, hotels, taverns, factories, schools, and churches; an ice-storage facility, a tinsmith, an awning company, the headquarters of the American Relief for France, and the brand-new School for Handicapped Colored Children; and the homes of 19,000 people, most of whom were Black.[77] But for Moses, all this was a virtue. "The more of them that are wiped out," he said, "the healthier Baltimore will be in the long run."[78]

People who weren't Robert Moses tended to put this sentiment a little less bluntly, but they shared it. As long as you were building in an "overbuilt metropolis," something was going to have to be wiped out no matter what. It might as well be something powerful people didn't want around. So, as Richard Rothstein writes in his 2017 book *The Color of Law: A Forgotten History of How Our Government Segregated America*:

> In 1943, the American Concrete Institute urged construction of urban expressways for "the elimination of slums and blighted areas." In 1949, the American Road Builders Association wrote to President Truman that if interstates were properly routed through metropolitan areas, they could "contribute in a substantial manner to the elimination of slum and deteriorated areas." An important influence on national legislation and administration of the highway system was the Urban Land Institute, whose 1957 newsletter recommended that city governments survey the "extent to which blighted areas may provide suitable highway routes." By 1962 the Highway Research Board boasted that interstate highways were "eating out slums" and "reclaiming blighted areas."[79]

Fair enough, but how did this logic pilot the Jones Falls Expressway through Tyson Street, that (per the *Sun*) "pocket-sized compound of Greenwich Village, the Left Bank and Old Baltimore"?[80] Simple: the men who drew the maps weren't arty enough to know better. According to Eddie Rosenfeld and his cohort, when Tyson Street was still a poor Black-branded neighborhood "every house in the block was substandard and violated all the health laws that have ever been heard of."[81] A 1949 article in *Living for Young Homemakers* reported that just one house on Rosenfeld's block had had indoor plumbing. None had gas, hot water, or heat, and "cook stoves of the wood-burning variety were found in such inconsistent places as a cellar, on a second-floor landing, and smack inside a front door."[82] And people who hadn't been paying attention wouldn't know that the stoves in the doorway had been replaced by low-slung chairs and, allegedly, Picasso. In other words, Baltimore's Department of Planning thought it was doing garden-variety slum clearance, not shredding a slice of bohemia.

Shelley Murphy came home from the beach and joined her neighbors on a hastily convened Save Tyson Street Committee. City officials, the *Sun* reported, sent it a message: "Expect the worst." "It was a question of whether the highway is more important than Tyson street," the paper explained, and "the highway was the primary consideration."[83] Nobody seemed to care that, as one Tyson Street neighbor told a reporter, "a highway could be as bad to us as a bomb."[84]

But the roadbuilders had miscalculated. "Not only does the 900 block of Tyson Street represent Baltimore's most famous example of the elimination of slums through private enterprise," the president of the Save Tyson Street Committee wrote in a letter to Mayor D'Alesandro, but "tax assessments and consequently revenue to the city have risen several hundred per cent over the last ten years."[85] At first D'Alesandro shrugged the Tyson Streeters off—his watery nonresponse, that he "sympathized with the plight of the Tyson Street residents" but didn't "want to be in the position of urging the expressway and then hindering it," presaged many later ones—but the logic of their position was inescapable.[86]

Especially now. Inspired by a code-enforcement plan pioneered in Baltimore and celebrated by its most enthusiastic apostles of private enterprise, the Housing Act of 1954 required cities that got urban-renewal money from the federal government to show that they were using code enforcement and housing rehabilitation to revitalize "blighted" residential neighborhoods. (This was instead of bulldozing them and building public housing projects in their place, as under the earlier version of the law.)[87] Even though the money for the expressway would be coming from a different federal pot, as housing official Albert Cole pointed out at an event in September 1957, "surely it would be ironical if [urban renewal and urban highways] should operate in opposition to each other."[88] "Ironical" was one way to put it. Fundamentally, the federal government could hardly ask private enterprise—such as, in this case, the members of the Save Tyson Street Committee—to pay for residential rehabilitation in its stead if it was going to bulldoze their investment as soon as the paint dried. What the newspapers called "privately financed urban renewal" would only work if officials would leave private financiers and their properties alone.[89]

Cole's argument was fair, but it isn't what saved Tyson Street. The residents mustered the magazines, schmoozed the newspapers, threw parties and open houses and fundraisers, and hired their own contingent of highway engineers to, the *Sun* reported, "devise satisfactory and constructive alternatives to wiping out the Pastel Block."[90] Most important, they also put a coterie of lawyers on the case, and within weeks the state legislature passed a "Tyson Street Rider" that forbade the city's using state-issued bonds to pay its share for any highway whose route touched the street.[91]

That was the end of the expressway through Shelley Murphy's kitchen.[92] A community had routed the roadbuilders, and Baltimore's "freshly painted patch of antiquity" was spared.[93] Indeed, it thrived. "I wish I had about twenty [Tyson Streets] in a row," one real estate man told the newspaper in 1964. "I'd show Georgetown up."[94]

Mapping the 10-D

Every one of the countless highway maps Baltimore had produced since 1942 featured some version of a lateral expressway along the Franklin-Mulberry corridor through Old West Baltimore. Each one swung its version of that expressway down and out of town toward Washington, DC.[95] But the 1957 expressway plan did the opposite. On the map the Department of Planning drew, the east–west transect slid *up* around Fulton Avenue and crept out of town, the 1960 *Study for East–West Expressway* reported, "via Leakin Park."[96] The preposition's blandness obscured its consequence. In fact, the road was going to slice right *through* Leakin Park, burying Baltimore's largest green space under acres of concrete. Along the way, it would bury Rosemont.[97]

Highways are politics. That's especially true in Baltimore, where by happenstance the city council was the legislative body that had to crank through the arduous process of passing separate condemnation ordinances for every "leg" of every proposed expressway. Since a leg was usually 10 or 20 blocks long and a block or two wide, this process required dozens of individual condemnation ordinances, each of which was supposed to follow its own public hearing.[98] But even before things got to that point, road maps were horse trades like anything else. A leg that carved up one man's district at lunchtime could peel through another's by dinner. It was easier where there was no one to speak up. For instance, as Johns Hopkins sociologist Douglas Hauber pointed out in 1974, Robert Moses's Franklin Street route through Old West Baltimore had traced over the crack between two city council districts, making it "a kind of political 'no man's land' . . . leaving some question as to who is responsible for the welfare of the people living there."[99] Likewise, in the middle of the 1950s Rosemont sat at the very eastern edge of its city council district, and its residents were outnumbered by all the white voters in all the white neighborhoods to its north and west, all the way out to the city line.

But weren't Baltimore's highways also supposed to be clearing its slums? Wasn't that the argument for Robert Moses's Franklin Street Expressway, and the argument for—and then against—the Tyson Street route? As was perfectly obvious to anyone who visited the place, and as was right then being corroborated by the fight over demolishing the R.N.I.A.'s houses to build the Belmont Avenue elementary school, Rosemont wasn't a slum. Was it?

Most of the time, when people talked about "slums" and "blight," they were picturing something real: the stoves on the landing, the yard hoppers out back, peeling paint and akimbo fences and rickety porches. These conditions multiplied in Black neighborhoods, where they were also what the writer Walter Johnson calls "an index of racist exploitation in a segregated housing market."[100] ("Many landlords" in Baltimore's Black neighborhoods, Fanny McConnell Buford explained, "have refused to reinvest any portion of their rental returns for the upkeep or repair of slum property—either out of indifference, greed, or simply because it has not been necessary in order to hold tenants.")[101] Framed this way, "slums" and "the blighted areas that tend to produce slums" were the predictable (and profitable) result of shoving one-fifth of a city's population into one-fiftieth of its housing. Thus, as far as most white people were concerned, "Black" and "blighted" became interchangeable adjectives. Buoyed by the transitive property, Baltimore's planners drew their maps accordingly.

Because they had the bad luck to be sitting in between the suburbs and downtown, and because of their relative lack of political power in the city council and the state legislature, and because of the pervasive subconscious supposition that any Black neighborhood must have been a blighted one, even places like Rosemont were vulnerable to being carved in two. Referring to a small change the Department of Planning made to its 1957 maps, one booster gave away the whole game. Compared with the original route, he wrote, the new one was much improved: the neighborhood it would take now was "inhabited by negroes, is a slum and is not considered as much of a political obstacle."[102]

In brand and in fact, Rosemont had been a white neighborhood in 1942. Not one of the routes the advisory engineers suggested for the East–West Expressway that year came anywhere near it.[103] It was a white neighborhood in 1943, and the same thing was true.[104] It was a white neighborhood in 1945, in 1946, and in 1949.[105] But by 1957, Rosemont was a Black community. Now it was a target.

But the people who lived there happened to be preoccupied that summer, with the box-factory crisis and the Belmont Elementary debacle. If anybody in the R.N.I.A. registered the threat the expressway posed, the archives don't reflect it. Mary Rosemond even wrote that the R.N.I.A. became "a social group" because it had no "crisis around which to mobilize."[106] And in fact there *was* no crisis, not that anyone could see. After the mayor spurned the Department of Planning's 1957 maps for being too "controversial" and not sensitive enough to "the effect of the Expressway upon existing residential neighborhoods" like Tyson Street, Baltimore's expressway-planning process crumbled into chaos.[107]

For almost a decade, while the city lurched anarchically from one map to the next, a sword swung low over Rosemont—but all the swinging blurred the blade.[108] For instance, according to the route that appeared in the *Study for East–West Expressway* the City of Baltimore Planning Commission published in 1960, a driver headed toward downtown on the six- or eight-lane expressway would have left Leakin Park at ground level, plunged into a moat two stories deep under Lanvale and Poplar Grove, then shot out of the ground on a skyway that towered over the houses below before dipping into another moat between Franklin and Mulberry Streets.[109] It was ridiculous, and it would have been annihilating. But that same year, Baltimore got a new mayor, the former state's attorney J. Harold Grady, who understood that he stood to lose far more than gain by being (as political scientist Douglas Hauber later explained) "the first mayor of Baltimore to make a 'final' decision regarding the expressway system."[110] So, Grady ditched the 1960 plan and called for a new one, to be produced by the expressway consultants—an outfit led by engineers from the J. E. Greiner Company, the construction firm that monopolized roadbuilding in Maryland.[111]

Two years and $600,000 later, the expressway consultants announced a new set of alignments, the "Baltimore 10-D Interstate System." In and around Rosemont, the 10-D elevated some of the previously depressed segments, depressed some of the elevated ones, and slid the crosswise band a little to the south, through what planners called a "poorer quality residential area."[112] (This was, in fact, the old Edmondson Terraces development at the eastern end of the neighborhood.) These were fractional changes, until you consider that the lines on the consultants' map, which were mostly unlabeled, represented hundreds of houses and businesses, a whole different roster of properties now in the path of the highway bulldozer.

Still, not many people really noticed. The newspapers covered the 10-D with gusto, but they focused on the parts of the route that hung over the harbor and promised to displace hundreds of working-class white families in South

Baltimore. There the expressway consultants, like the Department of Planning before them, had made a bet that wouldn't pay. "If you look at the way expressways are planned in Baltimore and the way expressways are planned around the country, they always put them through the neighborhoods that are considered the powerless neighborhoods," then-Councilwoman Barbara Mikulski explained in 1974, looking back at the 10-D route. Those white waterfront neighborhoods were filled with (the *Sun* explained) "steel workers and . . . housewives" and (Mikulski elaborated) "European ethnic people who had bought their houses, who had thought they were going to stay next to Saint Casimir's Church the rest of their life."[113] They were white, but otherwise they were not like the people who lived on Tyson Street at all.

The expressway consultants assumed that this part of South Baltimore was not the kind of "existing residential neighborhood" that the roadbuilders were now sworn to protect. They also assumed that the people who lived there would buckle in the end to the interests of their employers: the factories in Dundalk and Curtis Bay drooling over any expressway that could get trucks in and out more quickly than the traffic-choked status quo. But a person's home was her home. "The idea of an east–west expressway is beguiling," the *Sun*'s editors wrote in October 1961. "It is only when a line is laid down on the map of the city that the doubts begin to shape up for most of us."[114]

The city council's system of segment-by-segment condemnation made it impossible to build an expressway by fiat. It also made it impossible for elected officials or anyone else to block the entire project, because there was no "entire project" to block. The best a neighborhood could hope for was that its representatives could nudge individual segments of the road into someone else's district, which was generally the goal. (The idea of an east–west expressway *was* beguiling, so long as your kitchen wasn't the one in its path.) But federal rules also required a public hearing on the entire system, and so on January 30, 1962, the expressway consultants held one.

All of Baltimore had seen what happened when you tried to exterminate a place like Tyson Street. Now it was time to find out what happened when you tried the same thing someplace else.

The auditorium of the Eastern High School in Waverly was packed that night, mostly with white homeowners from South Baltimore and their representatives—including State Senator "Soft Shoes" McGuirk, whose district was due to be pulverized. Nobody from Black West Baltimore was there. For one thing, Waverly was about five miles and a half-hour drive, and more than an hour by public transit, away. More important, the people in the path of the East–West Expressway part of the road didn't know the hearing had anything to do with them, because the maps the newspaper printed showed an expressway through Federal Hill and Fells Point that was completely separate from the one through West Baltimore. Also, although federal rules said the hearing needed to be advertised to everyone the road would affect, it wasn't. Few people north of downtown knew it was happening at all.[115]

In any case, the meeting was a catastrophe. According to the newspaper, more than thirteen hundred sweaty, furious protestors "heckled a small band of city officials and business leaders who generally backed the route . . . despite pleas for order." "Many of the neighborhoods affected have already been earmarked for slum clearance," the expressway consultants' PR man said, idiotically.[116] "What did the consultants say in private when such diplomacy was not needed?" one reporter wondered.[117] Everyone else wondered the same. The room erupted. Per the *Sun*'s account, "A chorus of boos greeted this remark, interspersed with shouts of 'Who says?' and 'My home's no slum.'"[118]

Not long after the disastrous hearing at Eastern High, the head of the Maryland State Roads Commission announced that the agency would not "rubber stamp" the 10-D plan.[119] The roads commission started a study of its own, interrupted when Mayor Theodore McKeldin, returning to city hall in 1963 after two terms as governor, hired a third—or was it a fourth?—consultancy to restudy all the previous ones.[120] In 1964, the federal government demanded a study of its own.[121] Plans came and went, elusive as lynx. "If the East–West expressway had been built along every proposed route," one reporter noted later, "at least a quarter of the private property in downtown Baltimore would be paved today."[122]

Other cities, which did not have the complication of the segment-by-segment condemnation process, were getting *their* interstate highways built. Other cities were cashing checks from the federal government and, in theory, using that money and those expressways to revitalize their downtowns. Baltimore's Charles Center was under construction, but to get there visitors had to endure traffic like library paste on the horse-and-buggy grid. The GBC and its allies were losing their minds. And so, in 1965, planners resurrected the expressway consultants' 10-D map, not because they liked it best but because the public hearing the federal government required had already taken place. Construction could begin.

But not in white South Baltimore, where McGuirk and his allies in the legislature and city council had persuaded the roads commission to replace the 10-D route with, at least, an asterisk. Instead the State Roads Commission gave the go-ahead to start building the other part of the system, the East–West Expressway part, the part that ran through Rosemont. The reason why was obvious. "Highways are routed on a political and economic basis," West Baltimore activist Esther Redd explained a few years later. "The [expressway] snake, if not racist, most certainly seems to know that white is more threatening to it than black."[123]

Thus the people in Rosemont were about to find out what the people on Tyson Street already knew. A highway could be as bad to them as a bomb.

5

"Crime in the Street":
How the Highway Robbed Rosemont (1967)

In June 1967, Baltimore's city council held its first hearing on the condemnation lines for the 10-D version of the East–West Expressway (now also known as I-170) through the Rosemont neighborhood. As mapped, the highway would have plowed a furrow across Edmondson Avenue from Bentalou Street to Franklintown Road, then northwest to and through the park. En route, it would swallow more than eight hundred homes. It would also dispatch hundreds of shops and offices—the radio repair, the TV sales and service, Robinson's clothing store for men and boys, the Ideal Carry-Out, Ben's Shoes, liquor stores, candy stores, grocery stores, barbershops, bakeries—along with a big handful of churches and the Alexander Hamilton Elementary School.[1]

"Hundreds At Council Meeting Object to Route," the *Sun*'s headline said. "Refuse to Be Soothed."[2]

One of their objections had to do with money. What, neighbors wondered, could they expect to get in exchange for giving up their homes? West Baltimore Councilman William Donald Schaefer, whose enthusiasm for expressway construction would one day earn him the nickname "the cement king of Baltimore," waved the State Roads Commission's land-acquisition chief to the lectern more than a dozen times to explain; and more than a dozen times, the official repeated the same mind-bending answer.[3] Homeowners would get "fair market value" for their condemned houses, he said, or "the price a willing buyer would pay to a willing seller."[4] Bishop James I. Doswell, the pastor of a church in the road's path, interpreted the garble. "What you will give us," he said, "will not suffice for us to relocate."[5]

Other objections were more existential. "When we had to fight to get into this neighborhood, we bought our houses," said Clement Glenn, one homeowner in the expressway corridor. "We own our houses—what you said we wouldn't do—and now you want to take it away from us."[6] Then one of Glenn's neighbors, Bill Butler, stood and turned to Councilman Schaefer.

"I want to know one thing," Butler said. "If all these people are opposed to your highway, what can you do about it?"

"The answer," said Schaefer, "is they can do what you are doing, express their opposition."

"The opposition to the expressway is not helping us a bit," Butler replied. "If we all got together and appealed this, what good would it do?"

"Mr. Butler," Schaefer snapped, "you obviously know the answer as well as I do. If the ordinance is passed it becomes the law and condemnation is enforced."

"Yes," Butler said—maybe patiently, maybe not. "But the thing I want to know is what can we do to stop the ordinance from being passed? Let's say everybody in the immediate area protests, every living soul protests . . . What good would it do us? Whether we protest or not is not the question."

"The council committee and the council itself will consider the overall good of the expressway for the entire city," said Schaefer. "This is not just an area, this is a city-wide project. This is the answer."[7]

Whether or not they'd been present for the meeting with school officials ten years before about Belmont Elementary, every Rosemonter at the highway hearing heard the echoes of what board member John Sherwood had said then. Once again, sacrifices had to be made; and once again, they found themselves elected to be the sacrificers.

Not many people in the audience that night had come to defend the expressway, but there was one: the Greater Baltimore Committee's William Boucher. "We believe," he said, "that the expressway system of which this is a part is absolutely necessary for the physical and social welfare of the city."[8] Men like Boucher still saw in the Federal-Aid Highway Act of 1956 an opportunity to get what they badly wanted: the renewal of downtown. Now, ten years and as many plans later, their camp had expanded to include the roadbuilders themselves, all the engineers and functionaries and cement brokers and rebar manufacturers whose entire raison d'être was expressway construction. These men cared less about a route's particulars and more about building anything at all.

Yet so far, all Baltimore had to show for its decade of agita was the 10-D map nobody was happy with and the $51 million, nine-mile Jones Falls Expressway radial from downtown north to the beltway that (almost everyone thought) had to be connected to some other part of the system soon.[9] Meanwhile, as one *Sun* reporter wrote in 1963, the endless will-they-or-won't-they-and-where "tie[d] up private property owners: those who do not know whether to move or stay, modernize or let slide."[10] This was as true for developers in white neighborhoods as it was for homeowners in Rosemont. And so, in the mid-1960s, the confederacy of people who wanted to see Baltimore's interstate highway system built decided to get it done.

In January 1966, the Maryland State Roads Commission created the Interstate Division for Baltimore City to "expedite the completion of the Interstate System of Highways" there.[11] The next month, the city council voted 19 to 1 to approve the first condemnation lines for any part of the 10-D system, one segment to the east of Rosemont: fifteen hundred homes and businesses along a fillet of Franklin and Mulberry through the Harlem Park neighborhood.[12] In June, officials signed an "advance right-of-way acquisition agreement" for all the properties in that corridor.[13]

Especially after the Supreme Court's 1954 *Berman v. Parker* decision stretched officials' power to take private property for virtually any "public purpose" they cared to name, eminent domain brooked no argument. As one young poet explained in "(on urban renewal)," published in the late 1960s in the Baltimore literary magazine *Chicory*:

> when the city puts a stamp on your house
> you know you goin' somewhere.[14]

"The rights of . . . property owners are satisfied," Justice Douglas wrote in *Berman v. Parker*, "when they receive that just compensation which the Fifth Amendment exacts as the price of the taking."[15] But as the people who lived in the Harlem Park expressway corridor were about to learn, "just" was like the wet shimmer on the highway on a hot day: an impression, not a fact.

The Myth of the Fair Market

The letter hissed into John Wells' mailbox in September 1967. "As you are aware," it said, "it is necessary that your above captioned property be acquired in connection with the aforesaid Interstate Highway Project. Your property has been appraised, the appraisal has been reviewed, the just compensation to which you are entitled has been determined, and this Bureau"—the Interstate Division for Baltimore City—"is now in a position to acquire said property."[16]

John Wells, who lived in the neighborhood that was condemned the previous February, *was* aware of all that. The city had sent someone out to the little house on Pulaski Street where he lived with his wife Ada and their seven children: "taking a survey," she'd said, to see if the family would be interested in moving.[17] They would not. They'd bought their house in 1955 for $7,000, plus $84 in annual ground rent, and they had just finished paying it off; with interest and improvements, the total came to more than $13,000.[18] Although they knew something about the expressway plans—they'd been hearing about them, Wells later told a reporter, "off and on" for years—they hadn't paid much attention. "We just went on paying for our property," he said, "and hoped it would never come through."[19] But now, in the fall of 1967, it looked like it was.

"It is our sincere hope," the letter from the Interstate Division said, "that an amicable settlement will be had."[20] The state was offering to buy John and Ada Wells's house for $5,200.

As the roads commission's man would later remind the people at the Rosemont condemnation hearing, state law said highway officials couldn't pay any more for a property they took than what "a willing buyer would pay a willing seller on the fair market."[21] But a fair market for a condemned house is a sluggish one at best, and from the beginning few understood the system for defining or divining it. "What exactly is the city's method in getting appraisals?" West Baltimore Councilman Reuben Caplan asked at a meeting in February 1966, after the first East–West Expressway condemnation lines were approved. Were houses evaluated "on the basis of their condition [after] the area came under the threat of condemnation or before"?[22] Could owners appeal or negotiate? "There ought to be an element of fairness," added one of Caplan's colleagues. "They ought to have to offer the top dollar."[23]

But there wasn't, and they didn't—at least not in the 1966 East–West Expressway corridor. Instead, more than a year after the city council approved those condemnation lines, independent appraisers from all over Maryland arrived in the neighborhood, hired by the Interstate Division to assign value to its houses.

These appraisers used two approaches to calculate what they called the "before" or fair market value of the properties in the condemnation zone. In the first, which officials called the "market" approach, appraisers identified comparable properties "sold recently in the same or competing areas" and used them to extrapolate "the probable price at which [the condemned house in question] could be sold by a willing-seller to a willing-buyer."[24] (This is a typical approach to real estate assessment, except that here the "subject property" was condemned and often the "similar properties of the same type and class" were too. This condition limited the pool of willing buyers, even imaginary ones.) The second, the "income" approach, boiled down to an estimate of the rent a condemned property would have been able to produce in the future had it not been condemned. Every appraiser did things a little differently, and some were more generous than others, but usually the value appraisers submitted to highway officials landed somewhere in between these two numbers.

Along the way, the appraisers filled out a very long form. On the first page, there was always a neighborhood analysis, which in John Wells's case read:

> The major portion of the dwellings in the area are tenant occupied as single family dwellings, some have been converted to multi-family use. The age of the properties, which are approximately 50 years old, in connection with primarily tenant occupancy and proportionately high maintenance costs, indicates future neighborhood depreciation.[25]

Next, a description of the property.

> (1) The subject is an inside, 2 story, row brick dwelling on the East side of N. Pulaski Street, between W. Franklin Street and Mulberry Street. The lot is 13' 8 3/4" = 925.089 S.F.
> (2) The subject dwelling has a full basement, six rooms and bathroom. The roof is flat, built-up and tarred.
> (3) The subject has a 2nd story rear frame porch.[26]

Then the appraiser listed the details about the house, some of which he could have learned from city records or from the neighbors (since all the houses in a row were, generally, the same), and some of which he would have needed to go inside to learn. How old was it? What were the interior walls made from? How about the floors? The downspouts? The foundation? What was its interior and exterior condition? What kind of furnace did it have? What about the electrical panel and wiring? Pipes? Water heater? Were there storm windows and doors? Was the basement finished, and was there an extra "flush," or even a whole bathroom, down there? Was there wallpaper? Was the kitchen renovated? Had the original claw-foot tub been replaced by a modern built-in? Some appraisers were more thorough than others, but there was always a floor plan penciled on graph paper and a black-and-white photo of at least the front of the house. In this case, the snapshot shows a dark brick inside row with white marble stoop and cornice and arched brick-and-marble lintels above the windows. It's identical to its neighbors except for the shiny storm door and the small child standing out in front—one of the seven Wellses or a neighbor, presumably—holding a sign with the house number scribbled on it in chalk.

The value appraiser W. F. Miley settled on for John and Ada Wells's house was $6,250. But that number included the $1,050 the Interstate Division was going to have to pay the suburban dentist who held the ground rent on the property. (In Baltimore, it is possible to own a building—an "improvement," in legal terms—but not the land it sits on, in which case building owners must pay an annual "ground rent" to the landowner.) This is how officials came to offer John and Ada Wells $5,200 for a house valued at $6,250 and purchased twelve years before for $7,000 (or, with ground rent included, more than $8,000), not counting all they had put into it. "They thought we were ignorant enough to believe that they could take our houses, and not pay us enough to replace them," one Franklin Street homeowner explained, "just so some white people who moved to the suburbs could get themselves to work on time."[27]

"They" were wrong. A few months before those appraisers started coming around, in November 1966, John Wells and hundreds of his neighbors had gotten together to form the Relocation Action Movement (R.A.M.). (Wells was the group's first president.) R.A.M.'s initial goal was to protest the "negligent method of condemnation" that had left the people living in the highway's wash for months—and then a year, and then more than a year—with, one member pointed out, "no plans, no hearings, no studies, no nothing" for what came next.[28]

Then the letters from the Interstate Division started to arrive, and the people in the neighborhood started to learn just how (in R.A.M.'s words) "unreasonably low" its offers were.[29] For example, the *Sun* reported that Harlem Park construction worker Richardson Dingle-El and his wife, a piano teacher, had bought their three-bedroom house in 1952 for $6,250. In July 1967, the Interstate Division bought the house from them for $4,600. (As the newspaper noted, the house's 60-percent property-tax valuation that year was about $4,000, which meant that by the city's own math the house's market value should have been more than $6,600—and then, "to add insult to injury, the city took out the 25 days' worth of property taxes for the new fiscal year before paying.")[30] Officials offered Ella Rowe $5,000 for the Mulberry Street home she'd bought for $7,000 15 years before, then painted and paneled and sided and roofed for $10,000 more.[31] A seamstress down the block got less than $2,000 for her house. An elderly widow got almost nothing.[32]

The problem of inadequate payment for houses in Baltimore's expressway corridors would not be limited to Black homeowners. The "fair market" price of a condemned house is rarely going to be fair to the person who owns it, no matter who they are. But Black people got the worst of it.

Because of the self-serving real estate industry mythology about "declining" property values in their neighborhoods, appraisers offered Black owners less money for their homes in the first place. Then, Black owners needed more money to replace their houses. One city publication gushed that the people who lived in the path of the East–West Expressway could see in it an opportunity to move "wherever they wanted to!"[33] This sounded nice, but it wasn't true. Just the week before it passed the first condemnation lines for the East–West Expressway, Baltimore's city council had voted against an open-housing ordinance for the third time in three years.³⁴ This vote was preceded by a televised hearing at the War Memorial building at which thousands of white people jeered and heckled the archbishop of Baltimore while he urged the council to vote for the law on the grounds that "the dignity of the individual requires that no prohibition be placed against any person with respect to his place of habitation simply because of his race, religion, or ancestry."³⁵ A police guard swept the archbishop out of the building, and the open-housing bill was defeated 13 votes to 8.³⁶

So long as sellers, landlords, and realtors were free to discriminate, they could raise the price of the housing available to Black families by choking off its supply. In 1967, BURHA officials did the math and found that the average white homeowner in the 10-D corridor through Fells Point would have needed $2,500 to close the gap between the "fair market" value of his house and what it would have cost to buy another. The average owner in the first East–West Expressway corridor, by contrast, needed $3,900.³⁷

Yet during the spring and summer of 1967, agents from the Interstate Division prowled the Harlem Park condemnation corridor, trying (John Wells explained) to "talk people into selling for the price the city wanted to pay."³⁸ Homeowners couldn't afford to stay, and they couldn't afford to leave. All the roadbuilders needed to do was wait, while more and more families found themselves (one R.A.M. publication reported) "stranded in block[s] of vacated, boarded-up, garbage-infested city owned houses causing increased problems of vandalism, rats and an unreasonably large amount of additional upkeep on their own homes."³⁹ Paint blistered. Neighbors bled away. Occupied houses crumbled, and empty ones burned. Drifts of broken glass were everywhere. Nobody came to pick up the trash, even from the houses people still lived in, and the police wouldn't come, either.⁴⁰ The whole place, reporter James Dilts later wrote, was becoming "a dead example of the damage these mere lines on a map can do."⁴¹ "Their houses are all they've got," R.A.M. member Clarence Landrum said of his neighbors. "Talk about crime in the street."⁴²

Then, in the summer of 1967, the Congress for Racial Equality (CORE)—which, like many civil rights organizations at the time, was taking a radical turn—named Baltimore its first "Target City" for concentrated action.⁴³ CORE had many targets in the Target City, from housing discrimination to segregated labor unions to whites-only taverns and racist strip clubs.⁴⁴ At first, the East–West Expressway wasn't among them. On the contrary: CORE's position now, the *Afro-American* reported, was that the "colored middle class" was "trying to escape the reality of rampant segregation [with] the illusory comforts of private success."⁴⁵ By that logic, the homeowners of West Baltimore were not really a part of the group's remit.

But once CORE staff came to understand what was really going on in the 1966 East–West Expressway condemnation corridor—"white men's roads," activists put it, "through black men's homes"—they changed their position.[46] "The Relocation Action Movement believes that the Government owes it to displaced families to help them find houses on a par with those they left behind," field secretary Danny Gant told the *Sun* in September 1967, and he "refused to say his group would be quiescent ... if no help were forthcoming." "Asked what his group planned to do," the reporter wrote, Gant replied: "For me to tell [Mayor McKeldin] that would be like Rommel telling Patton what he planned to do in the African desert before he did it."[47]

With CORE behind R.A.M.'s cause, Baltimore's policymakers began appreciating the gravity, or at least the bad optics, of the situation unfolding in the expressway condemnation corridor. In October 1967, Mayor McKeldin told reporters that the Interstate Division's "fair market" standard was in fact "very unfair and has always been unfair."[48] The mayor, the *Sun*'s headline explained, vowed to "Fight to Aid Relocated Home Owners" by helping R.A.M. persuade roadbuilders to drop the "fair market" standard in favor of one activists called "replacement value." Neighbor Clarence Landrum explained what this meant: "enough money so they can go buy another house."[49]

By the end of 1967, the people whose homes the city had condemned some twenty months before finally had some leverage. Handwritten notes on the "Record of Negotiations" form in the file the Interstate Division kept on John Wells reflect this changing context:

11/20/67
　　We assume owner wants to negotiate.

11/21/67
　　Spoke to Mrs W—she, and she says her husband also, expect the present agitation for "replacement costs" as opposed to "fair market value" will sooner or later get them more money—and they will certainly not negotiate—says she's sure her "husband will still be in the house when the bulldozer comes into the yard."[50]

Highway officials up and down the line started forswearing their own approach. The "fair market" they'd created for the houses they condemned, they now conceded, wasn't fair after all. But when it came to changing the way they did things, they kept finding reasons to delay. In the winter of 1968, federal highway officials agreed to cover increased payments, but only if the Maryland General Assembly first changed its law to allow them. In the spring, the general assembly did change the law, but wouldn't implement it until the federal government amended the Federal-Aid Highway Law. Finally, in August 1968, the stars aligned. The new federal law went into effect, Maryland changed its law, and owner-occupants in the path of an interstate highway could now qualify for a "supplemental" payment of up to $5,000 "where that is necessary to secure a comparable dwelling that is determined to be decent, safe, sanitary, adequate to accommodate the displaced owner."[51]

It was a victory, but it wasn't absolute. Maryland's law said a homeowner was only eligible for the supplemental payment if "he has continued to own and physically reside in said dwelling until negotiations for acquisition in the project area commence."[52] Since a homeowner had no way to predict when those negotiations *would* commence, he was effectively trapped in his condemned house indefinitely if he wanted the extra money. (The first losers in this game of chicken were the neighbors who had done what officials asked and sold for "the price the city wanted to pay," foreclosing any further negotiation.) Maryland's law also restricted payment of the supplement "only to a displaced owner who purchases and occupies a dwelling within one year subsequent to the date on which he is required to move from the dwelling acquired for the project."[53] A person who chose not to buy another house would only receive "fair market" value for the one the state was taking.

In this way, the people who stuck around in the 1966 expressway condemnation corridor until they won the supplemental payment in 1968 might have been financially better off than their neighbors. Still, they lost money on the deal. For example, in September 1968, the Interstate Division agreed to pay John and Ada Wells a $4,950 "supplement" on top of the original $5,200 they'd offered for the little house on Pulaski Street.[54] This was about $3,500 less than they'd put into the house over the years. The next month, the family bought a house on Liberty Road in Baltimore County for $17,500. This was $12,300 more than the Interstate Division first offered them to take their house and $7,350 more than the state paid them in the end.[55] They made up the difference with a mortgage from the Augusta Building and Loan Association.[56]

Still, R.A.M.'s victory was swamped by incalculable loss. Now when the rest of Baltimore looked at the "jungles of boarded up houses, rats, and Fire Department sirens" in the 1966 condemnation corridor, one newsletter pointed out, they saw what all those years of expressway planning guaranteed they would: a "slum."[57] "Since the neighborhood was deserted," John Wells said at a meeting with State Roads Commission officials in the summer of 1968, "people from other neighborhoods started using it as a dumpyard. Rats started coming around. The condition of the houses is just not fit for people to be in." "My roof is leaking," he said. "My plaster is falling. Pay us and let us get out, now."⁵⁸ "I'm one of only two people in the block," another neighbor said to Jerome B. Wolff, the director of the State Roads Commission. "All the windows are broken and I can hear the glass fall out at night. I'm afraid." Somebody yelled: "How would you like to live like that, Mr. Wolff?" "He said," *Sun* reporter James Dilts wrote, "he wouldn't like to live like that."⁵⁹

Repeating the Process in Rosemont

Some fifteen months after Baltimore's city council condemned the first segment of the East–West Expressway, in June 1967, it turned its attention west to the next one. Rosemont, from Bentalou Street to the Gwynns Falls Park, was the target now. Generally speaking, following the condemnation corridor north and west brought just a little *more*: more money, more office jobs, more college degrees, more homeowners, more expensive houses, more renovated bathrooms and basement wet bars, and a more exclusive, and exclusionary, sense of who belonged and who didn't. These class distinctions may not have been visible to someone like William Boucher, but they were meaningful all the same. In fact, they're why it's possible to give the Interstate Division some of the credit for making the place we now call "Greater Rosemont." The 1967 condemnation lines slit West Baltimore into pieces, but they also stitched together the people who lived in and near their path, turning patchwork blocks into a quilt in peril. The things that had separated them from their neighbors to the south and east now dissolved into the existential threat that linked them together. No matter how much they earned or what they'd paid for their house, they shared the same slippery grip on their homes and neighborhoods, and the same keen awareness that the roadbuilders were about to take almost everything they'd earned.

By the time the appraisers got around to the neighborhood more than a year after that first contentious hearing, many of its homeowners were eligible for the supplemental payment in addition to the market price, about twice as much as they would have gotten before. Yet what had really changed?

A decade and a half had passed since Black people had started to move here, but everyone in Rosemont was still stuck in the same speculators' market. Even during the 1960s, the Activists, Inc. computer database showed that only about a quarter of the Black people who had bought homes anywhere in Baltimore had been able to obtain the legitimate bank loans or other financing necessary "to buy at a fair market price."⁶⁰ In West Baltimore at the end of the decade, the Activists calculated speculators' markups as high as 85 percent.⁶¹ The *Sun* reported an average markup of nearly $5,000 on every home a Black family bought from a speculator.⁶²

Even *before* the homes in the Rosemont corridor were condemned for the East–West Expressway, their owners had been the marks in what the Activists called "a gigantic conspiracy . . . to rob black families of millions of dollars in the purchase of homes."[63] Now they were being robbed twice more, once to leave the neighborhood they'd built and once again to settle in a new one.

Notwithstanding the supplemental payment, the appraisal process across the 1967 Rosemont condemnation corridor worked much as it had in John Wells's neighborhood. Except for the end rows, which were bigger and sunnier, the bones of the houses on a given block were mostly identical to one another. The Interstate Division charged its appraisers with looking inside the houses, sizing up their kitchen and bathroom renovations and basement bars, to assign individual prices for each one.[64] (The supplemental payment worked the same way. As a 1969 brochure from the Interstate Division explained, how much of the $5,000 maximum a homeowner received was "determined upon a finding that the City is paying you less than the <u>average</u> of comparable replacement payments, which are <u>available</u> on the market"—whatever that meant.[65])

This discretion could be predatory. "THIS YOU WILL HAVE TO WATCH," John Wells warned readers of the *R.A.M. Observer* newsletter in July 1968. "If you should let them appraise your home, be with them and make sure that nothing is left out—all the repairs you have done tell them about them. Leave nothing out, because they will if you are not right behind them, and this lowers the price of your home. Ask to look at the appraisals sheet. Speaking from experience I know, because this happened to me."[66] In fact, both the option price and supplemental payment differed markedly—and unpredictably—from appraiser to appraiser and house to house. At 2400 Lauretta, the Smiths got $5,930 plus a $5,000 supplemental payment; at 2402, the Hensons got $7,333 plus a $3,200 supplemental payment; at 2407, the Perkinses got $5,975 plus a $4,100 supplemental payment; at 2408, the Nickelsons got $6,950 plus $3,200; at 2409, the Queens got $6,525 plus $3,550.[67]

As is typical, the Interstate Division paid creditors who had placed a lien on the property first. Then, families with minimal or no outstanding loans got most of the money they were owed. The unluckiest ones were so deep in debt that even after they lost their houses, they still owed money to their lenders. At 2410 Lauretta, Johnnie and Larene Simmons had bought with their unrecorded land-installment contract from the Rafferty Realty Company for $7,950. When they sold to the Interstate Division in July 1969, they still owed $10,152 on it. So, although they were supposed to get $5,500 plus a $4,700 supplemental payment for their home, in fact they had to pay the state of Maryland two cents for it to buy their house.[68]

So, the math didn't work. Neither did the process.

The Interstate Division (and other public agencies in Baltimore) had a lot of condemned properties that needed appraising in 1968 and 1969, a limited supply of appraisers, and no incentive to do anything quickly. People frustrated with the appraisers' slow pace might be likelier to move out before negotiations for the acquisition of their property began, rendering themselves ineligible for the supplemental payment. Suddenly, a house that might have cost the roadbuilders $10,000 could be had for $4,500.

In October 1968, more than a year after the city council approved the Rosemont condemnation lines, one homeowner from the 2800 block of Harlem Avenue wrote a letter to the man in charge of the Interstate Division's Bureau of Right of Way Negotiations. "I have been waiting some time," he wrote, "for the city to buy this property from me for the expressway."

> The delay is causing a great hardship on me and my family, since I cannot make any improvements to the property; nor can I rent the store portion of my property. Whenever anyone is interested in renting it, they change their mind when they learn of the expressway coming through my property.
>
> I have had a wonderful opportunity to buy a house in the suburbs, and I could not let this opportunity go by, since I know I will have to move eventually, and who knows what I will be able to find in the future.
>
> I understand the city can buy a property from people in my position. I, therefore, urgently request you to purchase this property now because of the hardships these delays have caused me.[69]

The Interstate Division still waited more than a year to send his appraisal. Other exchanges went on for even longer.

> July 11, 1968
>
> I would like to have my home appraised at an early date if possible. I understand the Expressway will be coming through this section which I live. I, Mrs. Mary G. Briscoe 2724 Edmondson Avenue on corner of Glenolden Avenue. Please let me hear from you soon as possible.
>
> Yours truly
> (Mrs.) Mary G. Briscoe

The agency soon replied.

> July 15, 1968
>
> Dear Mrs. Briscoe:
> In response to your letter of July 11th, I wish to advise that we will attempt to assign an appraisal contract for your property within the next 30 days.

More than a month later:

August 31, 1968

Dear Sir;
My letter was written to you in July. I received an answer on July the 16th, 1968. Stating that you would if possible, make an appraisal of my property within thirty days. Since that time I have not heard anything. Therefore, I would like to know something before the winter sets in.

Thanking you kindly,
Very truly Yours,
Mary G. Briscoe

And the reply:

September 3, 1968

Dear Mrs. Briscoe:
To date, we have been unable to make the appraisal assignment. However, we will make the assignment as soon as an appraiser is available.

It went on like this for months.

January 1, 1969

I would love to sell my house to the City. Would you please negotiate with me as soon as possible. This is my third letter since July. One man has been here.

Yours truly
(Mrs.) Mary G. Briscoe

January 13, 1969

I would love to sell my house to the City. Would you please negotiate with me as soon as possible. I was told by Mr. Donald Schaefer that my letter to him had been forward to you. Hope to hear from you soon as possible.

Yours truly
(Mrs.) Mary G. Briscoe

January 15, 1969

I am writing to have an appraisal of my house and enter into negotiations. This is the third or fourth letter to you since July, one man has been here to appraise the house and no one else. I have seen some homes but could not do anything until you all do something. Please give this matter an early attention. I will be waiting to hear from you.

P.S. I am home in the mornings until one P.M. after that someone else hear in the evenings.

Sincerely
(Mrs.) Mary G. Briscoe

January 25, 1969

I am interested in appraisal of my home and enter into negotiation as once. This is the fourth letter to you since July, and only one man has been here to appraise. I called your Office Tuesday morning your secretary said that you had one appraisal in your Office waiting for one of your men to take care of it and bring you the report, then you would get in touch with me. I have been waiting and no answer. Please give this your attention at once please. I would like to get straight to March 1, 1969 is the dead line. I hope to be on my way in a new home by then.

Sincerely yours
Mary G. Briscoe[70]

Finally, in April 1969, Mary Briscoe's offer from the Interstate Division arrived: $6,434.00 in "fair market" value plus a $4,900 supplemental payment, for a house she and her husband had bought in 1954 for $9,000 plus some $1,500 more in ground rent.[71]

Homeowners, trapped in limbo, begged for somebody's attention. "I am very anxious to sell and get settled in an apartment. I wrote a letter and a man came out several months ago but haven't heard anything since," one wrote.[72] "Since I have received a notice of the Expressway coming through this area I would like to get paid for my house as soon as possible as I have seen another house that I would like to buy and I am anxious to move," said another.[73] "My husband and I have been scanning around for houses; however, it is a dubious situation, not knowing how much we'll have to spend on a down payment for another house," a third explained. "We were wondering, if we could possibly find out what our settlement is going to be?"[74]

Absentee owners did not qualify for the supplemental payment, but many landlords who sold quickly came out closer to whole in the end than homeowners did. One was paid $6,025 for a house he'd paid $5,500 for in 1956.[75] Another got $3,634 for a property that had cost him $3,600.[76] (And this was after more than a decade of wringing out profits from it in all kinds of ways.) However, in some cases absentee owners did experience the same administrative disregard from the Interstate Division. In the summer of 1968, one wrote:

> I have a property at 2702 Edmondson Ave. It is in the East-West Expressway. I have to put tenants out. They are not paying. It will be difficult to rent now knowing they will have to move in the near future, and if I do rent it I will have to spend around $500 to $600 for painting and fixing. I am requesting immediate appraisal, or would you suggest I spend money and try to rent this house. Would appreciate it very much if I can hear from you soon.[77]

A year later, the Interstate Division sent the appraisal.

> My tenant is moving Thursday Nov 1-1968. I cannot afford to allow a long vacancy. I am a widow + also don't approve of leaving the empty property without heat during the winter months.[78]

This one took a year and a half.

Just as their neighbors to the east did, the people who lived at the western end of the Rosemont condemnation corridor often found themselves upside down in the end. Houses purchased for $10,000 eight or ten years before were valued at $6,100 or $6,300.[79] Meanwhile, the Interstate Division found every loophole it could to avoid paying the supplements people were owed. People who moved out before the rules said they could—even just a month or a few weeks before—did not qualify. People who moved out but whose relatives stayed behind in the homes they owned did not qualify. People who traveled a lot for work did not qualify.[80] Even some of the Interstate Division's own men thought a little more generosity might be in order. "The writer must comment that it is his feeling that the strict interpretation and application of the law appears to place a burden upon the owners in question," an official wrote in one case, in which a mother had died and her daughter, a (white) "deaf-mute" who had lived in the home since 1944, had moved out before settlement "because of the fact that the neighborhood was not a very safe place for someone in her condition to live."[81] "It is my personal opinion that the law was not intended to cause hardship and/or burden," he wrote in another case, in which a husband had neglected to add his wife to the deed before he died, leaving her a tenant in the eyes of the law. "There is a distinct possibility that a moral obligation exists."[82]

Sometimes these appeals worked, and people got something closer to the money they were owed. Most of the time, though, they did not. A homeowner was free to push back on the Interstate Division's offer, and ultimately free to refuse to sell altogether. But the appraisers' discretion to set the prices for negotiation gave the roadbuilders all the power. As far as the East–West Expressway was concerned, the people who lived in the Rosemont condemnation corridor were numbers in a ledger, data on a punch card—and, still, vehicles for transferring even more wealth to speculators.

A New Market

If they wanted to keep their supplemental payment, a person who sold their house in the Rosemont highway corridor needed to buy another one someplace else within the year. The phone book shows that for most, this meant moving north and west, often following in the footsteps of the white people they'd bought their houses from in the first place. It meant spending what it cost to buy more expensive houses in newer, more suburban neighborhoods, snaring themselves once again in a real estate market that was built to bleed them dry.

By the late 1960s, some things *were* fairer about Baltimore's housing market. For example, blockbusting had been outlawed in Maryland in 1966.[83] In April 1968, President Lyndon B. Johnson signed a new Civil Rights Act, often called the Fair Housing Act, which prohibited the racist "steering" that limited housing options for Black families while driving up their costs. Yet the difference these changes made on the ground was limited. For Black shoppers in and around Baltimore, the supply of options was still constrained. And although the loans' terms may have been better, the sellers and the lenders were all the same: the Kappelmans, the Goldsekers, Straw Man, Baltimore Federal, Uptown Federal, New Michael's. Consequently, even the Rosemonters who had managed to pay off their mortgages and escape the speculators' trap before they lost their homes to the highway were pulled right back into it.

According to one Activists, Inc. report, two federal laws signed into law in 1968, the Fair Housing Act and the Housing and Urban Development Act, made that "the last big year for wheeling and dealing in real estate in Baltimore."[84] Yet the East–West Expressway ensured it was a big year indeed. Across the Rosemont condemnation corridor, the Interstate Division paid speculators every dollar they were owed before homeowners saw a cent, then served those same speculators thousands of customers for more expensive homes and bigger loans at higher rates on recently busted blocks in Edmonson Village, Gwynn Oak, and Woodmere.[85]

That spring, R.A.M. activist Clarence Landrum and his wife, Elizabeth, had sold their house on Lauretta Avenue to the Interstate Division. Appraisers had valued the place's "fair market value" at $5,175, $445 less than the Landrums had borrowed from Baltimore Federal to buy it in 1952. Their "supplemental payment," the extra money R.A.M. had gotten included in the 1968 highway bill, was $3,600—more than many of their neighbors got, but less than the $5,000 maximum.[86] The Landrums cashed their check, paid off the $1,084 remaining on the Lauretta Avenue mortgage, then put a big down payment on a new place: a three-bedroom semi-detached on a quiet lane in

Hunting Ridge. It was about three miles west of the old place, past Edmondson Village, in a cozy suburb whose streets looped and whorled.[87] It looked like the Landrums were moving up in the world.

But if the Landrums had wanted to leave the house on Lauretta Avenue, they would have left it on their own terms. They had not left, not until the expressway forced them out. Adding insult to injury, now the family was more in debt than ever. On Lauretta Avenue, they paid $52 a month. They had kept up the payments, repaid most of the money they owed, and acquired a significant amount of equity, unlike their neighbors who bought on installment. In the new house, even with the big down payment the Interstate Division's check made possible, they paid twice as much every month.[88] "I was victimized by the highway," Clarence Landrum told a *Sun* reporter. "I'm further in debt now than I was 18 years ago."[89]

6

"If You Are Dead, You Are Dead": How the Highway Stalled in Rosemont (1968)

Early in 1968, activists from all over the city gathered in the Archdiocese of Baltimore's sleek new office tower downtown "to decide," the meeting's organizers wrote, "whether the city of Baltimore is to live in or to drive through." Its result was a new coalition, a multiracial alphabet soup of thirty-five neighborhood groups from all over the city—including the Relocation Action Movement (R.A.M.) and the Rosemont Neighborhood Improvement Association (R.N.I.A.)—known as the Movement Against Destruction (MAD).[1] MAD's goal was straightforward but not simple: to stop Baltimore from becoming a "motorized wasteland" and make it, instead, "a decent place in which people can live."[2]

A report from the conference reminded readers where things stood.

> At issue in Baltimore are 21 miles of proposed interstate expressways. The trunk line of the system is the 13.4 mile East–West Expressway. It enters the city on the west side as I-70N, traverses one of Baltimore's stream-valley parks, Leakin Park, bisects a stable, middle-class Negro community called Rosemont, travels down the Franklin-Mulberry corridor, and dips down through South Baltimore where it connects with the 3.7 mile Southwest Expressway, I-95, coming in from Washington.
>
> Then it slices off a corner of Federal Hill, a historic city park and vantage point, crosses the Inner Harbor by means as yet undetermined, and heads through the heart of Fells Point, an area of the 18th century architectural charm and contemporary diversity, which is the last remaining waterfront residential neighborhood in Baltimore and one of the oldest, according to preservationists, on the east side and heading north toward Philadelphia.[3]

"It is obvious from their actions," the report continued:

that the "road gang," made of politicians, highway technocrats and lobbyists for car, oil, concrete, and other special interests, is not concerned with transportation. Their real interest is in road-building and what concerns them is not people but profit.

Besides bribing and browbeating the cities into accepting the expressways, the road gang has also insisted on deciding where they were to go. Usually this meant laying out the shortest route between two points and bending it when politics requires. In Baltimore, the routes favor suburbanites and industry and the poor people downtown pay the price. It is a clear case of "white men's roads through black men's homes."[4]

It was true. If everything went to plan, some three thousand families, most of them Black, were going to lose their homes. More than seven hundred already had. The city was also going to lose some hundred acres of park land, when it didn't have any to spare. And the whole thing was going to cost more than $400 million.[5]

"It would seem," the activists concluded, "that a better way of running a road could be found than this."[6]

Two years earlier, and a few months after Baltimore's city council voted to condemn the first segment of the East–West Expressway, the R.N.I.A. held its first meeting in almost a decade. But it wasn't about the highway. "It has come to our attention," recently elected president Joseph Wiles wrote, "that plans have been proposed for the establishment of HIGH RISE APARTMENTS AND MULTIPLE DWELLINGS" on the lot where the Board of School Commissioners had first tried to build the Belmont Elementary School nine years earlier, and on the wedge of land next to the railroad tracks where the Bryant Packing Box factory now stood.[7] "We have reorganized our neighborhood association in order to protest and find legal means to divert the building of these type dwellings in our community," the R.N.I.A.'s mailer said. "WE MUST ACT NOW!! Won't you attend our next meeting and become a part of this organization to help maintain the integrity of this neighborhood and protect the value of our homes?"[8]

At the time, Baltimore had twenty public housing developments, most of which were arranged in a pair of decaying parentheses around the city center. Each was big enough to house hundreds of families. Four were the enormous high-rise tower complexes so many cities had used federal urban-renewal money to build after 1954.[9] None was especially old, but Baltimore's Urban Renewal and Housing Authority (BURHA) had quickly proved to be a terrible landlord, and the high-rises especially had begun to feel stark, dispiriting, and dangerous.[10] "The image now," planner Anthony Downs said in 1968, "is of high-rise buildings that are unsafe to be in and filled with broken Negro families. The term 'public housing' conjures up a vision of thousands of unstable people concentrated in huge buildings so that they swamp surrounding neighborhoods and schools."[11] In a conversation with historian Rhonda Y. Williams, one former resident of a Baltimore public housing development put the same image in blunter terms. To outsiders, she said, her neighbors were "lazy, no-good, dumb, ignorant, don't want nothing, want somebody to give them something." "People look down on you," said another.[12]

Joseph Wiles knew that Baltimore's housing authority was not actually going to build any high-rise apartments in his neighborhood. Zoning rules prohibited the construction of anything taller than four stories there.[13] More to the point, officials were explicitly planning an experiment in a *new* kind of public housing: "scatter site," in bureaucratese. Instead of stuffing a city's poorest people into a few huge complexes, the idea went, housing authorities would contract with private developers to build smaller apartment buildings all over the city. These, officials explained a little too candidly, would "take the people out of the slums, and the slums out of the people."[14]

The R.N.I.A.'s members found much to dislike in BURHA's plan. As they would later explain in a letter to the *Sun* newspaper: "The objections raised by our association have been based upon 1) population density and overcrowding of our area, 2) inadequate school and recreation facilities, 3) insufficient sanitation and police services, 4) deplorable traffic and transportation conditions, and 5) the fostering of 'de facto' segregation and establishment of a ghetto."[15] Also, when it came down to it, the people who lived in Rosemont didn't want to share their blocks and schools with, they said, "the type of people that occupy these project homes."[16] They also didn't think they should have to, just because they were Black. "This plan," one Rosemonter said, "is out of [the] general complexion of the neighborhood."[17]

The people the R.N.I.A. represented still had the same vision of who they were, what they had, what they were owed, and why they were owed it: because, as they said, they were "citizens, tax-payers, homeowners."[18] And in their defense of the neighborhood's "general complexion"—and in an example of what historian N. D. B. Connolly calls the "contradictions of self-interest and black solidarity"—the R.N.I.A.'s members said the same kinds of things about the people who lived in Baltimore's public housing that white people like Helen and Herbert Bowers might once have said about them.[19] "The majority are of questionable character," Gwendolyn Mickle said at one meeting, and "are idle living on welfare, therefore free to roam the area, which can lead to crime and trespassing on private property."[20] "Public housing is mainly populated by people who have many more children than they can care for or supervise properly," added attorney Archie Williams. "This is an influx on the community."[21] "We're not against housing," Mary Rosemond told a reporter later, but the people the new buildings would bring into the neighborhood "can't take care of themselves." That, she added, is "why they're there."[22]

Part of this response was simple snobbery. "Regardless of one's color," Connolly writes, "the suburban ideal included a discernible distance from poor black people," and "propertied Negroes had long held as one of Jim Crow's greatest evils . . . the elision of class distinctions" that made it possible to tell, and keep, "riffraff" apart from their betters.[23] Certainly there was an element of what Dallas Nicholas had said in the disagreement over Belmont Elementary in 1957. Couldn't BURHA just choose some other site involving cheaper houses instead? But solidarity with the poor Black people BURHA wanted to make their neighbors would have cost Rosemont's homeowners a great deal, too. It would have meant yielding again to the same old idea that *they* should always be the ones to sacrifice for Baltimore so people like the Bowerses would never have to.

At the end of the year, the R.N.I.A. mailed out its first annual report since 1957. "Have we been able to create or instill some interest in the urgent need for a unified neighborhood?" R.N.I.A. President Wiles asked in the report's introduction. "Have we increased the desire among our neighbors to be our brother's keeper; to help preserve, beautify, and protect each other's property and belongings?"[24] This idea—that being "our brother's keeper" meant preserving and protecting our brother's property—was as American as anything, as American as an expressway. Yet when it came to Rosemont, the people who held the power in Baltimore still didn't share it. Would they ever?

The Urban Design Concept Team in Rosemont

What one neighbor called "this fight to prevent public houses from being built in our neighborhood" would drag on for years.[25] In the meantime, something else came up.

The man in charge of the new Interstate Division for Baltimore City was an engineer named Joseph M. Axelrod. Axelrod was not, at least according to his boss at the federal Bureau of Public Roads, a "bull-dozing maniac in a black hat tearing everything apart just for the sport of it," though he was given to telling reporters things that made him seem this way.[26] He was just clear on what his job was: to finally get Baltimore's 10-D expressway system built.

Joseph Axelrod didn't think the 10-D plan was perfect. On the contrary, he explained in a later speech at the Engineers Club while activists took notes.

"He admitted," one scribbled, "that, although the East–West Expressway was first planned 30 years ago, and seemed like a great idea at the time, if it were planned today it would be done much differently." "But," he said, "if you don't build the expressway, downtown Baltimore will die. . . . And while the in-city expressway concept is old, it is too late to change it now."[27] From Axelrod's point of view, it was time to stop dithering and start bulldozing.

In the middle of 1967, at around the same time the city council passed the 10-D condemnation lines through the Rosemont area, officials at the Interstate Division and the Bureau of Public Roads assembled an outfit they named, not very precisely, the Urban Design Concept Team (UDCT). The UDCT was an "interdisciplinary team of experts" that included city planners, environmental scientists, sociologists, architects from the tony out-of-town firm Skidmore, Owings, and Merrill, and eventually a complement of engineers from roadbuilders J. E. Greiner.[28] Its purpose, one of the architects wrote, was to devise a "systematic, total process" for the design and construction of urban expressways, "to plan the urban highway not in isolation, but in full relation to the needs of the surrounding area and the city as a whole."[29]

Another architect on the team, the famous Nathaniel Owings, made the same point with a little more pizzazz. As far as he was concerned, he wrote in 1969, the UDCT was supposed to be finding a way "to lace tubes of traffic through vital parts without unduly disturbing the living organism of the city."[30]

It sounded great in theory. It wasn't going to work in practice. In particular, as became clear to the UDCT's non-engineer members almost immediately, it wasn't going to work in Rosemont. As James Dilts explained in the *Sun*, if the team's brief was to "blend the expressway" into the neighborhood's fabric as "the warp and woof of a priceless tapestry," here the operation was going to be something much closer to "'blending' a buzz saw into a Persian rug."[31]

The UDCT spent the 1967 Christmas season in the neighborhood: wandering through and around the condemnation zone, meeting neighbors, taking photographs, and collecting facts and figures. The group's *Rosemont Area Studies*, published in February 1968, introduced the situation in the 1967 condemnation corridor to highway officials and other readers who had never visited the place or even, clearly, thought much about it. "The Rosemont area is a stable, middle-class neighborhood located in West Baltimore," the report explained.[32] "The impacts of this alignment would be severe; the proposed road would (1) bisect the neighborhood, severing important linkages and isolating some 500 households from the rest of the community, (2) dislocate 68 businesses and institutions which form the focal point of the community and which provide some 490 jobs, and (3) dislocate approximately 880 dwelling units with difficult relocation problems."[33]

In Rosemont's defense, the UDCT's report reproduced familiar assumptions about the kinds of places, and people, that usually found themselves at the sharp end of urban renewal in Baltimore.

> Home ownership—Rosemont has a substantially higher rate of home ownership than Baltimore City as a whole. In 1960 its proportion of homeowners was 71 percent, vs. 55 percent for the city. The Concept Team's 1968 survey indicates that this level of ownership has been maintained, with 72 percent of all households interviewed owning their residences. A high rate of ownership exists generally throughout the area, both within the condemnation zone and outside it.
>
> Investment in properties—One important measure of attachment to home and neighborhood is extent of <u>recent</u> investment in improving the property. Of almost 300 owners responding to the question, 57 percent said they had done some remodeling (other than painting) since 1960. About half of these (46 percent) had spent $1,000 or more; 14 percent, $2,500 or more.
>
> Age of residents—Rosemont is predominantly an area of middle-aged and elderly householders. Sixty percent of all household heads are age 50 or over, and one-fifth are past 65. These facts are doubtless related to the high level of stability; middle-aged and elderly households are among those least likely to move.
>
> Plans to move—In the Rosemont area as a whole, only 18 percent of residents have plans to move from their present homes. This figure is well within normal limits of mobility for urban neighborhoods. Within the condemnation lines, however, 43 percent plan to move. But when asked if they would still move if the freeway were not coming through, fully half of these said they would prefer to stay.

In interviews, the people who lived in and around the condemnation zone echoed this point of view.

> We keep up our property and we take pride in it. We're fighting this expressway. We don't want to face the expressway, but if it pays me a fair amount, I'll have to move rather than look out with the expressway under my nose, but we don't want to move. If it was a blight area, we wouldn't care, but we all worked hard for what we have and don't want to move unless I am forced to.
>
> We are too old to move. We just have a few dollars to pay and it's all ours. And nobody will sell to old folks. They won't give us a mortgage. It's just awful. I hope we don't have to move. I didn't want to, but if they're building the expressway, we'll have to.
>
> We're getting too old to buy another. After you live in a home for 17 years, you don't want to move! We have our house paid for . . . so it would be a terrible hardship on us unless they gave us an awful good price for this house. I don't want no apartment—I've had a house all my married life and I couldn't stand to be cooped up in no apartment.

ANALYSIS OF THE OFFICIAL INTERSTATE EXPRESSWAY ROUTE

The 10-D expressway through Rosemont, Urban Design Concept Team, *Rosemont Area Studies*, February 1968. Courtesy of University of Baltimore Special Collections and Archives.

We're trying to find out just how close it will come to us. Nobody seems to know exactly. We wouldn't like living so close to an expressway, but we're too close to retirement to think about buying another house.

Don't want to leave unless we have to. Children are close to school and we hope to be all paid for soon and it's awful to leave when you're used to things.

We've put so much money into the house.[34]

The *Rosemont Area Studies* and the R.N.I.A. were making the same basic argument. The Rosemont condemnation corridor wasn't "a blight area." It was just Black. And there was no way to blend or weave or lace the 10-D expressway into its warp and woof. "So severe were the dislocation and disruptive impacts of the established 'given' highway right-of-way," the report concluded, "that only a different road location could provide a reasonable solution."[35]

The Holy Week Riots and the 3-A Map

It's impossible to say what would have happened to the UDCT's report under ordinary circumstances, because ordinary circumstances were not what happened next. Around dinnertime on April 6, 1968, two days after James

"IF YOU ARE DEAD, YOU ARE DEAD" 99

Earl Ray shot Martin Luther King Jr. in Memphis, someone smashed the window of the Fashion Hat Shop on Gay Street in East Baltimore.[36] Then somebody else heaved a firebomb into the display at the Ideal Furniture Store, and the Baltimore riot began. Police scrambled to cordon the streets while teenagers squeezed past carrying whatever they could grab from the open storefronts: clothes in plastic from the dry cleaner, melting bricks of ice cream, television sets, a matched pair of lamps. All night long, burglar alarms clanged.[37] The next morning, Palm Sunday, the protests had reached "old" West Baltimore, turning it into (the *Sun* reported) an "ugly no-man's land."[38]

Impact of the 10-D expressway through Rosemont, Urban Design Concept Team, *Rosemont Area Studies*, February 1968. Courtesy of University of Baltimore Special Collections and Archives.

By Monday afternoon, "the looting [had] spread out of the Negro slums . . . and into middle-class shopping centers."[39] Rioters "scourged" every store on Edmondson Avenue west of Fremont: only a few burned, but almost all were sacked.[40] Years later, one neighbor remembered the bus ride home from her after-school job that day. In Rosemont's commercial corridor, she said, "all you could hear was screaming, breaking of glass."[41]

"The coming of violence to Baltimore's ghetto," the American Friends Service Committee's *Report on Baltimore Civil Disorders, 1968* began, "was no surprise."[42] And the East Baltimore neighborhoods where the riot began were just the kinds of places people thought of when they thought of "Baltimore's ghetto." They were among the oldest parts of the city, and the poorest. They were also surrounded by another dismal sickle of urban-renewal projects—the Latrobe Homes, the Jones Falls Expressway, the Somerset Court Homes, the Orleans Street Viaduct, the Douglass Homes, and the 59-acre Johns Hopkins hospital campus under construction that neighbors called "the plantation"—which together had dislodged thousands of Black families from their homes.[43] What housing remained was overcrowded, neglected by its landlords, and much too expensive. Police were abusive, shopkeepers were exploitative, and on and on. "When one accumulates a list of the complaints" of the people who lived in neighborhoods like these, the committee's report concluded, "one tends to wonder why the retaliation was not worse."[44]

Also, as the National Advisory Commission on Civil Disorders (often called the Kerner Commission) would explain in its report later that year, the nation's most combustible neighborhoods were often the same ones "cut up by ribbons of superhighways," neighborhoods where, one resident put it, "planners make plans and then simply tell people what they are going to do."[45] The 1967 Rosemont condemnation corridor was not remotely "Baltimore's ghetto," but it did make it easy to see how the East–West Expressway—the meat-axe maps, the desultory condemnation processes, the property owners turned into prey—contributed to the fury on display that week. In fact, geo-referenced maps of "incidents of looting, arson, and vandalism" show them following the 10-D's path as clearly as if they'd had its coordinates and a compass in hand.[46] Gay Street and Rosemont looked very different from one another, but they were both places white Baltimore had already declared expendable, places where "ugly no-man's land" had been public policy for thirty years. The expressway that connected them embodied what the Maryland Crime Investigating Commission called "a sort of 'cold-shoulderism' toward the Negro that excludes their feelings and their rights": cold shoulders, in Baltimore, made of concrete.[47]

For years, roadbuilders had been pressing the same case for a transitive property of urban renewal. If expressways were for slum clearance, and if a neighborhood was to be cleared for an expressway, then that neighborhood must be a slum. After the 1968 riot, white Baltimore started to see that equation was a lie, or more than a lie. Rosemont, a reporter wrote in *City* magazine that fall, was what "every explosive American city would most like to have: a highly stable and cohesive neighborhood."[48]

In front of this backdrop, the Urban Design Concept Team proposed an alternate route for the Rosemont segment of the East–West Expressway known as the 3-A. The 3-A linked the western end of the 1966 condemnation corridor to Leakin Park just as the 10-D had, but it twisted out of plumb at Pulaski Street and followed the railroad tracks diagonally south and west through disused industrial tracts. Then it burrowed under the Western Cemetery before lurching up into the park.[49] In other words, it avoided residential Rosemont almost entirely.

The 3-A would take just 160 houses instead of nearly 1,000. It would also require (Dilts wrote) "the relocation of some 3,600 bodies, as against roughly the same number of live ones in Rosemont."[50] These were 3,600 reasons why the roadbuilders hadn't drawn the route this way to begin with: In 1850, the Maryland General Assembly had declared that the land was "to be used as a public cemetery forever, for the burial of the dead, and for no other purpose." Also, more to the point, "no road, canal, or public highway, shall be opened through the said Cemetery."[51] But the assembly had said a lot of things in 1850, and policymakers in 1968 weren't treating all of them as immutable truths. In the *Afro-American*, one Black member of the UDCT guessed why this one was so enduring: "You can't disturb the dead white folks in Western Cemetery in an effort to spare the homes of the black folk in Rosemont."[52]

In December 1967, when the UDCT started its work, the Interstate Division had made no promises about the outcome. It had only agreed to consider the team's presentation and "decide whether alternative alignments could be investigated."[53] Had the events of Holy Week changed the context enough that the Interstate Division would agree to investigate the new route? At first, the answer appeared to be no. "I think we create more uproar by considering other routes," Interstate Division Chief Axelrod told the R.N.I.A. in the summer of 1968. "We were reluctant to consider it in the first place. That route there"—the 10-D—"is the final one."[54]

But this was Baltimore, where (the *Sun* editorialized) "expressway plans . . . are 'final' only until such time as a determination is made to have a fresh study."[55] "Is it going to bypass Rosemont or not?" Fifth District Councilman Alexander Stark asked in October. "The influential people know what the proposal is, but those people whose homes are going to be demolished don't know."[56] "We are right at the verge of a definite answer," the mayor responded.[57] "As far as I'm concerned, all the options are open," federal highway administrator Lowell Bridwell said in November.[58] Finally, on Christmas Eve 1968—and on the theory that "I don't want to be responsible for what may be regarded as idiocy or worse in years to come"—Mayor D'Alesandro announced that he was going to back the 3-A plan, steering the East–West Expressway around Rosemont instead of through it.[59] In January 1969, the State Roads Commission, the Bureau of Public Roads, and the Federal Highway Administration approved the new route. Now, at least officially, it seemed like Rosemont would be spared.

Yet it was still condemned.

The 10-D Condemnation Lines

By January 1969, when the State Roads Commission decided to adopt the 3-A expressway route bypassing Rosemont, the 880 houses in the 10-D expressway corridor through the neighborhood had been condemned for a year and a half. So far the Interstate Division had purchased 249 of them. Also, according to a memo from the Department of Public Works, it "had under active discussion the acquisition of a number of other properties."[60] In this context, the 3-A map wasn't purely a win. It also made things more complicated.

Nobody thought it was fair for officials to leave homeowners in the lurch by withdrawing offers they had already made or refusing to continue negotiations, especially since (the Department of Public Works explained) "a number of owner-occupants were actively engaged in the purchase of another home or other re-location."[61] On the other hand, the Interstate Division no longer had any need for the properties in the path of the 10-D route, and it wasn't made of money. And as Joseph Wiles explained to a reporter, an open-ended process of property acquisition could easily become "a leeway and a loophole to city officials who want to come back to this route."[62] So the Interstate Division split the difference. As of January 16, the day the Federal Highway Administration approved the 3-A route, it stopped buying commercial and landlord-owned properties in the 10-D condemnation zone. Owner-occupants, on the other hand, had until March 1 to decide whether they still wanted to sell.[63]

The March 1 deadline ratcheted the sword over the neighborhood a little lower. From the beginning, it had been clear that (as the UDCT's report noted) the 10-D plan had the potential to "tip the entire neighborhood into rapid decline, if those residents of sections adjoining the route who leave as a result of disruption and inconvenience caused by the freeway are replaced by others not of the same high calibre."[64] But until now, homeowners' agency had been limited to *when*, not if, they were going to sell. This new choice was much thornier, and it reintroduced that familiar tension between self-interest and solidarity.

From one point of view, "high calibre" people needed to stay in their homes if Rosemont was to remain *Rosemont*. "It is important," the Concept Team urged in the *Interstate Expressway Newsletter* in December 1968, "that homeowners in the Rosemont area . . . stay where they are unless they have already made plans to move." "Which route the Expressway will take in relation to Rosemont is not known at present," it continued. "There is still a good chance that it will remain . . . an appealing community to those who live there."[65] "When Should a Home Owner in a Condemnation Area Sell His Home????????" a flyer posted by the Citizens' Planning and Housing Association (CPHA) asked. "If you desire to live in your home, there is no reason why you must sell your home now," it answered.

> Just because a home is within the condemnation area, it does not mean that the city will require that home for an expressway or boulevard.
> In some condemnation areas, the city is considering alternate routes for the expressway and it is possible that the adoption of a particular route may mean that fewer houses are required.
> . . . if you desire to live in your home there is no need to sell your home, unless and until, the Interstate Department tells you, it needs your home for a right of way and that it needs it soon.[66]

From another point of view, though, letting the March 1 deadline pass was a risky gamble. First, the 3-A expressway through the neighborhood was still an expressway through the neighborhood, and many people didn't want to live in a neighborhood with an expressway through it. Second, as the *Sun* pointed out, "whole generation of Baltimoreans have grown up, married and become parents while hearing 'once and for all' decisions as to the mythical East–West expressway."[67] The people who lived in Rosemont knew better than to trust that this decision was going to be *the* decision. Third, hundreds of neighbors had already moved away, or were preparing to, so the place was already changing. Fourth, the neighborhood had been condemned for a year and a half, and had been slated for condemnation for years before that. Despite activists' best efforts to encourage neighbors to keep investing in their houses, things were starting to look a little frayed.

Some neighbors had also recently lost their homes to the speculators they'd bought them from, which is part of the reason why Rosemont now had more landlord-owned properties than it ever had. This problem made the others worse. "People around here are letting their property go down," one

Rosemont renter had told an interviewer from the UDCT. "Landlord keeps saying no use to do anything because of the expressway, and you know they just don't do like they would if the expressway wasn't worrying them." "I like the neighborhood," another said. "I get along with everyone here, but the house is going to pieces, and I can't get the landlord to do a thing."[68]

Also, the place was getting *more* crowded instead of less. "Dislocation and relocation of families because of Urban Renewal Projects and the East–West Expressway has caused a tremendous population shift into our area," R.N.I.A. officers Joseph Wiles and Rose Gallop wrote the *Sun* in June 1969. "Many houses were converted to multiple family dwellings. There was a fifteen percent increase in population between 1961 and 1967 and the trend is toward an increase rather than a decrease in 1969 and 1970," and "along with this great influx of housing and people into the area, there has not been a proportionate increase in facilities and services to the Community."[69]

For all these reasons, neighbors told a reporter that January, "because of the destructive years of decay and indecision, some of us [still] wish to leave."[70] In January and February 1969, they flooded the Interstate Division with letters. "I am very much interested in selling my home to the City," one read. "I am in the Rosemont Area and according to your statement, I have to let you know before March 1969."[71] "I would like to enter into negotiation for acquisition of my property," said another. "I understand that March 1 is deadline for those who wish to sell."[72] "March 1, 1969 is the dead line. I hope to be on my way in a new home by then."[73] "I am in the path of what was to be the proposed East–West Expressway. Although the route has been changed, I would still consider selling my property."[74]

Because of the extra time the owner-occupants got that the speculator landlords didn't, for once the landlords were the ones stuck taking the bigger loss. For example, at the end of February 1969, a representative from the Goldseker firm wrote the Interstate Division asking it to buy seven properties it owned in the Rosemont condemnation zone. "Since the enactment of the Condemnation Ordinance and the publicity it received," he wrote, "it has been impossible to retain the better type resident and in many times, new tenants are reluctant to move in the dwelling because of the decay caused by the boarding and vandalization of the vacant properties in this area."[75]

"Please be advised that this Division is working under explicit instructions received from Mayor D'Alesandro's office," the chief of the Bureau of Right of Way Negotiations replied. "These instructions require that all property in the area involved, which was not owner-occupied, must request acquisition in writing by Jan. 17, 1969. This date, unfortunately, is firm. . . . Obviously, since your initial request is dated February 27th, we are unable to purchase any of your property involved at this time."[76]

In April, the Ranch Realty Company filed a complaint in Circuit Court on the grounds that the city was "discriminating against non-resident owners of property in the Rosemont area" by granting owner-occupants but not landlords the extra time to sell.[77] "Discriminating" was pretty rich, but it was true that once the Federal Highway Administration approved the 3-A route, absentee owners had only had a few days to respond. This, no doubt, is the simplest reason so many more landlords than homeowners hung onto their properties even after they were condemned. Another reason may be that speculators felt freer than homeowners did to push back against the Interstate Division's initial offers, prolonging negotiations. Correspondence in the Department of Public Works' files suggest that when the clock ran out, the Interstate Division simply stopped haggling.[78] But also, even though the real estate men complained the condemnation ordinance had caused a "serious decline" in property values in the neighborhood, the math was different for them.[79] They had paid less for their properties to begin with, and they weren't trying to build homes and lives in the Rosemont condemnation corridor; they were trying to find tenants to exploit. And in Baltimore, expressway or no expressway, there was no shortage of those. That meant that when speculators decided whether to sell or not, they were solving for different variables, and many concluded that hanging on to their properties was a good bet.

In any case, even though city, state, and federal officials all agreed in principle that the East–West Expressway was going to take the 3-A route around Rosemont instead of the 10-D route through it, by the end of 1969 the Interstate Division had acquired 486 of the 880 residential properties in the 10-D condemnation zone. 105 of these came from absentee owners who had sold early. The rest came from owner-occupants.[80] Consequently, highway officials started to back away from their commitment to the 3-A route. "Individual owners took the money and ran," Joseph Axelrod said in a sour speech at the Engineers Club, "leaving only absentee landlords which deteriorated the neighborhood."[81] So long as that was the case, he told a reporter that spring, "maybe it doesn't make so much sense to not go through the [10-D] corridor after all."[82]

Without an official promise that their homes would be safe from the expressway, nobody could live comfortably in the Rosemont area. In May 1969, new R.N.I.A. president Rose Gallop wrote a letter to Mayor D'Alesandro asking him to lift the 10-D condemnation lines. "Since it has been repeatedly stated by you that there would not be an East–West Expressway route through the Rosemont community," she wrote, "we can see no reason for, or understand why these ordinances are any longer required." "Residents of this community still feel insecure and uneasy, when a threat of an expressway is ever present and imminent as long as these ordinances still exist," she continued. "Removal of these ordinances would be a gesture of good-faith by the administration and would also give tangible evidence that you have a sincere desire to preserve and re-establish the stability of this neighborhood."[83]

The mayor refused. "It is not feasible or politically possible to remove the existing condemnation ordinances," he replied, "unless, at the same time, the new line is fixed and a new ordinance is introduced simultaneously."[84] He implied that his hands were somehow tied by the federal government, but this wasn't true, and the R.N.I.A.'s members knew it. Mary Rosemond took the pen. "In order to present a complete report to the Rosemont Neighborhood Improvement Association," she wrote the mayor, "I have tried to locate and identify that Federal law which states the condemnation line cannot be lifted until a new route is chosen. To date I have been unsuccessful in finding this information. I am now asking your direction concerning the specific identity of the law and where a copy of it may be secured."[85] In response, D'Alesandro mailed a copy of his earlier letter to Rose Gallop back to her, with a peevish cover note reiterating its contents. "It is not feasible or politically possible to remove the existing condemnation ordinance unless, at the same time, the new line is fixed and a new ordinance is introduced simultaneously," the mayor snipped. "This is a matter of practical necessity and therefore administration policy at this time."[86]

What "practical necessity" meant was this: The highway's advocates thought if they lifted the 10-D condemnation line before securing condemnations for the 3-A route, they would never get those new condemnations, and Baltimore's entire expressway system would die. They were probably right. And so, as an insurance policy for themselves, the roadbuilders kept Rosemont's houses condemned. The neighborhood's problems kept multiplying. And "if you are dead," one official said in 1969, "you are dead. It doesn't matter what kind of poison you die from."[87]

The 3-A Hearing

In response to the citizen uprisings of the previous years, in January 1969 the federal Department of Transportation had begun to require "corridor public hearings" "to ensure that an opportunity is afforded for effective participation by interested persons in the process of determining the need for, and the location of, a Federal-aid highway."[88] The 3-A was a new highway, which meant it required new public hearings—but nobody at the State Roads Commission seemed to be in any rush to get them scheduled. "What is the hold-up on the hearings??" MAD's note-taker wondered in April.[89] When they *were* scheduled, for the middle of a workday in June, they needed to be canceled at the last minute when officials failed to make the informational materials the law required available to the public. They failed to make news of the cancellation available to the public, too. ("NEWS FLASH!!!" MAD's minutes read. "The Office of the State Roads Commission notified MAD they were unable to cancel the ad in the newspapers for the June 4 Public Hearing. That hearing is cancelled, however, and citizens are to disregard the announcement.")[90] Finally, the 3-A Corridor public hearing got an official date, time, and place: August 6 at 7 p.m. at Edmondson High School, more than two miles away and across the park from Rosemont. Preliminary briefings were scheduled for the same time and place on July 29 and 30. Yet "newspaper reports in all Baltimore papers stated that the Hearing would be held Aug. 6 at 7 PM at the Lafayette Elementary School #202 and that briefing meetings would be held there on July 30 and August 1," MAD reported. "Would the real By-Pass Public Hearing please stand up!!"[91]

All these things made clear that the roadbuilders were not especially moved to learn what "interested persons" might have to say about "the need for, and the location of" the 3-A expressway. Still, more than six hundred people showed up to the first night's hearing at Edmondson High. Many came because they'd seen MAD and R.A.M. fliers stapled to neighborhood telephone poles ("PEOPLE DON'T NEED THIS ROAD. HELP US FIGHT THE EXPRESSWAY"[92]) or gotten a call from someone on the R.N.I.A.'s telephone tree.

The 3-A corridor public hearing, the *Sun* said, was "a time for Negroes to tell what the still unsettled, years-old road issue has done to them and to their families and neighborhoods. And it was a time for white and black militants to tell city and state highway officials what could happen if the interstate, East–West expressway is built through Baltimore."[93] This was true: Anyone could speak. It was also false, because there weren't many "city and state highway officials" present. The mayor was absent. He had, he allegedly said, "heard all that stuff from the public before."[94] Most of the city council was absent, too. In fact, the only four elected officials anyone could point to in the crowd—State Senator Julian Lapides, House of Delegates representative Walter Orlinsky, and City Councilmen Robert L. Douglass and Stark—were there to protest the road, not defend it. Joseph Axelrod did show up that first night, but the *Sun* reported the episode proved such a strain that his doctor told him not to come back.[95] One activist from South Baltimore wondered where the mayor and his "City Hall Mafia" were. Then he turned to

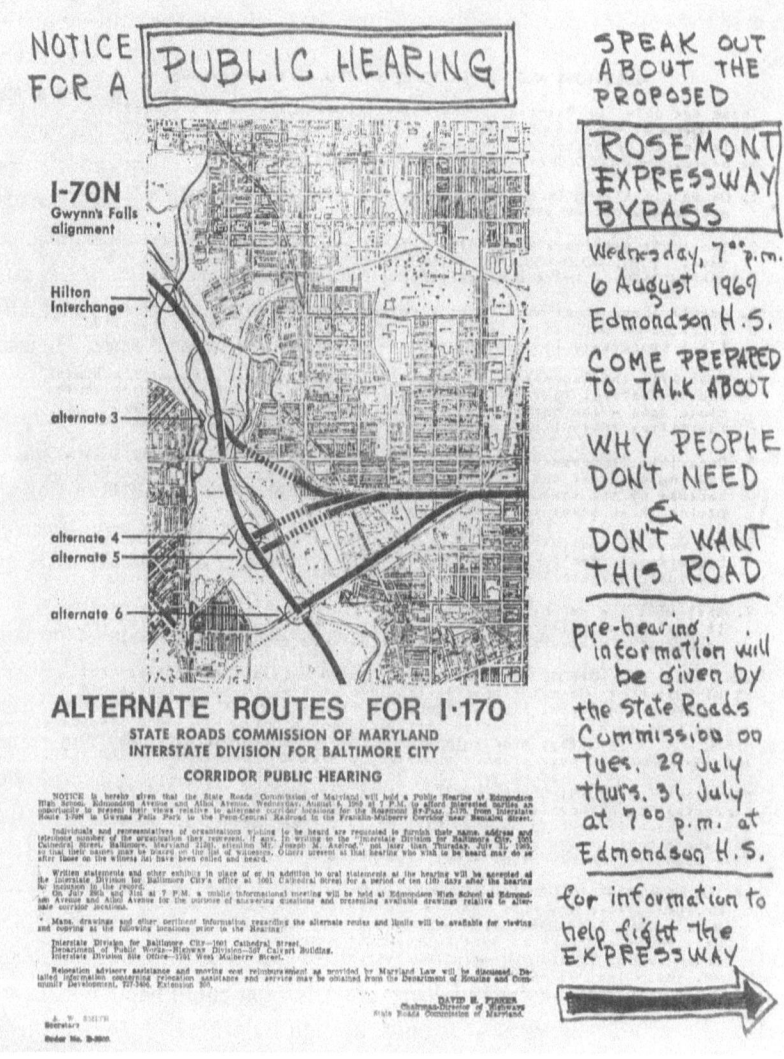

Movement Against Destruction (MAD) public hearing notice, Rosemont expressway bypass, July 1969. Courtesy of University of Baltimore Special Collections and Archives.

the bureaucrats on the stage: "But since Tommy has seen fit to send you out, boys—you're going to catch it."[96]

The meetings *did* have a full complement of armed police officers. "What kind of government is this?" Stu Weschler asked. "When people seek to be heard, instead of listening they send men with guns on them." "You talk about law and order," West Baltimore activist Esther Redd said to the mayor's empty chair. "You do your jobs, and you'll get law and order."[97]

The State Roads Commission claimed that its notes from the hearings, which went on for three nights, were "lost" not even six months later. (According to the R.N.I.A., the lost transcript was a foot tall at least.)[98] Still, surviving excerpts set the scene.

BARBARA MIKULSKI [*then an activist from East Baltimore*]—"First of all, everybody knows who I am but I don't know who you guys are. I would like to know who you are. Would you stand for the purpose of introducing yourselves so we know who we will be talking to? (Applause) And your addresses?"

WALTER J. ADDISON (hearing chairman)—"I have identified myself."

(Cries of "Where do you live?")

MR. ADDISON—"Sitting to my left is Mr. Joseph Axelrod, who is chief of the Interstate Division of Baltimore city."

(Loud boos.)

VOICE—"Where do you live?"

MR. ADDISON—"Next to Mr. Axelrod is Mr. Richard Trainor, chief of the Bureau of Transportation of the Interstate Division. On my right is Mr. Hugo Liem. Next to him C. Edward Walter, chief of engineering of the Department of Public Works."

VOICE—"Where do they live?"

(Pandemonium followed.)[99]

It seemed like everyone in the room joined the glissando of insults. "Edgar Allan Poe would have loved to have this thing to write about," said the lawyer for the church that owned the Western Cemetery. "It's macabre. It's grisly."[100] Sammie Abbott from Washington, DC's National Commission for the Transportation Crisis informed the few officials present that their colleagues were "dehumanized technocrats," "pip-squeaks," "finks," "knuckleheads," and "smiling idiots," and he sneered at the obfuscating language they used. "Instead of saying they're going to bulldoze," he said, "they're going to 'impact.' Instead of saying they're going to grave-rob the dead, they're going to 'impact' them. God damn these impacters."[101]

On the third night of the hearings, State Delegate Orlinsky rose to speak. "We don't have the real options before us," he said. "We have options of roads or roads."

> You are all surrounded with roads and roads money, and all you can think about is roads and roads money, and you are divinely attached to roads and roads money.

Orlinsky went on:

> If you want your road, remember we want our city. We want our city to be a place fit for human, not vehicular, habitation. You show us what you will do for our city and we will listen. But you come here with the notion that your prime responsibility is to move traffic with the saint-like Highway Trust Funds and we must say, as General McCauliffe said to the Germans at Bastogne, "Nuts." It is our money you are using. You have no right to keep secrets from us.

"Either we are part of the process of arranging our lives," he said, "or democracy loses its meaning."

Finally, he pointed to all the Rosemonters in the audience. "They are human beings," he said. "They deserve consideration as human beings, and you are not giving it to them."

> Escalate, and you are going to bear the responsibility. You are not going to get out of that tomorrow, and you will cry with everybody else for our own stupidity of not listening to human beings when they cry out in need, when they cry out in desperation, having spent lifetimes doing everything that America says you should do in order to be a citizen, and then watch out when here comes the concrete.

"For what, and for whom and why?" Orlinsky concluded. "This is not government. It is stupidity of the highest sort."[102]

It was a beautiful speech, but it didn't make much difference. It seemed like nothing did. Maybe nothing would. Planning for the 3-A went on, and the 10-D condemnation lines stayed in place. In October 1969, Councilman Stark introduced an ordinance that would have lifted the 10-D condemnation lines through Rosemont, but the city council declined to pass it.[103] "City officials stress that the destruction to be wrought by the expressway has already run its course," one political scientist explained. "Now the city may as well reap the benefits."[104] In a meeting with MAD activists, Secretary of Transportation John A. Volpe made the same point. MAD's notes interpreted: "Idea that since road plans have already made wastelands of many areas of the city, only good effects can result now, since all the bad has been done, is like saying that 'too bad you got a bad cut, we'll just have to let you bleed to death!'"[105]

By the end of the year, the *Sun* reported that Mayor D'Alesandro was back to choosing among eight different expressway plans: six new ones, including one known as the 6-A and one known as the 3-D; the UDCT's 3-A through the Western Cemetery; and the old 10-D through Rosemont.[106] "It's a ticklish situation," his aide told the newspaper in June 1970.[107] That November, Mayor D'Alesandro introduced a bill establishing a new condemnation line around Rosemont and through the cemetery, and promised that once it was approved, he would finally lift the condemnations on the Rosemont houses.[108] The city council scheduled another hearing, and the whole business started again from the beginning. Neighbors packed the War Memorial building. "Why don't you use the money for schools?" one asked. "Why don't you just cancel the whole thing?" said another.[109]

"WHO WANTS THIS ROAD?" Stu Weschler from MAD had asked the crowd on the last night of the expressway hearings in August 1969. "Only the road builders, highway lobby, and a few politicians. WHO DOESN'T WANT IT? The PEOPLE don't want it. It will now be a question of whose will is the strongest: the people of Baltimore who wish to save and better their city or those interests which stand to profit from the destruction of it?"[110] "We will defeat this road," Weschler continued. "The fact is, the truth is, that the people of Baltimore do not want, do not need, and will not have this proposed road!!!"[111]

By the end of the 1960s, it was starting to look like this might be true. But if it was, what would the people of Baltimore have instead?

PART III

The Aftermath

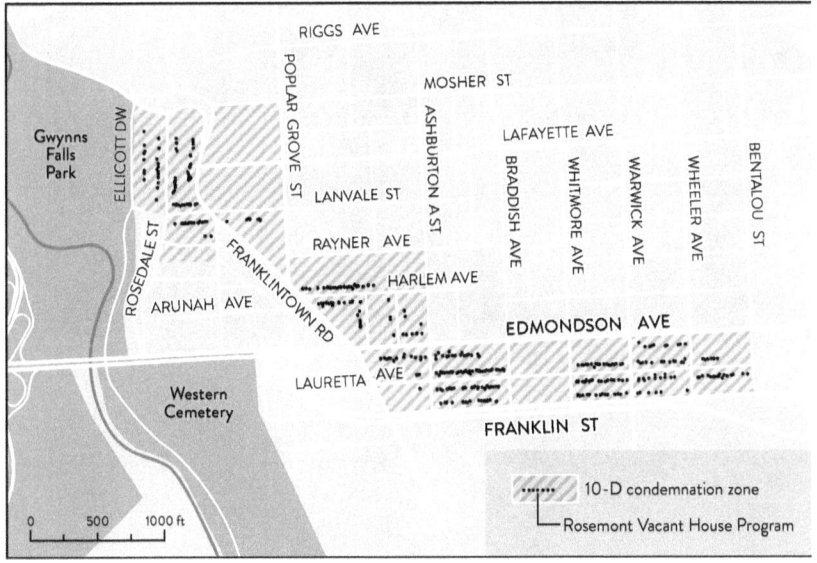

7

"The Rosemont Dilemma":
How Baltimore Reinvented Rosemont (1968–1971)

While most of Baltimore's eyes were on Rosemont, the roadbuilders saw an opportunity in the neighborhood next door. They had no plans to start construction on any part of the I-170 highway system, nor did they have anything like a complete route for it. All they had was the 1966 condemnation corridor across the bottom of Harlem Park, to Rosemont's east, and no guarantee they'd be able to keep even that. But they also had bulldozers and wrecking balls—both excellent tools for turning an open question about urban renewal into a fait accompli. And so by the end of the summer of 1969, the Interstate Division had razed hundreds of houses in the Harlem Park corridor into rubble, scraping them clean off the face of the city and creating what neighbors called "the world's longest vacant lot."¹

That August, just a few weeks after the mutinous expressway hearings at Edmondson High, activists from the Relocation Action Movement (R.A.M.) staged a protest at the very western end of that lot, near where John and Ada Wells had once lived. They called it a "talent show," though what was really on display was the mess the road plans had made. The event's coordinator, Rosemont resident and R.A.M. secretary Esther Redd, was an old hand at this kind of protest. To take just one example, in 1960 the May Department Store Company had sued her for picketing the segregated Roof Top Restaurant at the segregated Hecht's at the segregated shopping center near Morgan State, on the grounds that Redd had "persuaded the restaurant kitchen staff to walk off their jobs" while carrying a large sign that said "We Will Never Stop Until You End Segregation."² And just a few months before the talent show, the *Sun* reported, she'd led "a flock of teen-agers" to Mayor D'Alesandro's office because he'd offered summer jobs to dozens of Rosemont youths and then stopped taking their calls. When Redd and her flock showed up at city hall for their assignments, the man in the employment office offered a compromise: jobs for the boys, but not the girls. "Girls," she said, "I guess it's time to see the mayor." (In short order, all the promised jobs materialized.)[3] In fact, Redd had invited the mayor to the world's largest vacant lot that day, along with Vice President Spiro T. Agnew and Secretary of Transportation John A. Volpe to the event, but all three men declined the invitation. In his stead, the *Sun* reported, the mayor "did send three Negro aides." "The Mayor's stooges," Redd told the reporter. "Little Black City Hall."[4]

In any case, it wasn't much of a show. The stage wobbled. The loudspeaker died. There was only one rickety bench to sit on. The Interstate Division had pledged to build a playground on the cleared site, but had not done it. Instead the littlest audience members had to improvise a sandbox for themselves out of the dirt and debris the bulldozers had left behind. Without a microphone, the emcee had to yell. "This is what the Mayor calls a playground," he shouted.[5]

Things did not look quite as apocalyptic in the Rosemont condemnation corridor, where at least the houses were still standing, but they were getting pretty bad. Not long after the talent show, Esther Redd wrote a letter to the commissioner of the city's new Department of Housing and Community Development (HCD), a young white tax attorney named Robert C. Embry Jr., asking for his help. Embry was just thirty years old then, a graduate of Williams and Harvard who had served on Baltimore's city council for all of nine months before he took the wheel at HCD: "an extremely bright young man," the *Sun* reported, who "assumes the housing post at a time when top city officials are at last taking an aggressive interest in correcting Baltimore's substandard housing conditions."[6] Until now, the increasingly substandard housing conditions in the Rosemont expressway corridor had not been part of Embry's remit. They weren't even supposed to *be* housing for much longer. But the mayor had pledged to replace the 10-D route with one of the seven (or was it eight?) others he'd asked the Urban Design Concept Team (UDCT) to study, the ones that swung the highway down away from the neighborhood's houses and through the Western Cemetery. Maybe the place had some kind of future after all.

The question was, what kind? "Dear Sir," Esther Redd wrote in her 1969 letter to Robert Embry. "Members of the 2300, 2400, 2500, 2600, and 2700 blocks of Edmondson, Lauretta Avenue and Franklin Street petition the Commissioner to take steps, immediately, to bring relief to our deprived neighborhood." "Mr. Embry," Redd continued, "the physical and psychological effects this continued deterioration has on the lives of youths and adults is untold.

"THE ROSEMONT DILEMMA"

Only in years to come will we be able to note the true results of such deterioration and it will not be good. The time is that all men should be concerned."[7]

By this time the Interstate Division owned nearly half of the 900 houses it had condemned in the Rosemont 10-D corridor. Though it had installed rental tenants in some, most were empty.[8] Many of the condemned houses the Interstate Division did not own were now owned by absentee landlords, and most of those were empty, too. The homeowners in the highway's path, the people who had made so much of Rosemont what it was, had left. Clarence and Elizabeth Landrum had moved to Hunting Ridge, near the Edmondson Village Shopping Center.[9] Their neighbors Frank and Frances Clements moved to Hunting Ridge, too. The Wainwrights on Edmondson moved to Windsor Hills. The McBrides moved to Pimlico, the Tarvers and the Hawkinses to Woodlawn.[10] "It was just like taking a double-barreled shotgun and shooting into a crowd of people," one Rosemonter told a reporter from the *Sun* a few years later. "Everybody just scattered."[11]

The maps and drawings in the *Rosemont Area Studies* report the UDCT published in 1968 had already shown what planners called "immediate deterioration" in the condemnation corridor and "increased blight" around the condemnation lines at the eastern end of the neighborhood. (The team found that other parts of the neighborhood, like the blocks to the north and west where the members of the Rosemont Neighborhood Improvement Association (R.N.I.A.) lived, still evinced "exceptional high quality.")[12] Two years hence, those distinctions were starting to blur. Even the parts of the Rosemont area relatively far from the condemnation zone, like Mary Rosemond and Gertrude Corbett's "exceptional high quality" block, now suffered for the planners' map. Residents there reported streets and alleys freckled with dead rats, dog waste, and trash because city sanitation crews had stopped cleaning them.[13] Nobody could take out an insurance policy or get a home-improvement loan, and planners reported that residents dared not spend much on upkeep "for fear that the Expressway would make that investment fruitless."[14]

All this compulsory neglect guaranteed that routine maintenance issues that homeowners and We Workers would have resolved in a day or a weekend in 1957 or 1962 swelled into big, complicated problems now.[15] According to the *Sun*, in the spring of 1970 more than five thousand of the neighborhood's houses were in violation of the city's building code.[16] As Mary Rosemond explained in a meeting with city officials, the entire neighborhood waited "in limbo [as] residents valiantly try to keep from becoming a near slum . . .

900 block of Franklintown Road, Baltimore Department of Housing and Community Development, 1971. Courtesy of Baltimore City Archives. Department of Housing and Community Development Records, Land Development Division, Vacant House Program Real Estate Files, box 1, folder 9 [OR BRG48-40-1-9].

because no one is sure whether the area will become a great asset to the city or a two minute short cut."[17]

It was obvious, as a MAD spokesman said at the end of 1969, that in Rosemont "the state has created chaos." The expressway map had turned a "viable area" into "blighted scar."[18] But how to resolve what the R.N.I.A. newsletter was calling "the Rosemont Dilemma," and for whom, was much less clear.[19] The people who had owned homes in the condemnation corridor, the Landrums and the McBrides and the Tarvers, could never get back what they'd lost. But the people who persevered in Rosemont still saw a path forward: As Mary Rosemond said, they knew their neighborhood could yet be a great asset to the city. But the people who had the power in Baltimore, the ones who had created Rosemont's chaos and would be charged with fixing it, didn't seem to see the value in what had been, nor in what remained. They set out, now, to build something entirely new.

Well—not *entirely* new. In the end, the people who profited from the new Rosemont were the not that different from the people who profited from the old one. And the people who paid the price were awfully similar, too.

Home Ownership for the Poor

Discrimination in mortgage lending was among the many things the Kerner Commission's 1968 *Report of the National Advisory Commission on Civil Disorders* blamed for the uprisings in cities nationwide in 1967 and 1968.[20] Generous credit made it easier for most white people to buy what they wanted and live where they pleased, the report explained, but Black people were stuck in place, excluded from the consumer freedoms that had become the essence of the postwar American dream.[21] And because federal policy had caused this problem, officials thought, then federal policy could solve it—or at least it could stop insisting upon it.[22] "We have got to recognize that stimulating a flow of mortgage funds into the inner city, yes even into the slums, for the transfer of houses, for rehabilitation, and for new construction, is an FHA mission of the highest priority," Federal Housing Administration (FHA) commissioner Philip Brownstein told his staff in 1967.[23] Besides, Wisconsin Congressman Henry Reuss explained, "a man who owns his own home is not likely to burn it down."[24]

Accordingly, 1968's Housing and Urban Development (HUD) Act replaced the federal government's blatantly discriminatory Depression-era standards for mortgage lending with fairer, more accessible ones. Under the new rules, FHA would insure any mortgage a bank would issue "in a location which is judged to be reasonably viable, considering the need for housing for low- and moderate-income families and the objective of upgrading older, declining neighborhoods."[25] The only properties *ineligible* for FHA-insured bank loans were those "so deteriorated . . . [that] the livability of the property or the health or safety of its occupants are seriously affected."[26]

Along with that year's Civil Rights Act, which prohibited housing discrimination based on race, religion, national origin, or sex, the HUD Act of 1968 relaxed speculators' grip on the housing and home finance market for Black homebuyers. From now on, in theory, the market would treat every potential buyer the same. Black people would finally be able to get conventional, regulated mortgages from banks instead of predatory schemes from double-dealing lenders who made up the rules as they went along.

The real estate industry supported the HUD Act because, in the process of making the housing market fairer, it also made that market bigger. It insured more mortgages, so more lenders were guaranteed to make money whether borrowers paid their bills or not. It also offered to enable "the construction or rehabilitation of 26 million housing units, 6 million of these for low- and moderate-income families," over the next decade.[27] In other words, President Johnson said, the law "summon[ed] the talents and energies of private enterprise to the task of housing low-income families" by offering private enterprise more opportunities to profit from it.[28] And private enterprise badly needed those opportunities. As historian Keeanga-Yamahtta Taylor notes, by the end of the 1960s the market for building and selling single-family houses to middle-class white Americans was shriveling.[29] In 1970, nearly 70 percent of white families in the United States already lived in homes that they owned, compared to about 40 percent of Black families.[30] The other 60 percent represented a huge and untapped customer base for builders, bankers, and other real estate men.

Not all those people were like the people who had lived in Rosemont before the expressway came through, middle-class buyers who could easily have qualified for a bank mortgage if a bank would have given them one. In fact, most of the people like that already owned houses they'd bought from speculators, just as the Rosemonters did. Those who didn't, in many cases, couldn't really afford to. (In 1968, more than one-third of Black families lived under the official poverty line, compared with 10 percent of white ones.)[31] Just ending redlining and racist steering wasn't going to be enough to get those people into houses that they owned. They would need an extra boost.

The 1968 law provided this boost via what one journalist called a "number soup" of low-income housing programs.[32] One of these, aimed at what HUD called "the frayed-collar worker," was known as Section 235. Section 235 made homeownership more accessible by subsidizing mortgage payments for anyone who earned less than 135 percent of the public housing maximum: In Baltimore City, that was $7,425 for a family of four.[33] With a Section 235 mortgage loan, buyers with just $200 for a down payment could now qualify for a federally insured $15,000 or $20,000 bank mortgage, and the federal government made up the difference between a 1 percent interest rate and the FHA market rate (7 percent, at first).[34] After the down payment, borrowers paid their lender 20 percent of their adjusted income each month and the government covered the rest. This way, a Baltimore family earning about $6,300 after deductions could buy a $17,500 house for $200 down and $101.35 per month. Without the subsidy, the monthly payment for that same house would have been almost twice as much.[35]

But from the beginning, the HUD Act trapped policymakers and everybody else in a snare of perverse incentives. Under Section 235 and the other programs aimed at subsidizing what policymakers called "home ownership for the poor," FHA insurance worked the same way it usually did.[36] If someone missed his mortgage payments, he lost his house, but the federal government made his lender whole.[37] This policy was always supposed to temper lenders' restraint and push them to issue more mortgages, and it still did—but now, there was no assurance that those mortgages were sound. Likewise, the 1968 law also created a secondary market for the new, "riskier" loans it encouraged banks to make.[38] When the Federal National Mortgage Association (FNMA, or "Fannie Mae") was chartered in 1938, it was a public entity that bought, bundled, and resold federally insured loans, increasing banks' liquidity so they could make more loans. The 1968 law spun Fannie Mae into a private business that bought conventional mortgages from lenders. It also established the Government National Mortgage Association (GNMA, or "Ginnie Mae") to guarantee the mortgage loans banks issued to low-income people. This new way of doing things, the sociologist Calvin Bradford writes, ensured "mortgage bankers had a ready buyer for any FHA loan they could get through the local FHA insuring offices."[39] It sluiced more dollars into the system and swamped lenders' restraint altogether.

"What the FHA does for the mortgage lender," one reporter wrote, "is to insure him against any possible loss in the event of foreclosure. It makes FHA loans a sure thing for investors."[40] In fact it effectively *paid* brokers, bankers, builders, and institutional investors "bent" (Taylor writes) "on profiting from the desperation of low-income urban residents."[41] "During the hearings on the HUD Act," the historian Rebecca K. Marchiel explains, "there was virtually no concern about possible consequences" of the recklessness the new law encouraged. "Members of Congress across party lines, representatives from the housing and mortgage industries, and fair housing advocates came to a near consensus that the primary goal of the legislation should be to recruit new capital into the urban mortgage market, and all other priorities were secondary."[42] "Private enterprise" could not lose, but rookie homebuyers cajoled into buying homes they could not afford could—and would.

With all that federal money sloshing around, buoying bromides about the transformative powers of homeownership, it quickly became "common practice in the inner city" (one 1971 report noted) for real estate men "to pick up houses for minimal amounts, perform a so-called 'paste-up' or cosmetic rehabilitation which, in many cases, amounts to a few hundred dollars and then resell the property under F.H.A. Section 235 for a profit of thousands of dollars."[43] If the buyers of these pasted-up houses found they were uninhabitable and defaulted on their mortgages, they would lose all the equity they'd built and destroy their credit. The bank would do it all again with a new patsy, and the federal government would swallow the cost.[44]

The way the Section 235 program was set up, builders, brokers, and bankers had no reason to treat buyers as anything other than marks in the con game historian Taylor calls "predatory inclusion." Selling defective houses for inflated prices made money for everybody: the cheaper the house, the higher the markup—and the higher the markup, the bigger the subsidies.[45] Thus the market HUD and its housing-industry partners built pressed desperate families to spend everything they had on (per *The Washington Post*) "decaying old homes they did not want and could not maintain," and also could not live in.[46] "It is not difficult to imagine the human agony of the home owner" under these circumstances, Texas Congressman Wright Patman told the *Post* in 1970. "He has been obligated on a long-term mortgage for a house worth far less than the amount of the note (he owes) and, worse yet, a house which will not last anywhere near the terms of the mortgage." "The federal government," Patman added, "is fostering slum housing."[47]

In 1971, the House Committee on Banking and Currency produced a sheaf of embarrassing documentation of Section 235 abuses in cities across the country. Almost everywhere, the committee found, real estate men were buying cheap houses in (political scientist R. Allen Hays explained) "neighborhoods which were changing racially or could be tipped toward racial change by skillful manipulation," then reselling them for preposterous profit.[48] For example, one speculator bought a house in Detroit for $8,500 and sold it a few months later, without so much as a new coat of paint, for $14,500. Another bought a house for $10,000 and sold it right away for $7,500 more. These houses sported dozens of code violations apiece, including leaky roofs, blocked plumbing, and broken stoves, sinks, and refrigerators. "Instead of buying a home," the report concluded, "people purchasing these houses are buying a disaster."[49]

After the House committee released its study, the Section 235 lending program stuttered. HUD Secretary George Romney froze its funds until, he said, the agency could root out the "incompetence, conflict of interest, favoritism, graft, bribes, fraud, shoddy workmanship, and forms of 'legal' profiteering that take advantage of technicalities to defraud the homebuyer and the taxpaying public."[50] These were strong words, but the freeze was only temporary. The FHA started issuing Section 235 mortgages again in April 1971.[51]

That's when Baltimore brought Section 235 to Rosemont.

Staying Alive with 235

In December 1968, Baltimore's Department of Housing and Community Development announced its first foray into Section 235. "Operation Rescue," also known as "Project Rehab," was a campaign to buy, rehabilitate, and sell 1,500 "vandal-prone" vacant houses across the city that would, the *Sun* reported, "form one of the nation's largest single efforts to date to get low income families into subsidized homes they can afford to buy."[52] However, at first the project used the federal funds at its disposal to buy derelict houses from landlords all over the city, which meant that in the best case it could only create what a Philadelphia housing reformer had once described as "islands of good in a sea of bad."[53] Its major accomplishment, one sociologist wrote, was to subsidize the purchase of abandoned properties from slumlords looking for "a way out of an impossible situation."[54]

But in Rosemont, the "sea of bad" was not a sea: It was more of a meandering stream along the 10-D condemnation corridor. What's more, the "impossible situation" the expressway map had created was not quite impossible yet. So, in April 1971, Baltimore announced it had gotten a grant from HUD to adapt the Operation Rescue/Project Rehab formula—buy, rehabilitate, resell—to the more concentrated Rosemont condemnation corridor. Using $6.4 million in federal money, HCD would buy the 486 houses the Interstate Division now owned in the 10-D corridor for $2,500 apiece and spend some $11,000 to rehabilitate each one, promotional materials promised, "from cellar to roof."[55] Then it would sell the rehabilitated houses to low-income buyers, who would pay for them using their own federal subsidy: Section 235 mortgages. (This campaign went by many names. For simplicity's sake, I'll call it the Rosemont Vacant House Program.)

Although the fair housing provisions of the Civil Rights Act of 1968 would (theoretically, eventually) open Baltimore's once-closed housing market to Black renters and buyers, in fact there was still almost no decent, affordable housing for poor Black people in Baltimore.[56] The Rosemont Vacant House Program aimed to chip away at this problem. But, of course, HUD's initial $6.4 million wasn't really for poor people's benefit. Some of the money went to the Interstate Division to reimburse it for the houses it had bought in 1968 and 1969. Most went right back into the pockets of real estate men: brokers, bankers, lawyers, and especially construction companies, for whom all those new roofs, new kitchens, and new bathrooms were about to add up to a windfall.[57] "Among builders," the historian Andrew R. Highsmith writes in his study of Section 235 in the Detroit suburbs, "the phrase 'Stay Alive with 235' became something of a mantra."[58] In Baltimore, it became an article of faith.

By the time HCD chief Embry introduced the Rosemont Vacant House Program, anyone who was paying attention could have spotted the many mousetraps and banana peels strewn in its path. But the supply side, the side of the bankers and builders who were first to cash the checks from HUD, was set up to succeed, and that was what mattered. As for the demand side, the people who would be buying and living in the rehabilitated houses and their neighbors—the city didn't have many alternatives, and neither did they. "Baltimore was fortunate to be selected" for the federal grant, Embry wrote to a group of Rosemont neighbors that year. "It is the only way we could get money to rehabilitate the Rosemont properties."[59]

In fact, Section 235 probably *was* the only way Baltimore could get the money to rehabilitate the condemned Rosemont properties, or at least the half of them the Interstate Division owned. (The fate of the rest was anybody's guess.) But there was a catch: Nearly every homeowner who had been pushed out of the condemnation corridor, and nearly every homeowner who had stayed behind there, earned too much to get a Section 235 mortgage. This fact required officials to misinterpret, even distort, the problem they were trying to solve. They had to finish erasing middle-class Rosemont so they could treat the neighborhood like the slum they'd always imagined it was.

It wasn't going to be easy, because middle-class Rosemont did not want to be erased; and as longtime neighbors might have put it, homeownership for the poor was "out of [the] general complexion of the neighborhood."[60] For example, the R.N.I.A. was still trying to stop the construction of the two "scatter site" public housing projects it had been fighting since 1966.[61] Even without the projects, the group argued, families dislocated from condemnation corridors across West Baltimore were already flooding their community, and "we now find ourselves with inadequate everything": schools, sanitation services, police protection, recreational facilities.[62] "We agree that the city has an obligation in its crusade to evacuate poverty, discrimination, ignorance, and illiteracy," the group's executive committee wrote in a letter to the mayor in 1970. "We further agree that public housing is needed as one way to help meet this obligation." But "the building of a public housing project on this site, located in the heart of a black community, would be perpetuating de facto segregation since these units would only house black citizens," the committee wrote. "We as concerned tax paying citizens demand protection of <u>our investments</u> in this stable ghettoized neighborhood."[63]

Of course, Rosemont had never been a monolith. Even now, the people the Rosemont Neighborhood Improvement Association represented were not the same as the people the Relocation Action Movement represented, who were not the same as the people the new Rosemont Coalition would represent, and so forth. But the threat of the expressway had drawn these communities together into one community of concerned tax-paying citizens who wanted the city to protect (or at least to *want* to protect) their investments, just as it would if they were white. But as the people who lived in Rosemont were about to learn, protecting people's investments in their neighborhoods was not—and could not be—among the Rosemont Vacant House Program's aims.

In April 1971, after HUD secretary Romney lifted the freeze on Section 235 funds, HCD officials called a meeting at the Doswell Temple, toward the eastern end of the Rosemont condemnation corridor, to introduce the neighborhood's new Vacant House Program.[64] HUD required cities receiving its funds to prove that they'd met requirements for "community participation," and it seems officials intended to invite only the relative handful of public housing tenants who were renting the Interstate Division's houses in the 10-D corridor. Those families would almost definitely have qualified for the Section 235 mortgages on offer, and officials wanted to get their answers to a short, intrusive HUD questionnaire. "How much mortgage payment do you feel you can pay per month?" it asked. "How much money would you have to make a down payment to purchase one of the Rosemont properties?"[65]

But somebody made a mistake, and everyone in the Rosemont area got an invitation to the meeting.[66] Many of the people in the audience were members of the Rosemont Coalition, a new organization representing the people who lived in the condemnation corridor as well as the people who lived around it: mostly longtime homeowners who had narrowly escaped losing their houses to the expressway. (For example, the group's president, steelworker George Terry, had lived on Arunah Avenue a block north of the condemnation zone since 1954.)[67] But as far as property values go, being one or two blocks away from an interstate highway is nearly as bad as being under one—and at least the people who had their houses taken had gotten a check from the Interstate Division in exchange. Appraisals showed that condemnation-adjacent houses bought for $8,000 or $10,000 a decade ago were now worth just $1,500 or $3,000—if anyone was buying, which they weren't.[68]

This was one reason for the anger that percolated in the crowd at the Doswell Temple that night. There were others, too. The Department of Housing and Community Development had been the agency in charge of renting the houses the Interstate Division owned in the condemnation corridor for more than a year now, and in that time the quality of their stewardship had not been impressive. A few months after the meeting, Rosemont Coalition president George Terry wrote to Walter Orlinsky, who was then the city council's president-elect, to explain some of the problems his neighbors in the HCD rentals were having. Families trying to survive the winter in those houses, he wrote, "will not have adequate heat, will not have roofs that can keep out winter's waters, will not have doors and windows that seal against wind, with flakes of paint falling, and electrical problems that have residents using unsafe extension cords."[69] In fact, Terry wrote, many of the houses were now "just pure sub-human shacks." And when tenants reached out for help, the city snubbed them. "If they keep complaining," Terry said, quoting HCD staff, "we will make them move."[70]

Then there was HCD's recently introduced Concentrated Code Enforcement Program, which was ostensibly designed to "undo some of the damage which the expressway controversy has caused the Rosemont area."[71] Starting in 1970s, code-enforcement inspectors patrolled all the blocks in Greater Rosemont except the ones in the condemnation zone, from North Avenue down past Franklin and Mulberry and from Monroe Street west to the park, looking for housing code violations: "serious fire and safety hazards, interior overcrowding, roaches and vermin, and electricity violations."[72] But inspectors often skipped the properties speculators and absentee landlords owned, even though on balance those were in the worst shape.[73] Instead, the *Afro-American* newspaper explained, they appeared on Black homeowners' "well-kept" stoops with "pages and pages of alleged housing code violations often needing thousands of dollars of repair work."[74] The 1968 HUD Act included another provision for low-interest rehabilitation loans for homeowners, and neighbors complained that city inspectors pushed homeowners to apply for those loans and use the money they got to hire particular contractors inspectors named.[75] If an owner hesitated, locals reported, city workers would return and demand more and pricier repairs.[76]

In short: As far as the hundreds of Rosemonters packing the pews at the Doswell Temple that night in April 1971 were concerned, when the city wasn't insulting their neighbors, it was shaking them down. And officials' dismissive behavior, starting with the fact that none of them even showed up to the meeting until a half-hour after its scheduled start, didn't do much to dispel the impression that as far as Baltimore was concerned, the people who lived in Rosemont were nothing more than a speed bump.[77] A local community organizer estimated that a third of the audience left in frustration before the meeting was over. "It was hard during the meeting to hear the questions because of the loud rumblings of discontent," the organizer's notes continued. "I found no real evidence of any HCD representative having a true interest in the residents of this community."[78]

In fact, they did not have any such interest, because "the residents of this community" had no place in the new Rosemont. The Section 235 income maximum for a family of four was less than what a typical teacher or steelworker would have earned, and much less than the combined incomes of two working adults in the old Rosemont. Responses to the HUD questionnaire showed that some 150 of the original Rosemont owner-occupants were temporarily renting houses in the condemnation zone, and that more than one-third of them *did* want to buy their houses back, but almost all earned too much money to do so.[79] Only 19 of the original homeowners in the Rosemont condemnation corridor both wanted to buy a rehabilitated home in the neighborhood and were eligible for the subsidized Section 235 mortgages that were the only way they could.[80] Even HCD officials conceded that "it is desirable to sell a reasonable number of properties to ... over income people in order to get as many 'standard' families in the area as possible," but FHA rules made no exceptions.[81] "Home ownership for the poor" meant what it said. By design, the Section 235 program in Rosemont excluded almost everyone who had once lived in the condemnation corridor, and almost everyone who still lived nearby.

Rather than tackle this contradiction head-on, city officials lied about it. They assured everyone assembled in the Doswell Temple that "all present occupants will be permitted to stay in their properties if they wish to do so," and that "all rehabilitated houses [will be] occupied by former residents of Rosemont."[82] Officials dissembled about other things that night, like that "part of [HCD tenants'] rent was going for the deposit on the home they're renting" (not true) and that "the purchase price of their home would not be over $7,500" (in fact the real price was more than twice that much).[83] But this first lie was most obnoxious, because it made it look like the Section 235 program was going to serve "the residents of this community" when instead it was going to keep on pushing them out.

Let Me Have My House Back

"I was once the owner at 2412 Lauretta Ave.," Ruby Maclin wrote Baltimore's Department of Housing and Community Development in May 1971. "The city want it for the Expressway, but fail. I would like to get my house back."[84] In 1954, Ruby Cain and her mother, Cornelia Offer, had bought the Lauretta Avenue house from LeRoy Kappelman, paid for in part with a $5,200 mortgage from Kappelman's own New Michaels Permanent Savings & Loan.[85] Over the years the family had poured many thousands more into the house, using loans from the Globe Home Improvement Company and County Loans, Inc. as well as a second mortgage from Leroy and Sarah Kappelman themselves.[86] But they'd paid back most of what they owed, and in May 1969, Ruby Cain—now, married, Ruby Maclin—sold the house to the Interstate Division for $12,042.18.[87] This was $8,000 in fair market value plus a $4,300 supplemental payment, minus a couple of hundred dollars for the Kappelmans.[88] That August, Maclin and her husband, Thomas, bought a bungalow on Liberty Road in Gwynn Oak from Straw Man, Inc., and moved to the suburbs, but the suburbs didn't suit the Maclins at all.[89] "Please help me to get out of this place out here," Maclin wrote in her letter to the city. "I was living happy on Lauretta Avenue until expressway came by with their mess. . . . So help me to get back, will you?" "I am going to get my house back," she wrote. "Let me have my house back."[90]

"Why," George Terry wrote in a letter to Robert Embry, "can't homes be turned over to residents at the same price the city paid for them with the stipulation that they meet standards after a period of time?"⁹¹ From a commonsense perspective, this proposition sounded reasonable. First, homeownership is what HCD said it was after, and homeownership is what it would get. Second, it would save money. City officials' private correspondence confirmed that "in all cases," a prospective buyer "would be economically better-off if he purchased 'as is,' and brought the dwelling up to code standards himself."⁹² Third, at least in theory, it was an opportunity to bring Rosemont back around to its old self again. Yes, many of the homeowners in the condemnation corridor were long gone now, started over in West Hills and Catonsville and Gwynn Oak and Arlington, but some were still around. Others, like Ruby Maclin, wanted to return, to move back home, to pick up where they'd left off.

But these were not the rules of the game Rosemont was playing now. The houses people wanted to buy as-is, like Ruby Maclin's, were in reasonably good shape compared with the others in the corridor. "From the Contractor's point of view," officials wrote in a confidential memo, "the reason that he has been willing to accept a contract price which is substantially less . . . , is that he has considered the total range of properties, knowing that he would not have to do everything to each one."⁹³ (In other words, the contractor earned $11,000 per house no matter what. If a house only needed a coat of paint or new doorknobs, that money was almost pure profit.) If people were allowed to buy easy-to-repair houses out of the Rosemont Sales Program, the memo continued, "it will so distort [the contractor's] contract, as well as the commitments which we have made to him, to the extent that the remaining deal will probably be unacceptable."⁹⁴ "The houses that are 'as is' to be taken out of the Morelite [Construction Company] contract are in good condition," another official wrote in November 1971. "Doubt if Morelite would agree" to give them up.⁹⁵

In fact, after months of negotiation, HCD did agree to sell six of the 486 houses in the Rosemont Vacant House Program back to their former owners, for a mysteriously derived "fair market value" of some $4,700 apiece. Then subcontractors went ahead and gutted one of the six houses, leaving only its exterior walls, and after this—in officials' words—"mishap," the prospective buyer quite reasonably decided she'd rather stay where she was.⁹⁶ And *then*, in March 1972, the Department of Housing and Community Development rescinded its offer to the remaining five buyers, including Ruby and Thomas Maclin. "We want to assure you that we have indeed tried," HCD chief Embry explained in a letter to the Rosemont Coalition, but "we have been unable to remove these . . . properties from the rehabilitation contract."⁹⁷

900 block of North Rosedale Street, Baltimore Department of Housing and Community Development, 1971. Courtesy of Baltimore City Archives. Department of Housing and Community Development Records, Land Development Division, Vacant House Program Real Estate Files, box 1, folder 9 [OR BRG48-40-1-9].

This was the principle that would hold sway over the new Rosemont: The "rehabilitation contract," and the Section 235 program itself, was king. And it was there to serve its own interests, not to serve Ruby Maclin or any of the other Rosemonters who had made the neighborhood thrive.

The Rosemont Vacant House Program could not repair the actual problem the expressway map created—at least not for the people who had suffered for it so far, the middle-class homeowners who wanted their community back the way it had been. Instead, it created a whole new set of problems, and it spread them around to a whole new group of people.

"When will the city recognize the foolhardiness of desperately spending money to build communities such as Rosemont," reporter James Dilts wrote in 1968, "while busily knocking down the ones they already have with a highway program?"[98] Three years later, when the Department of Housing and Community Development announced its plan to spend $6.4 million on the Rosemont Vacant House Program, Baltimore was no closer to an answer. On the contrary: Although the mayor had pledged to ditch the 10-D expressway route years before, he still refused to lift the condemnation lines through the neighborhood, which meant that the houses slated for rehabilitation were still condemned.

This choice served the interests of the roadbuilders most of all. "As long as this condemnation route is still in existence," the R.N.I.A.'s newsletter pointed out in 1971, "there is the constant threat that it can and will be used."[99] As long as it was still in existence, each week and month and year that passed only multiplied what activists called "the amount of deterioration which has already set in as a result of the threat of this road."[100] And as long as that deterioration multiplied, the people who wanted to see the expressway built could point to it as proof that the 10-D route through Rosemont was the right one after all. The price was paid, they argued. The die was cast. "We have already removed a couple thousand houses from the market," Greater Baltimore Committee director William Boucher said a few years later, explaining this point of view. "But that's been done, so wishing the expressway away doesn't bring them back."[101]

The decision to keep the condemnation lines through Rosemont in place even as the Vacant House Program began was not "ironical" in the same way as the tension between urban renewal and urban highways on white Tyson Street that housing official Albert Cole had identified in 1957.[102] If the money to rehabilitate Rosemont had come from its homeowners, and if those homeowners had been the kind of people whose interests Baltimore prioritized, then rehabilitating the houses and then knocking them down would be wasteful indeed. But the money came from the federal government, and the priority was spending it. Fixing the houses in the bargain would have been nice, but it wasn't necessary.

In December 1971—four years and five months after Baltimore's city council had condemned the 10-D alignment through Rosemont, three years after the Federal Highway Administration had approved the 3-A alignment to replace it, two years after Esther Redd wrote Robert Embry asking him to "take steps, immediately, to bring relief to our deprived neighborhood," and one year after the establishment of the Rosemont Vacant House Program—the condemnation lines for the 10-D route through the Rosemont area simply, and it seems accidentally, expired. A new era was set to begin. And like the expressway that produced it, it was going to be as bad to Rosemont as a bomb.

8

"Ripped Off": How Rosemont Paid
the Price (1972–1975)

At the end of the 1960s, the Baltimore mortgage banker and real estate developer James Rouse started to create what he called "a garden for the growing of people": Columbia, Maryland, on fourteen thousand acres of Howard County farmland some twenty miles from Rosemont.¹ "Not here your established suburban chic that proclaims, on scrolled metal signs, streets named Amherst, Bowdoin, Cornell, Dartmouth," *The New York Times* reported at the end of 1971. "On this broad swath of rolling Maryland greenery, the streets have names like Wild Bees Lane (after an Andrew Wyeth drawing), Forty Winks Way (after Fitzgerald) and Pale Orchis Court (Frost)."² Columbia, one resident explained, was meant to be "a new city, a new America."³

A decade before, James Rouse had played a big role in inventing two defining technologies of the American century: the shopping mall and urban renewal.⁴ Now, in Columbia, he was pioneering a planned community that seemed to have transcended the need for either one.⁵ In this new city, the *Times* noted, there were "no mail slots in the doors." Instead, "see the group mailbox at the curb; there's one for every 16 families. It's meant to encourage casual friendship. No outside TV aerials or permanent clotheslines. You can put up a fence or cut trees only if the architectural-review committee approves. No neon signs."⁶

> Ballet lessons for children aged 5 to 8 are on Wednesday at 4 in the Other Barn, which is a barn. Soul-dance classes for adults, Monday at 7:30. Judo for seniors, Thursday at 8:30. Open audition ("tech crews," too") for "Slow Dance on the Killing Ground." Rocketry. Chinese cooking. Sculpture. Macrame. Squash.⁷

Smallish Columbia townhouses cost around $30,000, and couples camped out for days to buy them.⁸ Whole houses went for $64,000.⁹ "If you can create an environment that is good enough," Rouse said, "people will pay for it."¹⁰

According to the novelist Michael Chabon, who grew up in Columbia in the 1970s, "the City was a discredited idea in those days, burnt and poisoned and abandoned to rot."[11] But out here on the old tobacco fields and iron ranges, among the oily smells of fresh blacktop and new paint, urbanism could be "reimagined, rebuilt, renewed."[12] Columbia, per the *Times*, was the "good city," soft with blandly curving streets and culs-de-sac and "swaying willows, old oaks and spreading greensward."[13] And its denizens, the people who were moving there from Baltimore and Washington, DC, and beyond, were there to pioneer something brand new. They were, Chabon writes, "colonists of a dream, immigrants to a new land that as yet existed mostly on paper": a foldout map in beige and bisque, toasted pumpkin and muddy avocado that represented an "ongoing act of architectural and social imagination."[14]

"Urban planning and development deal with highways, land uses, buildings, densities—even with crime, delinquency, disease and deterioration," James Rouse explained in 1971. "But they almost never begin with a simple question: 'How can we best provide for the growth and happiness of a man, his wife and family?'"[15] Columbia, with its swaying willows and exotic cookery and summer-camp arts and crafts, was one answer to this question. Rosemont was decidedly not. Yet the two places were related to one another by more than proximities of space and time: More than half of Rosemont's new homeowners got the Section 235 mortgages that would pay for their rehabilitated houses in the 10-D condemnation corridor from the Rouse Company. This made Rosemont and Columbia one another's siblings; and as siblings often are, they were also one another's antipodes. Even as their mortgage payments susurrated into the Rouse Company's pockets and subsidized its more utopian acts of architectural and social imagination, the people moving into the reimagined, rebuilt, and renewed version of Rosemont were the colonists of a different kind of dream—one that turned out to be much closer to a waking nightmare.

Starting in 1972, when Baltimore's Department of Housing and Community Development put the first refurbished houses in the Rosemont corridor on the market, the agency's real estate brokers began to advertise for buyers in the *Afro-American* newspaper.

BE A PROUD HOME OWNER[16]

TOTAL AMOUNT REQUIRED $200[17]

BEGINNERS LUCK[18]

WHERE THE NEW BALTIMORE BEGINS[19]

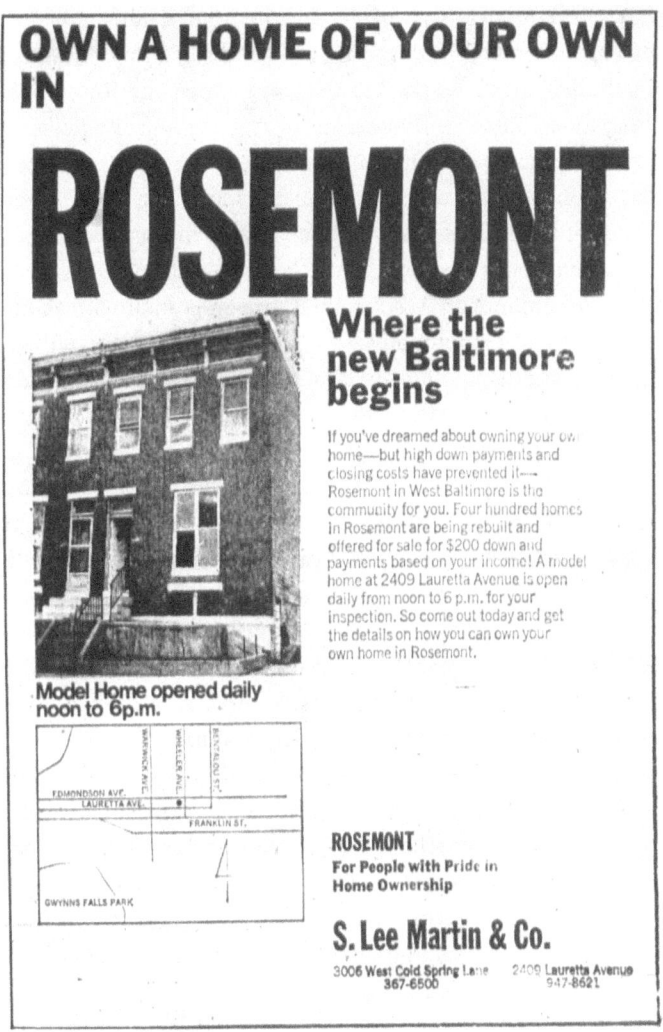

Advertisement for Section 235 homeownership program in Rosemont, Baltimore Department of Housing and Community Development/S. Lee Martin & Co. (1972). *Baltimore Afro-American*, February 12, 1972. Courtesy of the AFRO Archives.

"For the Two-Person Family," ads for the houses said, and typical buyers in the Rosemont Vacant House Program were meant to be young single mothers or retired couples whose children were grown and gone. The program's rules made sure they were poorer than the people whose homes they'd bought: In 1971, the maximum income the program allowed its participants was $6,075 for a family of two and $7,425 for a family of four.[20] They were different from the previous Rosemonters in other ways, too. Many hadn't gone to college. They didn't appear in the *Afro*'s social pages, and sometimes they didn't even appear in the telephone book. Between 1972, when the Rosemont Vacant House Program sold its first houses, and 1975, when the city pulled the plug on the program, records show that almost none of the people moving into the rehabilitated houses in the condemnation corridor came from Rosemont. In fact, just four of the families who had been living in Rosemont since before its condemnation would buy their houses back from the city: the Dorseys and the Burches on Edmondson Avenue, the Hairs on Franklin Street, and eventually the Maclins on Lauretta. Five of the families who were renting houses in the Rosemont condemnation corridor in 1970 ended up buying there, too.[21] The rest came from all over the city—many from public housing projects in East and West Baltimore and Cherry Hill.

According to the city's records, wherever they'd come from, almost all the new Rosemont buyers had been renters at their previous addresses. Whether they wanted to be homeowners now was immaterial, because by the early 1970s, the housing market for low-income people was in the process of turning inside out. Thanks in big part to the Housing and Urban Development Act of 1968, renting was harder, buying was easier, and if a poor family wanted a place to live, they often had to purchase it. And so Section 235 buyers nationwide "just grabbed," one official told *The Washington Post* in 1972. "They were desperate to get out. They would take anything that was available. And for people like them, renting possibilities just didn't exist and still don't."[22] "People were induced to purchase these homes because they were crying for housing," New York's secretary of state explained in his testimony on Section 235 before a Senate subcommittee in August 1972, and "because the unscrupulous people would say to them, 'Never mind renting a house, buy one. It won't cost you anything. What have you got to lose?'"[23]

1968's HUD Act and Fair Housing Act may have foreclosed many of the old opportunities for "wheeling and dealing in real estate" in the city, as the Activists, Inc. civil rights group had pointed out in its reports on the Baltimore housing market, but the "number soup" mortgage loans for low-income people it enabled had carved new avenues for the same.[24] For example, in Greater Rosemont, city code–enforcement operations made it seem like officials might push landlords to spend more than they wanted to spend—which was often anything at all—on maintenance and repairs. Thus in 1971, the Activists accused the speculator M. Goldseker Company of trying to "dispose of its rental properties" in the Rosemont Concentrated Code Enforcement Zone by "forc[ing] families to buy against their will" using those new mortgages—obtained, frequently, from the savings and loans it controlled.[25] If renters refused, they got evicted. But the Goldseker Company denied any malpractice. "Any accusation ... that we are forcing our tenants to buy their homes is absolutely and emphatically false," Sheldon Goldseker, the firm's spokesman, cooed in a prepared statement to the newspaper. "We have merely presented to our tenants a wonderful opportunity."[26] Yet one person's "wonderful opportunity" is another's booby trap.

In the summer of 1972, someone from the Rosemont Vacant House Program's real estate brokerage started pinning fliers advertising the program to the bulletin boards at city hall.[27] "Would you rather own a home," one asked, "or a box full of rent receipts?" "A house you buy is yours," read another. "When you buy it, you end up with something."[28] Indeed you did. But in Rosemont now, that something could be much worse than what you started with. To be sure, some of the people who bought the houses in the Rosemont condemnation corridor using the new FHA loans did so because they *did* want to own their own homes, and because they did want to live in Rosemont. But the rest, like the tenants who found themselves buying Goldseker houses they didn't want to own just so their families wouldn't be put out on the street, were making one of the only choices they thought they had. So: "We sell them," HCD's information officer told the paper in July 1972, talking about the houses in Rosemont's condemnation corridor, "just as fast as we can get them renovated."[29]

Brokers, Bankers, and Builders

A typical middle-class white person who wanted to buy a house might have started by hiring a real estate broker. Then, if they found a home they liked, they shopped around for a bank mortgage. They made an offer on the house and negotiated with the seller to get a price they wanted to pay. Of course there were sometimes hiccups in this process—no one *enjoys* buying a house, exactly—but in general, and in theory, parts of the market were set up to serve the buyers. If they didn't like their broker, they could get a new one. If their bank's interest rate or fees were too high, they could find another.

This was how the process usually worked, anyway. Almost none of it was true for the buyers in the Section 235 Rosemont Sales Program.

First, the program only had one real estate brokerage. S. Lee Martin was a local celebrity, a former track star at Morgan State renowned for his 1:53 half-mile.[30] His was not the only Black-owned firm to bid on the contract, but it was the one the Rosemont Coalition favored because, as part of his bid for the "Rosemont Sales Program" contract, Martin had pledged to donate a cut of his profits to local neighborhood associations and to give summer jobs to local teens.³¹ Also, he claimed to have extensive experience with the market the Rosemont Sales Program aimed to serve: 95 percent of the Martin company's clientele were Black.³² It's safe to assume that relatively few of those people were also poor, which was really the key to the Section 235 program and its trade—but that class distinction is one the people who had the power in Baltimore rarely bothered to make. On the other hand, before the Rosemont Vacant House Program, the city had not sold many houses under the "Home Ownership for the Poor" provisions of the 1968 housing law anyway, so nobody would have had much experience with their ins and outs.

In any case, HCD staff had wanted to work with the more established Black-owned R.L. Johnson firm, and they made no secret of their distaste for Martin and his salesmen. And to be fair, their complaints do seem to describe an unusually dysfunctional workplace.³³ For example, one Martin salesman apparently refused to "waste time" filling out forms. This quirk was understandable, if barely tenable under ordinary circumstances, but in a complicated federal program in which funds lumbered from one account to another on a bloat of documents in triplicate it was impossible.³⁴ Evidently, that same broker also "felt there was too much work involved in keeping track of sales" on the advertising map the Department of Housing and Community Development hung on the wall in the sample house.³⁵ Meanwhile, city reports indicate that although "our brokerage contract calls for Lee Martin to provide 'two competent salesmen' in the sample house," another salesman, a quarrelsome ex-boxer, could rarely be found at work. When he *was* in the office, one memo tattled, he "displayed an abrasive personality and [was] belligerent toward visitors."³⁶ According to another:

> buyers under contract or potential buyers no longer wish to have any contact with [that salesman]. . . . Apparently, Lee Martin has had some difficulty getting any of his people to work in Rosemont. How much of this is related to personality differences with [him] is undetermined.
>
> . . . some time last week Councilman Du Burns visited the sample house and in the course of the visit was confronted by [the salesman]. Apparently, in his abrasive manner, [the salesman] got into a heated discussion with Councilman Du Burns over who is the more knowledgeable person in real estate.³⁷

S. Lee Martin eventually reassigned that salesman to projects in other neighborhoods, but the problems in Rosemont continued. Prospective clients struggled to locate someone to answer their questions or show them houses, and no one ever seemed to be able to find any keys.³⁸ The brokers made more consequential mistakes, too. For example, and more than once, the real estate agents accidentally sold the same house to two different buyers.³⁹

In the grand scheme of things, the relative proficiency of a couple of Baltimore real estate salesmen in 1972 could not matter less, except that the buyers stuck in the Section 235 home sales program in Rosemont were also stuck with *them*. Even the tiny handful of buyers who hired their own real estate agents—like the Maclins, whose representative reportedly "had her pocketbook stolen by three young boys at gunpoint" in the Rosemont model home in 1971 and then quit the case—still had to deal with Martin's brokers at every step in the transaction.[40]

Likewise, they were stuck with whatever lender the program assigned them. The Department of Housing and Community Development divided the Rosemont condemnation corridor roughly in half, from east to west. At the eastern end of the condemnation corridor, Sidney H. Tinley's Chesapeake Financial Corporation provided all the Section 235 loans. At the western end, the Rouse Company did the same. In other words, the lender came with the house a buyer chose. The prices were the same, the terms were the same, and there was no negotiating. Records show that between 1972 and 1975, the Rouse Company issued around 190 mortgages to Section 235 buyers in Rosemont and Chesapeake Financial not quite 170.[41] (In the end, HCD sold the remaining 140-ish houses it renovated in Rosemont to Baltimore's housing authority, which used them as scatter site public housing and paid for them from a different pot of public funds.)[42]

Rouse and Tinley had built their fortunes on the ways of doing things that had made the old Rosemont. Now, together, they were poised to profit from ones that made the new.

Sidney H. Tinley was a notorious slumlord and big cheese in Baltimore: "a blue chip," the *Sun* once said, "among blue chips."[43] He'd graduated from Boys' Latin and Johns Hopkins. He'd served on the school board and the state planning commission. He'd been the president of the Real Estate Board of Greater Baltimore, the Mortgage Corporation of America, and the Maryland League of Building, Savings and Loan Associations and a director at the Maryland National Bank, the Central Savings Bank, the Union Trust Company, and the Title Guarantee Company.[44] He embodied many of the problems the Housing and Urban Development Act of 1968 was designed to solve.

Rouse, on the other hand, had a more complicated relationship to the exclusionary predation that was his bread and butter. After World War II, he'd established himself as a mortgage banker in suburban Baltimore—but he was also an active partner in the Baltimore Plan for Housing Law Enforcement, aimed at improving housing conditions for (mostly) Black renters in the aging neighborhoods near the city center.[45] The idea behind the Baltimore Plan was that housing code enforcement could show that "private enterprise can transform a run-down area as well as the government can," yet as one city report noted in 1957, "blight kept pace with all attempts to eliminate it."[46] Meanwhile, armed with Rouse Company mortgages their Black neighbors could never get, white buyers flooded out of the city. "Baltimore does not condone profiteering in squalor," the *Sun* said, but of course it did, and Rouse knew it.[47] He condoned it, too. After a stint as a lobbyist and political advisor in Washington, DC, Rouse returned to Baltimore and pivoted into property development: first shopping malls, then planned communities like Columbia.[48]

Rouse and Tinley were delighted to participate in the Rosemont Vacant House Program, because financing Section 235 loans for low-income people was a wildly lucrative operation. In Rosemont, it all started with the stupefying prices the FHA allowed the Department of Housing and Community Development to charge for the houses. The city had bought the houses in the Rosemont condemnation corridor from the Interstate Division in 1971 for $2,500 each. The Department of Housing and Community Development had told the potential "as-is" buyers that same year that their fair market value was $4,700. And officials had promised the Rosemont neighbors that the rehabilitated houses would sell for $7,500. However, in fact, the Department of Housing and Community Development (HCD) had persuaded the FHA to let them charge the "maximum allowable" price for the houses it was selling in the Rosemont corridor: an eye-popping $15,950 for mid-block houses and $16,500 for end rows, plus interest and fees.[49]

"Anyone with $20,000 to spend is not going to buy a house in Rosemont," Rosemont Neighborhood Improvement Association (R.N.I.A.) activist Rose Gallop pointed out, correctly.[50] Actually, anyone with $20,000 to spend did not even have that option. But the whole point of the Section 235 program was that the buyer herself never saw the whole bill at once. Because her payments were based on her income, not on the cost of the house, it was more like health care or college tuition today: priced, in theory, for an institutional payor and not an individual buyer. The city set the prices high because it had no reason not to: The bank paid them for the house, and then the federal government paid the bank back. And the banks would rather be paid some percentage of $17,000 than that same percentage of $7,500, $4,700, or $2,500.

Tinley and Rouse made their money from the interest subsidies HUD paid them, which rate crept steadily upward as time passed: first 6.5 percent, then 7.5, then 8.5.[51] This last rate, historian Rebecca K. Marchiel points out, was so high that it exceeded usury laws in some states, like Illinois.[52] But the interest was set so high to lure lenders to participate in the program—and the borrowers themselves didn't pay it. HUD did. Lenders were also allowed to juice their rate of return by discounting "points" from the face amount of the mortgage, so that the FHA insured a higher loan than the borrower got. When they sold the loans on the secondary market, they sold them for their full insured value.[53] Finally, Tinley and Rouse earned money from the front-end fees and closing costs they charged the federal government for each loan, which they could charge again and again on the same property when buyers defaulted. In sum: Banks, investors, and even brokers earned more money from the government when homeowners defaulted than they did when buyers paid their loans in full. Recklessness was its own reward. As legal scholar Harry B. Wilson explained in 1973, in the Section 235 program "the lender who makes a bad loan turns a high profit."[54]

The contractor who built a bad house did, too.

Construction contractors San-Dee (a local outfit) and Morelite (from New York City) started to renovate the condemned houses in the Rosemont 10-D corridor at the end of 1971.[55] In January 1972, before Morelite had turned a single house in the Rosemont corridor over to HCD for sale, company head Melvin Weintraub was indicted in New York City, charged with eighty-three counts of fraud related to the company's work for a housing-rehabilitation scheme in the Bronx.[56] "Sale of Houses Begins," the *Sun* headline read. "Developer Faces Charges."[57] The indictment was not Weintraub's first. In 1966, for instance, a New York court had accused him and his father of hiding the money they earned from rewiring old apartment houses in secret bank accounts so they wouldn't have to pay income tax on it.[58] It also would not be his last. In 1986, Weintraub would be ensnared in a Florida bribery scandal. In 2000, he would be sentenced to a year in prison for forcing undocumented construction workers to "scrape, cut, and claw asbestos with crowbars and with their bare hands" in a building renovation in New Haven.[59] (In his defense in that case, Weintraub's brother testified that he "was always a friend to minorities," even when "this was not a fashionable thing to do.")[60] Under ordinary circumstances, contractors' possibly fraudulent behavior might have been a worry to the people who hired them, but Weintraub's bosses in Baltimore had the luxury of serenity. "I am going to check with our attorney to see if this (the indictments) will have any effect on our relationship." HCD director Embry told the *Sun* that month. "We are very happy with [Morelite's] work."[61]

From the beginning, however, Morelite's negligence was hard to overlook. In January 1972, the same month Melvin Weintraub was indicted in New York City, a reporter for the *Afro-American* newspaper arranged a tour of the first model home for the Section 235 sales program in Rosemont, on Lauretta Avenue. Though Morelite had allegedly just finished renovating the house into "like-new condition" "from cellar to roof," the observers saw missing floorboards, cheap and broken appliances, windows that rattled in their frames when the wind blew.[62] Congressman Parren J. Mitchell, invited by the *Afro* to join the tour, banged his fist against the wall and shook his head. "A child will go through this in no time flat," he said.[63] The Rosemont houses, the reporter concluded, "were rehabilitated with such materials and such workmanship that they would fall into slum conditions way before the houses were paid for."[64] Mitchell echoed the point. "I don't want people to go into a home with a 30-year mortgage only to have it fall apart in 10," he said.[65]

After that first visit to the model home on Lauretta Avenue, Congressman Mitchell's aide, a young man named George Minor, did a little digging. The Department of Housing and Community Development, he learned, was paying Morelite $11,000 for each house it renovated in the Rosemont corridor, for which sum the company had promised "total rehabilitation": new walls and floors and new appliances, including washer-dryers, working stoves, and air-conditioning. But instead of total rehabilitation, Minor found, Morelite was doing "stop-gap" work—the barest minimum—and keeping all the cash left over when it was finished.[66]

Yet Robert Embry told the reporter that he had personally visited the model home "on a number of occasions" and found it in perfectly good condition.[67] When the *Afro* wouldn't let the story go, Embry agreed to push Morelite to redo its work, and the next month he accompanied Mitchell, Minor, and two reporters on an inspection tour. This time, the windows had been sealed against wind and water. The stove and vent hood clicked on. The electrical and telephone wires were new, and so was the green wall-to-wall carpeting. Congressman Mitchell thumped the wall again. "Okay," he said. "I am satisfied."[68] Aide Minor was less confident. "As far as Rosemont is concerned," he said, "[I] don't know what can be done to end up with a product [I] think should be on the market at that price."[69]

What Have You Got to Lose?

If they didn't read the newspaper regularly, Rosemont's Section 235 buyers could fairly imagine that since they were purchasing under an FHA program and not from a contract seller or a speculator, the houses they bought would meet FHA standards. In fact, that was not true. The 1968 Housing Act had loosened inspection requirements so that mortgages could be more equitably awarded: a "reasonable relaxation of standards," one political scientist wrote, "to reflect inner-city conditions."[70] But the new standards were so relaxed, and so vague, that individual inspectors could scrutinize properties as much or as little as they liked.[71] Some appraisers came inside the houses they were inspecting but didn't look at the wiring or the plumbing. Some didn't go inside and gave properties a desultory drive-by "windshield inspection" instead. Others did no inspection at all, because (as one reporter explained) sellers and lenders did not "want to know about problems that would prevent a mortgage."[72] Another report called this approach "the *caveat emptor* concept."[73]

All this went double in Rosemont. Buyers in the condemnation corridor could reasonably assume that since they were purchasing houses that the Department of Housing and Community Development's own contractors had renovated, those houses would be in good shape. And after the dustup over Morelite's model home, Robert Embry announced in June 1972 that the agency would spend $2,000 more on each Rosemont rehab, "to put up new dry walls instead of patching the old walls with plaster, to guarantee new plumbing and wiring, new bathroom fixtures, new baseboards and a hood over the stove."[74] Yet official records from meetings with contractors and subcontractors that summer document more of the same. "The finished products were something less than the standards of acceptability of HCD or of their trades," notes from one meeting read. "As an example, grease stains on the carpeting, grease smudges on freshly painted walls, etc."[75] Inspectors' reports show that HCD's contractors were still using the cheapest materials they could, tolerating or even encouraging sloppy work, and lining their pockets with the money they saved. For instance, investigators found Morelite's subcontractors cutting their lumber bill by putting only half of the required number of floor joists in each house they renovated, never mind what could happen to the people walking on them. When building inspectors did pay a visit to the Rosemont properties, one told the *Sun*, housing officials "made clear that we should not do anything about" the problems they found there.[76] Torn between preventing or fixing the problems with the Rosemont renovations or keeping buyers from finding out about those problems until it was too late, city officials made the easier—if costlier—choice.

"Why does the city tear down sturdy plaster walls and put in cheap sheetrock that any kid can put his foot through? Why do they tear out floors and ceilings that are sound?" the president of the Property Owners Association asked in a newspaper interview. "Any professional property owner could rebuild a vacant house for $8,000 tops"—compared to the (now) nearly twice that the Department of Housing and Community Development was spending—"by salvaging what's structurally sound and using his own men. We've told Bob Embry this many times but he hasn't listened."[77] This was a self-serving observation from a landlords' lobbyist who would have liked that money for himself, but it was also a fair point. The Rosemont homes were only about fifty years old. Piel and Keelty had built them to be good, solid houses. Most of the houses the Interstate Division bought—and therefore most of the houses in the Rosemont rehabilitation program—had been owner-occupied, and the people who had lived in them until the expressway map came through had taken great care to maintain them. But Morelite and San-Dee were taking these good houses and wrecking them, and using millions of dollars in public money to do it.

To be sure, the vehicle that delivered some of these new horrors to Rosemont was a familiar old jalopy: plain, simple graft. In 1973 and 1974, federal investigations of Baltimore's Department of Housing and Community Development started to show that its rehabilitation programs had been operating more like a slush funds. For example, in 1974, agents from the FBI's Federal Organized Crime Strike Force arrested and indicted Buddy Barnett, a major rehabilitation subcontractor in West Baltimore. According to the *Sun*, Barnett had used his $2 million in city contracts, which he'd gotten from his "close association" with the housing official who processed HCD's contractor payroll, to "launder gambling receipts" for the "reputed mobster" and hit man Bernard Brown.[78] (For his part, federal agents found Brown—on parole on charges of fraud and tax evasion—dead in a reporter's Mount Vernon apartment, surrounded by nineteen emptied Valium capsules.)[79] While Barnett was awaiting trial in federal court on his own fraud charges, his company won $120,000 in new contracts from the Department of Housing and Community Development. "We don't have the power to exclude people from bidding for moral turpitude," Embry told the paper.[80]

More to the point, that same year, a long investigation by the *Sun* revealed corruption in the Rosemont rehabilitation program orbiting around Robert Embry's second-in-command: Ottavio Grande, the city's chief of construction and buildings inspection. At first, Grande had doled out work to his associates using no-bid contracts; but starting in 1973, HCD began to require contractors to bid for their jobs.[81] Subsequently, as a *Sun* columnist explained: "Once every few months, nine contractors met in a motel to size up [the] contracts the city was about to put out on bid. They selected a contractor to do the job. He, in turn, submitted the lowest bid; all the others came in high. Grande got a 5 percent kickback."[82] "Collectively," the piece continued, "the contractors made about $5 million a year, and testimony showed that the conspiracy inflated the prices the city paid for its demolition work."[83]

In 1977, Ottavio Grande was tried in federal court on forty-eight counts of racketeering and extortion stemming from his work with the city's housing-rehabilitation programs, and he was convicted on thirty-eight of them.[84] The civic vandalism his trial transcripts describe seems to have stemmed less from any particular cunning on Grande's part than from a kind of blinkered gullibility on his boss's: According to the *Sun*'s account of HCD chief Embry's testimony, "being a lawyer, he had little background in construction. So he conceded it was natural for him to rely on Grande and those Grande assembled around him for technical advice."[85] ("Those Grande assembled around him," primarily his brothers and brothers-in-law and other friends, "called themselves the 'FBI,' for 'full-blooded Italians.'")[86] Even from a chair in the witness box, Embry couldn't bring himself to see the true dimensions of the plunder that had been going on right under his nose. "In my eight years in city government," he told the judge, "I never came across any official . . . who had more integrity than Mr. Grande."[87]

Maybe the Rosemont Vacant House Program was sheltering an unusually capable cabal of gangsters and conspirators. Alternatively, maybe behind every door at city hall a different Ottavio Grande was hornswoggling his own version of Robert Embry. Or, more likely, the Rosemont Vacant House Program was set up to work exactly as it did. Grande and Weintraub and their ilk may have taken every opportunity to hyperbolize the system, but even if everyone involved in it had been doing their jobs in good faith, the outcome would have been about the same: a grift. The HUD rehabilitation grant and the Section 235 loans that accompanied it had refilled Rosemont's coffers after the blockbusters and roadbuilders had drained them dry, so that a new group of real estate men could profiteer in squalor while creating more of the same.

Rosemont Is Now

The people who paid the price for all this malfeasance were the people moving into the Rosemont rehabs. For example, in April 1973, Thomas and Ruby Maclin were finally able to buy their Lauretta Avenue house back, not for the $2,500 the city had paid the Interstate Division or for the $4,700 it had initially offered for the "as-is" sale, but for $15,800, to be paid for by a Section 235 mortgage from James W. Rouse and Company.[88] "I sold my house [in the suburbs]," Ruby Maclin wrote in a letter to officials, "because I had good faith in living in my house at 2412 Lauretta Avenue." It soon emerged that her faith was badly misplaced.[89]

Conditions in the Maclins' "cellar to roof" renovated Lauretta Avenue house were so bad that the federal Department of Housing and Urban Development got involved. "The property was inspected by a member of our staff," one federal official wrote his Baltimore counterparts, "and he reports the following":

1. Wet basement.
2. Missing bathroom fixtures.
3. Damaged bathroom wall due to removal of fixtures.

4. Bathroom door does not close and lock properly.
5. Lock on front door insecurely installed.
6. Damaged kitchen tile.
7. Defective refrigerator.
8. Missing screens.
9. Inoperable door bell.
10. Inoperable exhaust fan (kitchen).
11. Leak under kitchen sink.

"This property is a recently rehabilitated home in the Rosemont Project Area," the official chided. "The above items are the responsibility of the contractor to correct and require immediate attention."[90] Baltimore housing officials agreed to make the repairs, and they did—but only some of them. Ruby Maclin had to write to HUD again. "ROSEMONT COMPLAINTS," she wrote:

1. Water running in basement
2. Repair leaking water pipe in kitchen
3. Install screens in windows (new man measured for them but measured wrong)
4. Approximately 30-40 rats are running in the backyard and running up people's steps on the front of the house.

**There were so many unfinished things to be done before.[91]

Other buyers suffered, too. For example, though the city kept paying for carpeting in the Rosemont rehabs, contractors simply stopped installing it. "On December 21st," one official wrote Ottavio Grande early in 1974:

we had arranged for five families to move in before the Christmas vacation to help avoid any vandalism that might occur. Carpet and move-in scheduling was coordinated between Mr. Burns of your office and Mr. Jaudon of my office. The following examples point out the problems that occurred.

Mrs. Imma Izzard was scheduled to move in after 3:00 p.m. on the 21st. At 6:00 p.m. this buyer called Mr. Jaudon at home to report that the carpet had not been installed and that she had to cancel the movers. This carpet was not installed until December 26th.

Mr. Jerry Ross was scheduled to move in after 3:00 p.m. on the 21st, but called this office at 4:00 p.m. stating that the carpet had not been installed. Mr. Ross had to chase down the Carpet Fair truck and convince them to lay carpet in his house. This carpet was installed by 7:00 p.m. with the movers waiting for completion and charging the family an extra waiting charge of $60.00.

On two other cases the carpet men ran out of carpet.[92]

The memo came back from Grande with excuses penciled in the margins: the installers were just late, they'd meant to be there, they'd run out of carpet and would return some other day, the family should just have refused to pay the waiting fee. More bluntly, Grande had also stamped all over it in cranky red letters: BULLSHIT BULLSHIT BULLSHIT BULLSHIT.[93] "Be that as it may," Grande's colleague replied, "my concern stems from the fact that we only need one such incident to cause us undue negative publicity and community relations problems." "As to the incidents reported being without fact," he added, "some conflict with your position is presented by the marginal notes made in your office on my memo to you."[94]

Federal reports on the Section 235 program saw problems like these for something like what they were. "The staff did find cases where homeowners failed to take care of basic maintenance responsibilities," one said: "However, no homeowner can be expected to cope with poor construction, cracked foundations, improper wiring, and a general failure of contractors to meet local building and maintenance requirements. A welfare mother with four or five children may well have a house that is in less than spotless condition, but they cannot be blamed because there is only one electrical outlet in the entire house."[95]

Yet when *city* officials looked at the neighborhood, they chose instead to see naive buyers overwhelmed by the responsibilities of homeownership. In 1972, the Housing Authority's financial counselors started to deliver a scripted lecture to every Section 235 buyer in Rosemont, half of which was dedicated *in loco parentis* to "the things that should be done" to "maintain your home in good condition and to give you continual pride in the property."[96] These included paying heat, electricity, cooking gas, and water bills; painting the walls; and cleaning the gutters. Turn off your lights, the counselor would say. Stop using the gas stove for heat. "We know you will keep your yard, porch, and window panes clean."[97] Under the umbrella of a hastily assembled Resident Family Services Division, officials from the city Department of Housing and Community Development got more than $100,000 from the federal government to put together a set of lessons on "how to live in a modern home."[98] "Occupancy coordinators" started teaching classes on money management, home repairs, caring for new appliances, cleaning a carpet, gardening, preparing nutritious family meals, and do-it-yourself decorating to some of the new homeowners.[99] "Are these people being trained as master plumbers, journeymen, electricians, or first class carpenters?" groused one letter-writer to the *Sun*. "Most assuredly it couldn't cost [this much] to teach a family to keep a house clean, replace a faucet washer, do general painting, and mow the lawn."[100]

A hand-drawn workbook, "Rosemont Is Now," would have been right at home on the shelves of the Columbia branch of the Howard County public library. It included lessons on cooking and cleaning as well as Home Beautification and Home Decoration.

LEARN—

To choose a splash of color or coordinate colors.
To solve your home decoration problems.
Window dressing and floor coverings.
Needle-craft and crocheting
Create candle molds and stencil silhouettes
Make 'Architectural' changes without altering the structure.[101]

"The possibilities," the book cheered, "are as unlimited as your imagination."[102] Yet Rosemont was not Columbia. Its possibilities were not unlimited, and its new homeowners' problems had nothing to do with uncoordinated cushions or unmolded candles or dirty windowpanes. They couldn't be solved by macramé or squash or "Slow Dance on the Killing Ground."

In fact it was simpler than all that, and more ominous. The problem the new Rosemonters had was that the houses they bought from the Department of Housing and Community Development were bad, and bad houses cost an enormous amount of money—money the homeowners by definition did not have—to repair. Loan records make clear that second and third mortgages were epidemic in the new Rosemont, as even people who could have comfortably afforded the payments on their Section 235 mortgage loan struggled to find the money for upkeep on their indifferently renovated houses. For instance, in July 1972, Julia Benjamin borrowed $16,250 from the Rouse Company to buy the three-bedroom, one-bath with a big porch at 2549 Lauretta.[103] In February 1976, she borrowed nearly one-quarter of that amount from the Globe Home Improvement Company, whose salesmen went door to door in the neighborhood peddling "KITCHENS ... BATHROOMS ... DECORATING ... CARPENTRY ... REPAIRS ... REMODELING ... PAINTING ... PAPERING ... ROOM ADDITIONS ... DORMERS ... STORM WINDOWS ... SIDING ... ROOFING ... ELECTRICAL ... PLUMBING ... CLUBROOMS ... ETC."[104] By August, her Rouse mortgage was in foreclosure and she'd lost her house. Likewise, in April 1977, State Home Remodeling Co. lent Nathaniel and Ruby E. Williams $8,950 to improve a house they'd spent $15,000 to buy not five years before.[105] The next year, they too were in default, the whole investment gone. Odessa Quickley had to borrow some $4,500 from Globe before she even moved into her supposedly "like new" house on Lanvale in 1974.[106]

Others in similar circumstances managed to hang on. In 1973, Richard and Dolores Wheeler bought their house on Edmondson Avenue for $16,200; by the end of the decade Globe and the Household Finance Corporation had loaned them more than $6,000.[107] In fact, according to city records, by November 1974 the Wheelers were already five months delinquent on their mortgage payment: "He got behind on his bills," a Housing Authority financial counselor wrote, "and used his mortgage money to pay some of them."[108] Chesapeake Financial recommended foreclosure. However, the family did what was necessary to keep the house—borrowing, refinancing, reverse mortgages—until at least 2020.[109]

The Household Finance Corporation, the subject of a 1978 Federal Trade Commission complaint for trying to "collect on loans that have been dismissed in bankruptcy proceedings by lending more money to the bankrupt consumers," lent Rosemont buyers thousands and thousands of dollars during the 1970s.[110] So did Thorp Credit, Belvedere Construction, FinanceAmerica Corp, the State Building Supply Co., Cadillac Construction Company, Colony Credit, G+E Contractors, Pittsburgh Aluminum, and Maryland Prime-O-Sash. And so did the Department of Housing and Community Development itself. Documents explained that these loans were meant to "alleviate harmful conditions which cause blight or deterioration within neighborhoods."[111] These were conditions that a buyer might reasonably assume HCD would have aimed to alleviate in the first place.

However, as city officials cheerfully pointed out, "the responsibility is different for homeowners than for tenants." Owners couldn't sell the houses for anything near what they'd paid, not to mention what they'd put into them.[112] Everybody who had bought a house in the Rosemont condemnation corridor from the Department of Housing and Community Development was stuck there.

"So often we're asked, 'How can people be so stupid?'" one Chicago tenant organizer said of the low-income buyers who used FHA loans to buy houses in that city in the early 1970s. "But the people aren't stupid. They're just so desperate to get out of the ghetto and they presumed they were dealing with honest people."[113] More important, they presumed they were dealing with an honest program. Instead, the new Rosemont homeowners were dealing with a way of thinking about the city, and about their new neighborhood in particular, that was inherited from an earlier time and adjusted to suit the new tools available to it. The plunder was the point.

By 1974, just two years after the first homeowners moved into their houses in the 10-D condemnation corridor, the Rosemont Vacant House Program was already winding down. About two-thirds of the houses the Interstate Division had sold to HCD were occupied by new buyers who had paid for them using Section 235 mortgages, and the rest had gone to the housing authority for use as rental public housing. This was in spite of the neighbors' clearly stated objection to public housing in Rosemont, but it only added insult to injury: On July 11, 1972, the zoning commission had approved the public housing development on the old box-factory site with no discussion.[114] The next day, bulldozers began to clear the land for the project's recreation center. "No notice of construction has ever been posted as required by law," the R.N.I.A. complained. "Your office did not notify us."[115] A few years later the project was finished: 136 units for Black tenants in a neighborhood that was by that time 98 percent Black.[116] "They call this planning a city," Joseph Wiles told a reporter from the *News-American*. "All you have to do is look at a map to see it's not planning. They're just dumping things here and there."[117]

Although the Section 235 program in Rosemont was short-lived, it still left a trail of havoc in its wake. In February 1974, the director of the Rosemont Sales Program wrote a letter to the vice president of the Rouse Company about the escalating number of mortgages nearing default in the condemnation corridor. "I am sure you recognize and appreciate the value of a personal meeting with a first time homebuyer on matters such as these," he wrote, but he had heard that Rouse's "collection staff did not visit the delinquent mortgagors because the collection staff was afraid to enter the neighborhood."[118] Not quite 10 percent of Rosemont borrowers lost their houses in the first years of their 235 mortgages, about the same as the national Section 235 average in 1974, compared with 2 percent of unsubsidized FHA borrowers.[119] But many more buyers had to take extra loans to keep their houses, and those loans eventually came due. In all, by my count, almost half of the buyers in the Rosemont Vacant House Program would eventually lose their homes.[120]

"It is probably inevitable," a 1974 report on the Section 235 program in the *Yale Law Journal* put it, "that in any government program, not all of the participants will be benefited to as great a degree as the program's proponents would have hoped. But the federal 'homeownership for the poor' program is unusual: thousands of participants actually were left in a far worse condition than before."[121] "I don't see how anyone who is black or Puerto Rican could have faith in the white system," one prosecutor said, "after being shaken down like this."[122]

FHA'd

In 1973, a reporter, insurance investigator, and detective novelist named Brian D. Boyer published a book on the Section 235 program nationwide called *Cities Destroyed for Cash*, whose title is a neat summary of its argument. Section 235, Boyer wrote, "was a deliberate program of urban ruin for profit, under the cover of government housing law and with an endless flow of federal money. The destruction of the cities can be understood if put in old-fashioned cops-and-robbers terms—there were a bunch of bad guys who stuck up the cities and rode away with the gold." "As they say in almost every big city in the United States," Boyer said, "the neighborhoods have been FHA'd. To be FHA'd is to be ruined."[123]

To be sure, some of the people who bought the houses in the Rosemont condemnation corridor using the new FHA loans were not ruined. For example, Drusilla Bunch learned about the Section 235 sales program in Rosemont through her job as an administrator at the Department of Housing and Community Development. She paid $16,250 for her house on a quiet stretch of Franklintown in 1974 because she wanted a garden, and because, she said, Rosemont was "known to be where schoolteachers would move"—a prized endorsement.[124] Leslie Carl Howard was working at Bethlehem Steel and living on the fourteenth floor of the Murphy Homes in "Old" West Baltimore with his wife and three children when he heard about the homeownership program on the radio. In 1974, the family packed their things into their yellow Super Beetle and moved into a $15,950 three-bedroom with a big, sunny bay window on Harlem Avenue.[125] For them, the program worked as advertised: Drusilla Bunch and Leslie Carl Howard thrived in their Rosemont homes for forty years and counting. But they weren't typical Section 235 homebuyers, either. (For one thing, they are still there.) And even they were kicking against the same undertow that was drowning so many of their neighbors. New and longtime Rosemonters alike now knew, as the scholar Peter Coviello puts it, "what it is to feel something cherished wrenched and jolted into something less, and then less, and then less."[126]

In 1977, a group of homeowners who had bought on Lauretta Avenue using the Section 235 program invited *Sun* reporter James Dilts out to the old Rosemont condemnation corridor. They wanted him to see, they said, how they'd been "ripped off by the City of Baltimore."[127] "Since I came in I've had problems," Shirley Fisher said. Fisher, an elementary school secretary, had bought her house with a $15,900 Section 235 mortgage in 1973, after the city's contractors had supposedly renovated it from "cellar to roof."[128] But her bathroom floor was spongy, and its tiles wobbled and popped loose. The living-room carpet puckered with tar the contractors had tracked in four years earlier. The porch wall leaked. "Normal wear and tear," city officials said.[129]

Shirley Fisher's neighbors had it just as bad. "Every week, I just put my paycheck right into this house," said Walter Thomas, a city sanitation worker. When it rained, the basement walls oozed. The front porch was peeling off. When Thomas's wife Martha took a bath, she said, "I can hear something crack," and she was sure one day she and the tub would both slump right through the floor. "See that?" Mrs. Thomas said, pointing to the daylight dribbling around her warped front door. "Look at the houses they sell you."[130]

As the Section 235 homeownership campaign in the Rosemont expressway corridor makes clear, the people who had the power in Baltimore were much better at breaking things than they were at building them. And so by the end of the 1970s, when outsiders looked at Rosemont, they did not see the "peaceful, clean, safe, attractive area of Baltimore" that had nurtured family and community life for decades.[131] They did not see the "stable, cohesive" hamlet that two generations of activists had worked so hard to preserve. Instead, they saw exactly what they had been expecting to see all along: just, as a 1980 article in the *Sun* put it, a "tree-lined slum."[132]

CONCLUSION

Roads to Nowhere

On an Indian summer Saturday in October 1975, the Sierra Club organized a "family day" in West Baltimore's Leakin Park. In muddy Hush Puppies and hiking boots, ornithologists, ecologists, botanists, and retired science teachers led parades through the forest, gesturing up with their walking sticks at the bright orange ribbons they'd looped from one tree branch to the next. The ribbons marked the path of I-70, the eight-lane superhighway the Urban Design Concept Team (UDCT)'s 1968 3-A plan sent crashing through the park on stilts as tall as apartment buildings.[1] "It is tragic and sad," one activist wrote in the *Sun* the next year, "that one generation of politicians and contractors should be able to destroy an irreplaceable resource that was centuries in the making."[2]

Starting in the late 1950s, activists in cities and suburbs nationwide began to mobilize in defense of American places. Unfettered capitalism, they argued, was pouring deadly chemicals into the air and water, destroying beloved old buildings, drowning rural communities under artificial lakes, turning national parks into hot-dog stands and open spaces into garbage dumps.[3] Activists like Rachel Carson and Jane Jacobs became celebrities. And for the flash of a moment historian Douglas Brinkley calls the "Silent Spring Revolution," policymakers started to embrace their causes.[4]

In this context, in Baltimore and in cities nationwide, people started to protest the construction of the "concrete monsters" on federal highway maps.[5] But before the late 1960s, those who resisted the construction of urban expressways in principle or in particular did not yet have many real tools they could use to stop them. Often, the closest thing they could get was the appointment of a multidisciplinary design team like the UDCT in Baltimore, as federal highway officials, increasingly sensitive to public criticism aimed at themselves, were persuaded to peel away and spread around some of the absolute power highway engineers had arrogated.[6] By contrast, the engineers managed thicker skins. Only a tiny handful of "so-called artistic and creative people" had a problem with urban expressway plans, one engineer told a congressional panel in 1967, and they were riling up everybody else.[7] The so-calleds were the problem, not the roads.

But even when cities like Baltimore and Chicago appointed them, the design teams and the "joint development" they brought did not actually solve many problems. For one thing, Baltimore neighborhood activist Barbara Mikulski remembered, "their idea of citizen participation, was for us to tell them what kind of shrubs we wanted alongside the highway, not whether we wanted the goddamn thing or not."[8] For their part, scholars Joseph F. C. DiMento and Cliff Ellis write, "more than a few architects resented their marginalization as decorators or salvage crews" for the freeways engineers had mapped willy-nilly a decade before.[9] Too often, the best outcome they could deliver was something like what the UDCT promised Baltimore: a butchered city in which, it is true, things could have been worse.

But urban expressway politics were about to take a new shape.[10]

The Fate of the East–West Expressway

In the late 1960s and early 1970s, a host of new federal rules and regulations aimed, historian Brinkley explains, to balance "the competing interests of economic growth and proper environmental stewardship."[11] Nobody was trying to shift the power too far, of course; and as President Nixon said a few years later, faced with "a flat choice between jobs and smoke" Americans would choose jobs every time.[12] Still, it was clear to many policymakers that to win voters, especially young people and (increasingly) women, they needed to put some legislative muscle behind their conservationist postures.[13]

In 1966, President Johnson had signed into the law the National Historic Preservation Act, which among other things required federally funded construction projects like expressways to account for and try to save the historic structures they threatened.[14] Also that year, the law that created the Department of Transportation prohibited roadbuilders from routing interstate highways through historic sites, wildlife or waterfowl refuges, or public parks unless "no feasible and prudent alternative" route could be found.[15] In 1968, the same Federal-Aid Highway Act that mandated relocation payments to homeowners like the ones in the East–West Expressway corridor reiterated that highway planners needed to consider (President Johnson said) "social and environmental factors in determining the location of urban highways—thus preserving many neighborhoods from the bulldozer and the wrecking ball."[16] And just before the 1968 presidential election, the Federal Highway Administration mandated at least a pair of public hearings for every highway project, one before any route decisions were made and one after.

Conservationists and city planners saw in this pivot "an opportunity for the ordinary citizen to gain some leverage," author A. Q. Mowbray noted in 1969.[17] State highway engineers and their allies saw the same thing, and they resented it mightily. "Our new interstate highways are anything but the atrocities the voices of opposition would have the public believe them to be," one state highway official said in 1968, and "to allow a single individual appearing in opposition to a highway project, to effectively tie up the project for an indefinite period of time" would be to cede the nation's economic future to those aforementioned "so-called" artistic and creative people.[18] From the roadbuilders' perspective, even a watered-down effort to mitigate some of the harm expressways caused was too much.

Still, the effort continued. In 1970, President Nixon signed the National Environmental Policy Act (NEPA). As the bill's sponsor, Washington Senator Scoop Jackson, explained, it was supposed to ensure that voters' concerns with "the integrity of man's life support system—the human environment" were "infused into the ongoing programs and actions of the Federal Government" by requiring all federal agencies to "assess the environmental effects of their proposed actions" *before* they took them.[19] In particular, it required any federally funded project that would adversely impact the environment, like an interstate highway, to produce a detailed environmental impact statement for public review and comment. NEPA was no guarantee a project could be stopped; none of these new laws were. It was, however, supposed to be a guarantee that citizens and activists could be involved in the federal decision-making process, and that government agencies would consider their choices in context before they made them. As a result, just as the roadbuilders anticipated, the balance of power between highway engineers and their adversaries shifted considerably.[20]

In Baltimore, where the 3-A system had tentacles that reached almost everywhere and snagged almost everything, these new regulations gave activists new tools to slow its construction.[21] In the early 1970s, journalists noted, activists sued the Interstate Division over "community disruption, destruction of historical sites, the loss of parkland, environmental pollution, the failure to demonstrate a need for expressways, the procedural defects, and the lack of public participation in expressway planning."[22] They started in 1970 in Fells Point and Federal Hill, eighteenth- and nineteenth-century neighborhoods along the harbor that would have been carved apart by the I-83 (through Fells Point) and I-95 (through Federal Hill) segments of the 3-A system.[23] Then, the next year, the Rosemont Neighborhood Improvement Association (R.N.I.A.) and the Movement Against Destruction (MAD) coalition joined a lawsuit aimed at another of the major weaknesses in the 3-A plan: the elevated superhighway through the park.[24] This lawsuit was filed by the Sierra Club and a new outfit calling itself the Volunteers Opposing the Leakin Park Expressway, or VOLPE. (The eponym referred to John Volpe, a Massachusetts construction magnate who served as Richard Nixon's Secretary of Transportation.)[25]

This lawsuit made good strategic sense. Section 4(f) of the Department of Transportation Act specifically protected public parks. And in 1971, in response to a lawsuit seeking to prevent the construction of I-40 through Overton Park in Memphis, the Supreme Court ruled that public parks could not be paved for expressways unless "the cost of community disruption resulting from alternative routes reached extraordinary magnitudes."[26] Nearly four miles of the 3-A's version of I-70 ran out of town in a waxing crescent through the parks, making it particularly vulnerable to legal action under this new standard.[27] What's more, without that segment of I-70, other parts of the 3-A system—and especially the I-170 connector through Harlem Park (the 1966 condemnation corridor) and Rosemont (its 1967 counterpart)—didn't make sense.[28] Killing the expressway through the parks also killed the "pass through or connect" rationale for the entire western half of the system.

But the parks' defenders had more than strategy in mind. They wanted to protect the park, full stop. Together, Gwynns Falls and Leakin Parks still constituted one of the largest urban green spaces on the East Coast. They were still mostly virgin forest, a "living museum," activist Barbara Holdridge wrote, "preserving the terrain and the natural beauties of Baltimore as it looked to the first settlers here."[29] The Federal Highway Administration's 1972 environmental impact study of the park would count hundreds of "spectacular" old-growth trees: 32 inches across, 44 inches across, 100 feet high, "larger than ever seen by [one dendrologist] in his U.S. Forest Service career."[30] Rare and ordinary wildflowers were everywhere. Jacob's ladder climbed, yellow lady's slipper tiptoed, tall bellflowers waved. Fish and bugs made their homes here along with snakes, groundhogs, coyotes, foxes, beavers, white-tailed deer, and more than 150 different kinds of birds.[31] Even more than a house or a neighborhood, the park was precious and irreplaceable, "the last scrap," Holdridge said, "of primitive nature left anywhere near Baltimore."[32]

To save the park, the VOLPE suit turned back the clock to challenge the legality of the 1962 10-D location hearing at Eastern High in Waverly. Because it had not been held or advertised in Rosemont, lawyers argued, it did

Brochure, Volunteers Opposed to Leakin Park Expressway, September 1972. Courtesy of University of Baltimore Special Collections and Archives.

not count as the "public" hearing the law had required even at the time. The judge agreed. He ordered the Interstate Division to hold three new location hearings: one for the entire East–West Expressway portion of the 3-A system, one for the segment of I-170 that ran through the 1966 condemnation corridor to Rosemont's east, and one for the "Rosemont bypass" alignment that slid underneath the neighborhood. Then the court enjoined further work on I-70 through the park until the Federal Highway Administration could prove there was no "feasible and prudent alternative" to the route.[33]

Even the expressway's proponents now conceded that the maps "are really no longer designed to serve the purposes that they were originally designed for 40 or 50 years ago when the expressway map was made."[34] (This particular proponent happened to be the erstwhile expressway *opponent* Walter Orlinsky, who had come around on the road once he was elected city council president in 1969. Observers surmised this was because he had borrowed a great deal of money from Mayor Schaefer and Governor Mandel to fund his campaign, and this change of heart was their repayment.[35] This may or may not have been true; but, not for nothing, Orlinsky did later go to federal prison for accepting a bribe from a Philadelphia sludge-hauling concern.)[36] Many pro-road policymakers made a simpler argument in its favor now: that there was, as one *Sun* headline put it, "No Way to Repeal a Destroyed House."[37]

At the 1972 hearing on the entire East–West system, most expressway advocates stuck to this basic argument. What was done, they said, was done.[38] To abandon the project now, the city's finance director explained, would be to leave "millions of dollars worth of 'tombstones' scattered throughout the City representing segments of the system starting nowhere and going nowhere." (One city councilor replied: "I question whether we are not better off with millions of dollars worth of tombstones rather than a mass of graveyards.")[39] Robert Embry testified that more than 80 percent of the families the 10-D system had displaced since 1965 were Black, which enabled the system's more cynical proponents to argue, as planning commission head George L. Jude later wrote in the newspaper, that "the poor and the black in Baltimore have already paid the costs" of the expressway system.[40] "It would be ironic indeed," he said, if "we were now to decide to forego [sic] the benefits."[41]

Which benefits? In 1973, the Greater Baltimore Committee solicited dozens of letters from local businessmen—from C&P Telephone, Black & Decker Manufacturing, Western Electric, Montgomery Ward, Monumental Life Insurance—to the Interstate Division. All testified that the city would die if the courts were allowed to pull the plug on the interstates. The 3-A system was "essential to the economic growth and redevelopment of the downtown core," the president of the Hecht Company department stores wrote.⁴² "Virtually the life of Baltimore City" depended on it, echoed the general manager of Bethlehem Steel's Sparrows Point.⁴³

Still, the Greater Baltimore Committee's William Boucher was often the only defender of the road who even bothered to show up at public meetings, and the public he met there was increasingly hostile. In May 1971, Boucher wrote Mayor Schaefer to complain that the city was hanging him out to dry. "The GBC will continue to explain [its reasons for wanting the expressway built] at public hearings because business leadership is in a position to appreciate their importance to the entire community," Boucher wrote. "We feel strongly, however, that the GBC should not be the only spokesman for what are city policies, conceived and developed by your administration and the departments of municipal government."⁴⁴

Many of the expressway system's most aggressive advocates were literally invested in its construction. Some owned the land near the rights-of-way. For example, a subsidiary of the Greiner Company engineering firm had bought up acres of land around the proposed path of I-95. Some were the people being paid to help build it, like the planning firm charged with designing the route through Leakin Park. That same firm also held the contract to write its environmental impact study. "Without great discussion of the wisdom of asking the wolves to guard the sheep," lawyers for the Movement Against Destruction (MAD) later wrote, "it does seem a bit much to expect an agency whose sole reason for existence is to build the 3-A System to conduct an environmental analysis of whether it <u>ought</u> to be built."⁴⁵ In fact, activists noted, the expressway faction was a whirling ouroboros of self-interest. Big donors to pro-highway politicians Spiro T. Agnew, Governor Mandel, and Mayor Schaefer had won the contracts to plan, design, and build fully two-thirds of the 3-A's mileage. One hand washed the other under a spigot of money. "A billion dollars, almost a billion dollars of federal money and two hundred and fifty million of city money," activist Carolyn Tyson explained. "I am not so naïve to think that anybody is going to let that slip through without a fight."⁴⁶ "It's a game they play" she continued, "and somebody is deciding who gets what. That's what it's all about . . . everybody gets a piece."⁴⁷

"BENEFITS FOR BLACKS FROM BALTIMORE'S 3-A SUPERHIGHWAY SYSTEM," read a flyer MAD activists distributed around this time.

> Blacks who own banks will make money as road funds go through their banks.
> Black politicians who favor the road will receive large campaign contributions from the road builders.

Blacks who own land in the counties will find it more valuable after the interstate road goes by it.

Blacks who own large construction companies can bid on multi-million dollar contracts.

Blacks will be able to obtain construction jobs such as superintendent, foreman, machine operator, concrete finisher and laborer.

Black-owned building supply companies can bid for contracts to supply steel and concrete for the roads.

Blacks will be able to move to the counties, then speed back into the central business district on the superhighways to tend their well-paid city jobs.

Blacks who own city property will be able to pay for the road through increased taxes.

"Note," the flyer concluded. "To obtain the true significance of the above statements, re-read them, substituting 'white' for 'black.'"[48]

Their position was growing more precarious, but the Interstate Division and their allies dialed up their impunity in Baltimore anyway. When the law forced officials to hold public hearings, activist Carolyn Tyson noted, they scheduled them for "inauspicious times" like Labor Day and Christmas Eve and barely advertised them. Then they posted armed police at the doors and required attendees to give the officers their names and addresses before they could enter. They suppressed environmental studies and failed to publish hearing transcripts. When activists went to city hall or Annapolis to try to find these public documents, they often met a stone wall. "Interstate has more trouble with its Xerox than any other city agency I know of," Tyson wrote.[49] MAD alleged the roadbuilders spread fearsome rumors about new road plans to frighten neighbors into signing off on old ones, executed contracts for work that hadn't yet been approved, bought houses in expired condemnation corridors and demolished them while the neighbors slept.[50] The regulatory environment might have changed, these actions seemed to say, but the balance of power had not.

Yet in 1968, highway historian Richard Weingroff explains, a federal rule known as the Howard-Cramer provision allowed states to adjust interstate highway routes, or substitute one for another, so long as they did not incur any additional costs. In 1973 a new Federal-Aid Highway Act empowered the Secretary of Transportation to withdraw approval of unbuilt urban expressways altogether.[51] This change was a real threat to the people who were betting on the momentum of the status quo. And the same year Congress passed the new highway law, 1973, the OPEC oil embargo and ensuing energy crisis started to push Americans out of their cars and off the interstates. Traffic on I-95 from Baltimore's northern city line to Delaware dropped by nearly half.[52] Day after day, photos of miles-long lines at gas stations—"bread lines on wheels," the *Sun* called them—filled the newspapers, underscoring for readers and policymakers in Baltimore and elsewhere that the age of the expressway had finally, and maybe permanently, ended.[53]

In February 1973, judges consolidated the 3-A lawsuits into a single class action, *Movement Against Destruction v. Volpe*, that aimed to answer two main questions. First, should the roadbuilders be enjoined in general from building any part of the 3-A until the environmental impact statement for the whole system had been approved? And second, should roadbuilders be enjoined in particular from building the I-170 part of the 3-A that ran along the 1966 corridor through and past Harlem Park, between Franklin and Mulberry Streets?[54] "The City of Baltimore feels strongly that the Franklin-Mulberry project should not be delayed because of the Leakin Park issues," city and state officials explained in a letter to the judges. "The entire corridor of some 15 to 20 blocks is vacant.... The city has displaced almost 1,000 residents for this corridor. Since 1966 the area has been a virtual wasteland." Again, what was done was done. "To leave this area fallow and to allow continued deterioration of this community any longer than absolutely necessary," officials wrote, "would be unthinkable."[55]

Highway officials had always led one another to believe that if construction on the I-170 segment along the 1966 condemnation corridor to Rosemont's east did not begin by the end of June 1973, the city would have to return more than $5 million to the federal government—money that had long since been spent on acquisition and demolition of properties in the expressway's path.[56] About a week before that deadline, two district court judges made their ruling. On the first question, they decided that each individual expressway segment, and not the 3-A system *per se*, was the appropriate "unit of approval" under NEPA. In other words, the potential illegality of any one part of the system could not be used to delay or stop the construction of other parts. On the second, they decided that construction along the I-170 corridor in Harlem Park, the place neighbors were now calling the "world's longest vacant lot," could proceed.[57] Just five buildings remained standing in the corridor, judges noted, so starting construction there "can be looked upon as an improvement." "The demolition has *already* occurred," they wrote. "The traffic *already* exists."[58] "If the alternative of not building the expressway were required," the opinion concluded, "it would be an exaltation of form over substance."[59]

But the court's ruling only allowed construction on the 1.3 miles of I-170 from Pulaski Street east to downtown—which, to their credit, federal highway officials recognized made no sense. "The Franklin-Mulberry highway would be meaningless unless Interstate 70 [to and through the park] also was built," one argued. "The city should not be allowed to begin work in the corridor until the suit over the parks [is] resolved."[60] But state highway officials and the mayor disagreed, and they were the ones in charge. "Mayor Schaefer maintained," the *Sun* reported later, "that the possibility of having to return the federal money was not a factor in his decision."[61]

This is how Baltimore got what people in the city call the Highway to Nowhere: the shard of expressway now known as Route 40 across the bottom of Harlem Park. It cost $100 million to build. It screamed through a thirty-foot concrete ditch whose walls echoed so loudly that nearby houses had to be condemned. And it ran out of gas on Rosemont's eastern doorstep, where the 1967 condemnation corridor started.[62] When the Highway to Nowhere opened to traffic in 1979, cars exited at Mount Street, but the expressway itself, an enormous empty concrete bathtub flanked by idle off-ramps, kept on going to Pulaski. In 2010, the city demolished the ramps and that unused portion of the highway, sending 51 tons of concrete and steel to the landfill.[63]

In 1974, the district court lifted the Leakin Park injunction and ruled that construction could proceed across the 3-A system. It was "bullshit," MAD attorney John C. Armor wrote one colleague. After everything, the Interstate Division and the courts still had "absolutely no interest in determining honestly whether it makes any sense in the current situation of the United States on all aspects of environmental concerns to spend billions of dollars on highways we can't afford, for cars we can't afford, using gasoline we can't afford (or maybe can't get), producing illegal air pollution, damaging irreplaceable parks and historic sites."[64] "It does not," Armor said in another letter, "make a God-damned ounce of sense," except "from the perspective of Maryland's candy-machine government. Put your nickels in the machine, and it produces the goodies—and Maryland's engineers and roadbuilders have fed a lot of nickels into the machine."[65]

By the middle of the 1970s, then, Rosemont was not that far from where it had been in 1967. Yes, the 10-D condemnation lines through the neighborhood had been lifted; and yes, the Section 235 homeownership campaign had rehabilitated and sold hundreds of the once-condemned houses to their new owners. But that campaign had been suspended. The houses were falling apart again. I-170, that enormous concrete-and-rebar bathtub, would terminate in a grim retaining wall at Pulaski Street. When I-70 through the park was built, which everyone now assumed it would be, some version of an expressway would have to connect it to that Pulaski Street stub through Rosemont, which would mean that some number of the people who lived there, and maybe even some of the people who had just moved in, were going to lose their homes after all.

What saved Rosemont, insofar as it was saved, was what scholars call the "financial vise" that was squeezing the interstate highway program to death—not just in Baltimore but nationwide.[66] Early-1970s austerity measures kept Baltimore less affected by the fiscal crisis of the 1970s than cities like New York had been, but the fact was, money was tight.[67] City Planning Director Larry Reich explained the math in his testimony at that 1972 hearing on the East–West Expressway system: "Between 1950 and 1970 the City lost—largely through migration—more than 130,000 white people and gained almost 100,000 black people, for a net population loss of 33,000. Many of the people who left the City were in the ages between 25 and 44 years—the people who were most likely to be productively employed."[68] Many of the white Baltimoreans who'd remained in the city were aging out of the workforce. Many of the Black Baltimoreans who'd moved in were children—"too young," Reich said, "for employment." "The young and the old require more services than those in the middle age groups," he explained, and "the increased costs are being shouldered by fewer people, both relatively and absolutely."[69] Moreover, the industrial tax base of the city had declined some 20 percent in the past ten years, representing "a loss of badly needed tax revenue" and "a loss in industrial jobs badly needed by the City's residents."[70] All this *before* the oil crisis, before stagflation, before the job market tanked nationwide, before the economy slid into (historian Meg Jacobs writes) "full-blown recession as unemployment rose and the gross national product stalled."[71] By the middle of the decade, Bethlehem Steel and the other firms whose letters filled the Greater Baltimore Committee's filing cabinets had other problems to worry about. They'd gotten their way on the expressway, in theory, but did it matter?

Scholars calculate the number of miles of new freeway opened nationwide between 1966 and 1976 was half that of the previous decade, and anti-road activism is certainly a big part of the reason why.[72] There would have been no costly environmental delays if there had not been environmentalists willing to cause them. But primarily, planning scholar Brian D. Taylor argues, it was "financial politics" connected to the oil crisis, and not anti-road activism, that neutered the American interstate highway program.[73] The federal gas tax, Taylor notes, was not indexed to rising costs, and fuel shocks and increasingly fuel-efficient vehicles were cutting tax receipts too.[74] At the same time, freeway construction and maintenance costs were soaring, especially in cities.[75] Labor, materials, and equipment all got more expensive. And Taylor attributes nearly half of increased freeway development costs during the 1960s and '70s to what he calls "the upscaling of freeway designs," including safety design features such as wider shoulders and larger, more sweeping curves. These design changes required more land to build, but land values had appreciated in advance of freeway development. Add the endless delays that new environmental regulations imposed, along with more spending on environmental impact studies, public participation, relocation expenses (in August 1971, a new federal law raised the ceiling on supplementary payments to $15,000) and legal fees. Especially in an inflationary context, all this turned expensive freeways into impossible ones.[76]

In Baltimore, too, penury finished what politics started. The anti-road movement slowed the expressway's construction, and by the time the district court gave Baltimore's roadbuilders the go-ahead to build I-70, the city just couldn't afford to do it. In 1980, Mayor Schaefer's transportation coordinator ran the numbers for a hearing with the Interstate Division: "I-70 and I-170 would appear to cost a total of $620,000,000 ($328,000,000–Leakin Park; $196,000,000–Lower Gwynns Falls; $96,000,000–Rosemont By pass)."[77] The local share, 10 percent of the bill, would be $62,000,000 for I-70 and I-170 alone. When officials multiplied those numbers by the rest of the 3-A system— by I-83 and I-95 and the Fort McHenry Tunnel and on and on—they were simply out of the question. The Maryland legislature agreed to move some vehicle excise-tax and corporate income-tax money from the general fund to the Transportation Trust Fund, increasing revenues by almost $3.5 million per year. But it just wasn't enough. "Continually decreasing motor vehicle revenues, due to reduced travel by the public and more efficient motor vehicles," Interstate Division officials wrote in a 1980 report, "adversely impacts Baltimore City's ability to meet its local share" of highway construction costs.[78] And if Baltimore could not pay for its expressways, it could not have them. "Because of the state and federal funding situation," the mayor's transportation coordinator explained that same year, "the city is no longer in a position to finish its total interstate system."[79]

City and state officials held one last hearing on I-70 in June 1980 and found almost no one left who would defend it. Even the Greater Baltimore Committee's steadfast William Boucher dropped his support, citing "present conditions and lack of funding."[80] "This segment [of the 3-A system is] expendable," City Council President Orlinsky conceded, "and should not be built."[81] In March 1981, Mayor Schaefer agreed to ask the Interstate Division to withdraw the Leakin Park expressway from the system. Almost forty years after Robert Moses first mapped one version of it and a decade and a half after Baltimore's city council had condemned Rosemont for another, the East–West Expressway was finally dead.[82]

Yet just because nobody ever built a highway through or under or around Rosemont does not exonerate the plans to do so, nor does it mean that they had no effect. On the contrary, exactly as reporter James Dilts predicted, "just the threat of an expressway overhanging Rosemont residents" turned out to be nearly "as damaging as the fact."[83] The 10-D condemnation lines had worked into the city's skin like the foxtails that still grew in the park, and the scars they left are still there.

Roads to Nowhere

Until now, we've told the story of the American interstate highway program using the concrete evidence we have: the expressways that we built.[84] *Those* are the choices that carved our cities into pieces, we say. *They* are what has branded inequality onto, and into, our urban landscapes. And we're right—they did. But as we've seen, their story is not the whole story. Almost everywhere, there is a road not taken—everywhere a Road to Nowhere—and those roads caused harm, too.[85]

According to highway historian Weingroff's arithmetic, 343 miles of interstate were removed from the system under the 1968 Howard-Cramer provision and Section 137(b) of the 1973 Federal-Aid Highway Act.[86] This number includes nearly nine miles in Baltimore: the 3.3 miles of I-70 through the park that were officially withdrawn in September 1981, along with 5.6 miles of I-83 and I-595 eliminated two years later.[87] This may not seem like much in a 47,000-mile system, but an enormous majority of those miles cross rural areas.[88] Of the miles in "urban areas," most run through suburbs and metropolitan areas that had not yet been completely developed when the roads were planned. And almost all the withdrawn miles were meant to be built inside city limits. In other words, to get a true sense of their impact, the fraction's denominator should be much smaller. Also, like squares and rectangles, all interstates are expressways but not all expressways are interstates. Weingroff's tally does not account for mileage that never made it into the interstate highway system to begin with, like the 10-D route through Rosemont, or that was never meant to.

Almost every city in the United States has at least one ghost expressway, though not every one of those roads tells the same story. In central cities especially, the scars left behind by roads never built have mostly faded. There is no Riverfront Expressway through the French Quarter in New Orleans, and no Golden Gate Freeway in San Francisco.[89] Could an observer tell there was ever meant to be? Maybe not. But in most places, if you know what you're looking at—and often even if you don't—the scars unbuilt highways left behind them are plain to see. And many of their stories reiterate Baltimore's almost beat for beat.

In Seattle, where I live, the six-lane R. H. Thomson Expressway was first mapped as the Empire Expressway connecting I-90 to the south and I-520 to the north in 1958. It would have carved right through the then–majority-Black

Central District, replacing Empire Way (now Martin Luther King Jr. Way) and the residential street to its west with a vast concrete trench.[90] The plans for the R. H. Thomson—which was not itself an interstate highway, so it would not appear on Weingroff's list of canceled miles—didn't linger for nearly as long as Baltimore's East–West plans did. For various reasons, it was clear by the mid-1960s that it would not be built, and the city council removed it from Seattle's Comprehensive Plan in 1970.[91] Few houses were ever condemned for it, and even fewer were demolished.[92] But the thousands of houses and hundreds of businesses in the expressway's path were allowed to decay where they stood, and many of them stayed that way for decades. Even in a gentrifying neighborhood in a rich city, the wound the Thomson Expressway caused is apparent. A fading scar is still a scar.

Milwaukee's story is even more dramatic. In 1951, the city hired a traffic-consultant firm to design an expressway system, some parts of which were built in the 1950s. Others reappeared in the region's comprehensive transportation plan, issued in 1965. However, according to local planner Richard W. Cutler, the exact routes of the planned expressways were kept secret until their condemnation hearings. At that point, homeowners had little choice but to sell, usually at a loss, and move.[93] Then freeway opponents stalled the construction process.

One of their main targets was the three-mile-long Park Freeway West. It was also not a designated interstate, but part of the in-town expressway loop system mapped, neighbor Roy Evans explained in a 2017 interview, to run right through the middle of a "strong, thriving, vibrant . . . economically stable African-American community."[94] Cutler writes (emphasis his): "[Anti-road activists] brought suit in federal court, claiming that an environmental impact statement had to be prepared under NEPA before construction could commence. They started suit notwithstanding the fact that *before the legislation was enacted in 1969* 99 percent of the land had been acquired and 1,590 homes had been cleared at a cost of $22 million."[95] A district judge ruled in the activists' favor in June 1972.

This dispute dragged on, through a 1974 county-wide advisory referendum on the expressway system in which 54.2 percent of county residents and 48 percent of residents in the affected wards voted YES on the plan.[96] Finally, in December 1977, the regional planning commission voted to remove the Park Freeway West from its transportation plan.[97] Yet all those acres of bulldozed right-of-way smeared across the northwest part of the city remained. Road or no road, the damage was done. "After they put the freeway through," Evans said, "the African-American community was all torn up. All that vibrancy was just destroyed. . . . After the freeway, you see what you see today, which is a fractured community without a lot of power."⁹⁸ It is, local historian John Gurda wrote in the *Milwaukee Journal-Sentinel* in 2022, a "scraped-bare corridor that redeveloped at a snail's pace."⁹⁹ Likewise, on the north side of downtown, a cleared right-of-way remained after officials de-mapped the Park Freeway East and demolished what little had been built.¹⁰⁰

Then there is New Haven, where the 500-foot-wide, ten-mile-long "Oak Street Connector" was mapped in 1959 to connect Route 35 to I-95 across the bottom of the city, making it easier for suburbanites to reach downtown department stores and office buildings and clearing an old and densely packed tenement neighborhood—a "slum"—where thousands of working-class Irish, Jewish, Italian, Eastern European, and Black families lived.¹⁰¹ "Not every structure in this area is substandard," city officials wrote in 1955, "but like cutting a rotten spot from an apple, some of the good has to be cut away too to save the whole."¹⁰² To build the highway, 886 families—more than 3,000 residents—and 350 businesses were displaced, and all the places they'd once called home were swept to the ground virtually overnight.¹⁰³ But the roadbuilders apparently spent all their money on the demolition contractors, and construction on the expressway stopped as abruptly as it had begun, turning a grand plan into, as Trinity College senior Harrison Silver put it in his 2022 thesis, a "glorified exit ramp."¹⁰⁴

In the end just one mile—four longish blocks—of the Connector was ever built.¹⁰⁵ In the vast clear zone, Yale political scientist Douglas W. Rae writes, "open space replaced a neighborhood."¹⁰⁶ For decades, all that remained there was more than a million square feet of dying grass, empty lots, a few ugly skyscrapers, and parked cars.¹⁰⁷ "That was gonna be part of the future of New Haven," one former resident told an interviewer, "and it just never happened."¹⁰⁸ In recent years, the city of New Haven has begun to try to reconnect the parts of the city that the Oak Street Connector tore apart. "We're undoing the last generation's sins of traffic work," one planner told a reporter from the *Yale Daily News* in 2022, by reestablishing the city grid where it's possible and building apartments and office buildings on the vacant land.¹⁰⁹ But it's not clear those sins can be undone so easily.

In California, the abandoned 238 Freeway through Hayward and 710 Freeway through the San Gabriel Valley have left hundreds of abandoned houses in the hands of the state.¹¹⁰ In Kansas City, U.S. 71 displaced more than three thousand people before construction stalled and the corridor, one neighbor told reporters, "became an eyesore and a dumping ground"—so much that construction resumed in the 1990s. The road, now more of a parkway than a freeway, was completed in 2001.¹¹¹ Then there are St. Louis, and Houston, and Boston.¹¹² Washington, DC, where gentrification and redevelopment have erased most of the evidence of the city's grand plans to carve expressways through its residential neighborhoods, is one of just a few exceptions.[113]

These cities are undoubtedly better off because these expressways were not built—just as Rosemont is, and just as the 1966 condemnation corridor through Harlem Park to its east would have been. But even where no house ever fell to the backhoe and the bulldozer, the places are not unscathed. Whatever their resolution, highway maps make policymakers' mid-century priorities as clear as the highways themselves do. As the scholar Benedict Anderson reminds us in the classic book *Imagined Communities*, a map is an instrument of power, a colonial grammar that reflects, shapes, and legitimizes the way its maker imagined his domain.[114] Anderson quotes historian Thongchai Winichakul, who explains: "In terms of most communication theories and common sense, a map is a scientific abstraction of reality. A map merely represents something which already exists objectively 'there.'" But in fact, Winichakul writes, a map is really "a model for, rather than a model of, what it purported to represent," a promise and a threat.[115] And as we've seen, threats have power too. Remember James Dilts: "plans for highways, if they are around long enough, become self-fulfilling prophecies."[116] As cities across the country seek to repair the damage done by all the urban-renewal expressways they built over the past seven decades, they'll need to include all the things they did *not* build in the accounting, too.

"The heart of the issue," MAD's Carolyn Tyson wrote in the 1970s, "is whether cities shall be places to live and to work in, or whether they shall be places to exploit."[117] So it was, and so it remains. *Road to Nowhere* is a book about something that never happened, a highway that was never built, "a monument to self-destruction" (as VOLPE's Barbara Holdridge put it) forestalled.[118] More important, though, it is about what got destroyed anyway.

Charm City

In the summer of 1974, Baltimore became "Charm City, U.S.A." That July, the Baltimore Promotional Council launched a $40,000 campaign aimed at luring tourists to town, placing ads featuring a collage of photos—rowhouses with white marble steps, the old sloop U.S.S. *Constellation*, iconic burlesque dancer Blaze Starr, and crabs—in *The New York Times* and other big-city papers. "While the wrecking balls of other cities have been busy leveling tradition in the name of progress," the ad read, "Baltimore has been meticulously rerouting progress around its history."[119] Whatever had or had not been rerouted, the ad—which only ran a handful of times before boosters pulled it—made clear that by the mid-1970s Baltimore was in the process of distilling its priorities. Charm City would be a city for the few.

This went for residents as well as visitors. At the same time the Department of Housing and Community Development had wandered away from the Section 235 homeownership campaign in Rosemont, it had started an "urban homesteading" program in other parts of the city in which, one official explained, "we are not trying to provide housing for people. We are trying to provide people for housing."[120] The program sold abandoned houses for $1, most of them in concentrated, and eventually literally fenced-off, eighteenth- and nineteenth-century neighborhoods in East and Southwest Baltimore.[121] (The houses were abandoned in the first place because of the 3-A expressway system: Most of the dollar houses in Otterbein and Barre Circle would have been within eye- or earshot of the I-95 segment of the 3-A, and some had been condemned for earlier versions of the route.) "The idea," another official told reporter Dilts in 1979, "is blitzkrieg—get the poor out quickly, fences up, sales for a dollar to a select group of upper middle-class people who can afford the renovations and the subsequent tax base."[122]

This was not very many people, because rehabilitating big, old, long-abandoned houses was *extremely* expensive: For example, renovation costs for Federal-style rowhouses in Otterbein and Barre Circle averaged about $36,000 per house.[123] "Homesteaders" needed to show they had most of the cash on hand to do the job.[124] As a result, especially in the concentrated dollar-house neighborhoods that made the headlines, Baltimore's urban homesteaders were mostly white, mostly upper-middle class, mostly (per the *Sun*) "split-level families" from the suburbs.[125] "To afford the costs of renovating in Stirling Street and Otterbein," the *Sun* reported, "black applicants earned too little."[126] Too, the Department of Housing and Community Development's guidelines for "homesteaders" and their contractors were quite unlike the ones Morelite and San-Dee had gotten in Rosemont. They urged property owners and their architects to make "restrained and dignified" choices that emphasized "proportion," "rhythm," and "harmonious design," preferably in exposed brick and earth tones.[127] Although there were only about 500 of these "urban pioneers," they attracted the same kind of fawning press that their forebears on Tyson Street had. Reporters goggled at their "rowhouse chic": stained glass, "expensive woodwork," club cellars and darkrooms, "plant rooms" and "sunlit art studios."[128] Homesteaders, one contractor told the paper, were sitting on a "golden egg in the ghetto."[129]

In fact, Baltimore's "dollar-house" program inspired a new economy of vandalism, now known as "salvage." Homesteaders and their decorators began to stalk other people's houses—usually, but not always, abandoned ones. Under cover of night, one newspaper article explained, they sometimes even broke in and helped themselves to "architecturally significant items that will make their restorations complete . . . like mahogany and oak doors, claw-footed bathtubs, stained glass, marble or slate fireplace mantels, old-fashioned molding, iron fencing or railings."[130] "Stained-glass windows are an obvious example," one official told *The Wall Street Journal*, "but people have also come home and found doors missing, porches missing."[131]

In 1971, the city had enacted an ordinance designed to stymie this kind of vandalism in places like Rosemont: it prohibited "the sale or transportation of stolen building materials" and prevented junk dealers from "carrying any plumbing or electrical fixtures through the city unless he is licensed as a demolition contractor."[132] Four years later, "to ensure that those who wanted or needed certain items could get them without breaking the law," Mayor Schaefer and HCD created the Baltimore Salvage Depot to sell "salvaged items which otherwise would have been lost": a use of the passive voice that obscured who was doing the salvaging, and who the losing.[133] White marble stoops, for which there was a terrifically long waiting list, went for $160 a set. Mantelpieces cost $200. Old sinks and bathtubs flew out the door. Cleaned-up old bricks sold by the gross. "The day we opened," the depot's manager told *The New York Times*, "200 people were waiting in line. Homeowners were elated to find just the matching baluster they needed. They were all looking for flooring, interior shutters, wood mantels, things you just couldn't go to the store and get."[134] In 1979, the Baltimore Salvage Depot won an award from *Environmental Monthly* magazine: It was, the magazine said, "a near perfect example of a municipally sponsored enterprise that makes excellent sense economically, environmentally, and esthetically."[135] It was also proof that Charm City would "salvage" some of its places by scalping the rest.

But all this was a blip compared to the centerpiece of Baltimore's ballyhooed "renaissance": Harborplace, a "festival marketplace" on the waterfront developed by Columbia and Rosemont's own James Rouse. Two brand-new glass cubes at the foot of Light Street were filled with restaurants, cafes, a gourmet food market, Laura Ashley and Pappagallo boutiques, shops selling handmade pottery, hand-tatted lace, and handblown glass, devoted to butterflies (Flutterby's), stuffed animals (Embraceable Zoo, where a person could buy a five-foot stuffed camel for $2,500), and gifts for left-handers (South Paw).[136] Boosters hoped the place would turn the whole city around. "The hoopla in this city's historic Inner Harbor on Wednesday night," *The Washington Post* reported upon its grand opening in 1980, "might lead an unsuspecting visitor to conclude that Baltimore is celebrating the Fourth of July, the discovery of

America, the resurgence of the Colts and a visit from the Pope—all at once."[137] There were fireworks, cannons and church bells, and 100,000 people milling around on the harbor's concrete apron while the "city fathers" waved to them from the decks of a 57-ship flotilla. There were also, per *The Christian Science Monitor*, parades of "kung fu specialists" and mimes.[138] Another old ship, the rechristened *Pride of Baltimore*, tooted into port while a crowd cheered.[139]

In 1981, the year officials finally euthanized the East–West Expressway, *Time* magazine published a glowing profile of this new and narrower Baltimore. "From early morning until well past midnight," reporter Michael Demarest wrote that August:

> natives and tourists by the thousands turn Baltimore's Inner Harbor into a continuous celebration: milling on the promenades, perching on the bulkheads, dangling feet in the drink, flirting on the benches, lounging in the outdoor cafés, ogling, jogging, strolling, munching, sipping, savoring the sounds and sweet airs. In their midst, jugglers hurl batons, mimes mime, clowns pratfall and dancers soar. At one time or another, the sounds of jazz, Mozart, marching bands, rock, Rodgers, Bach, bagpipes and bouzouki fill the air. The air is filled, too, with the fragrances of fresh-baked bread, cheeses, chocolate, roasting coffee beans, crepes, French fries, fruit, sausage, seafood, soul food, souvlaki, spices and herbs.[140]

Here, at last, Baltimore was (another reporter wrote) "rising phoenix-like from the ashes of . . . decay."[141] That the Inner Harbor project itself was an enormous undertaking—it took nearly $725 million, seventeen years, two bond issues, and two hard-fought ballot initiatives to complete—obscured the fact that it was a Potemkin city, and one that was almost unrecognizably small.[142]

Rosemont's Legacy

In the 1980s, austerity came to Baltimore, and to Rosemont. Many of the people who still lived in the neighborhood were municipal workers, as were many Black people in Baltimore: According to historian Jane Berger, more than one-quarter of all Black workers in Baltimore worked in the public sector in 1970.[143] As the city's leaders doubled and tripled down on downtown "revitalization," they undermined neighborhood public services and the workers who provided them. As one result, *The Washington Post* reported, during William Donald Schaefer's tenure as mayor between 1971 and 1986, Baltimore "went from 30th to eighth on the Census Bureau's list of the nation's poorest cities," and its assessable tax base declined by nearly 40 percent.[144] Between 1980 and 1990, Baltimore's municipal workforce likewise shrank by nearly

40 percent—and by 2010, Berger writes, Black workers' median income in Baltimore was "54 percent of that of whites, a figure that was worse than the differential had been during mid-1950s Jim Crow Baltimore."[145] For Rosemont, this meant fewer jobs, lower pay, less breathing room.

Empty houses and unemployed young people lured people who wanted to take advantage of both, and starting in the early 1980s Rosemont became a key battlefield in Baltimore's War on Drugs. In 1988, the *Sun* called that war "another Battle of Rosemont."[146] (The expressway was the first.) The presence of "customers and dealers clog[ging] the sidewalks" and the general sense of unsafety they carried with them, not to mention the overpolicing and violence that followed behind, reiterated class-based tensions in the neighborhood and made it even harder to thrive in the place the Rosemonters had fought so hard to keep.[147] Mary Rosemond's papers from the 1990s and 2000s include sheaves of letters from neighborhood organizations like the R.N.I.A. to city officials pleading for more drug enforcement, more sanitation services, more after-school programming, more job training—more of anything neighbors thought might make the community more livable than it was. Unfortunately, they didn't get much. As one result, Rosemont's subprime crisis predated the one that got the nation's attention in the early 2000s.

Too often still, we look at city neighborhoods like Rosemont and see only their struggles in the present tense. In Baltimore, it's easy to see what the scholar Lawrence T. Brown calls "the Black butterfly," two wings flanking a "white L" that stretches from Johns Hopkins University south to downtown and east along the waterfront.[148] It's harder to see, with apologies to Brown's metaphor, their caterpillar. And so we conclude that our neighborhoods must have plundered themselves.

But they didn't.

In June 2015, Maryland Governor Larry Hogan announced $2 billion in new highway spending aimed, he said, at "every single county in Maryland." On the internet, he posted a map of the state with blurry icons showing where all that money was headed: to improve traffic flow in Montgomery County, repair bridges and drains in Carroll and Harford Counties, repave the roads almost everywhere. But in the northwestern crook of the Chesapeake Bay, where Baltimore city should be, the infographic shows nothing at all—just water. Accidentally or on purpose, the city had disappeared.[149] In the same press conference, Governor Hogan announced that he'd canceled the Red Line light rail project, a 14-mile rapid-transit line that had been on the books since 2002. The Red Line was to run along the old "Road to Nowhere" corridor, connecting Black West Baltimore to downtown and drawing economic and residential development to the communities along its route. One of these communities was Rosemont.

More than sixty years had passed since the Board of School Commissioners had started to convert the neighborhood's schools to serve Black students, drawing Gertrude Corbett and her neighbors west into the new life they were determined to build for themselves and their children at almost any cost. Almost that many years had passed since the lines on highway planners' maps had first promised to eviscerate the neighborhood and swallow everything its new residents had invested in it. It had been fifty years since the condemnation lines through the neighborhood were passed, forty years since the last Section 235 buyer moved into her house in the condemnation corridor, and thirty-four years since the I-70 plan was killed for good in 1981. Still, all this had accomplished something. By the time Hogan canceled the Red Line, Rosemont had become more like the rest of Black Baltimore than it once was different. In fact, many data points suggest it had gotten comparatively worse. According to the Baltimore Neighborhood Indicators Alliance, the neighborhood's median income was (and remains) among the lowest in the city.[150] High-school dropout rates were (and remain) among the highest, as are unemployment rates.[151] The Postal Service reported that nearly one-fifth of residential addresses were unoccupied, more than almost any other neighborhood in Baltimore.[152] It could be hard to find a working streetlight.[153]

Here was the "irremediable urban blight" that policymakers had spent so many decades, and so many dollars, creating, and when they had a real chance to make up for it, they whiffed. The city, state, and federal governments had already spent nearly $300 million planning the Red Line, and construction was set to begin that year. But Hogan, a suburban real estate developer, had no interest in trying to fix what had gone wrong in West Baltimore, and he took the money set aside for the project and spent it building highways in Baltimore County. "Whites will receive 228 percent of the net benefit from the decision" to cancel the Red Line, the NAACP and ACLU noted in a complaint they filed with the Federal Highway Administration's Office of Civil Rights in December 2015, "while African-Americans will receive −124 percent."[154] But Larry Hogan wanted to spend money on the things he thought really mattered. "We're going to focus," he said, "on building *roads*."[155]

A few years later, in June 2023, a new governor, Wes Moore, announced that he was going to dust off the old plans for the Red Line and get the project built. "Government left the city of Baltimore . . . and the dreams of the people here behind," he told reporters. The Red Line, Moore continued, could carry Rosemonters and their neighbors "from where they live to where opportunity lies."[156]

Once these were the same place. Will they ever be again?

Acknowledgments

My first thanks go to the city of Baltimore, and to all the people I've met there over the years who generously welcomed me to their home and helped me to understand it—especially Drusilla Bunch, Ursula Cain, Christina Fraling, Helena Hicks, Leslie Carl Howard, Ed Orser, Eli Pousson, Roshanne Redmond, and Edward Rosemond. I hope the story I've told here rings true.

I wouldn't have been able to write this book without Baltimore's extraordinary archival collections, nor without the brilliant people whose work makes them so. Thanks especially to Rob Schoeberlein, Jeni Spamer, Saul Gibusiwa, and Ed Papenfuse at the Baltimore City Archives; Aiden Faust and Tom Hollowak at the University of Baltimore Special Collections and Archives; and all the staff in the Maryland Department at the Enoch Pratt Free Library, the Maryland State Archives, and the H. Furlong Baldwin Library at the Maryland Center for History and Culture. Thanks also to the terrific archivists at the Seattle Municipal Archives, the Hugh and Jane Ferguson Seattle Room at the Seattle Public Library, and especially the Seattle Public Schools Archives for being so kind to me and my students over the years. You've all been so gracious to me for so long, and you've made my work infinitely better. Thank you.

This book began its life at Columbia University many, many, many years ago. Thanks to Eric Foner and Kenneth T. Jackson for all of your support since then, and incalculable thanks to Betsy Blackmar for being the best and most patient reader and advisor I could ever have asked for. I'm sorry I didn't finish this in time for you to teach it! Thanks to Jeremy Derfner, Josh Wolff, and Kevin Murphy, then and now.

More scholars have helped this project along than I can count. Over the years, I have presented sections of the manuscript as papers at annual meetings of the American Historical Association, the Urban History Association, the Society for American City and Regional Planning History, the Journal of Policy History Conference on Policy History, the Boston Seminar in Immigration and Urban History (now the Dina G. Malgeri Modern American Society and Culture Seminar at the Massachusetts Historical Society), the Newberry Library Urban History Seminar, and the University of Memphis Graduate Association for African-American History. Thanks, too, to my brilliant colleagues at the W.E.B. DuBois Summer Institute at Harvard University; to Thaïsa Way, LaDale Winling, Mary Rizzo, and everyone else at the Connecting the Interstates Workshop; and to everyone in the urban historians' online writing group. Please know that every week, I am with you in spirit.

Thank you to all the funders who have supported me and this project over the years, including the American Council of Learned Societies, the National Endowment for the Humanities, the LBJ Presidential Library, the Maryland Center for History and Culture, the Society for American City and Regional Planning History, Columbia University's Department of History and Graduate School of Arts and Sciences, and the Jacob K. Javits Fellowship from the US Department of Education (RIP). This book wouldn't have been possible without your generosity.

Thank you to my students at Seattle University for asking good questions, looking at and living in the world with care and curiosity, and reminding me why this kind of work matters. Thanks to Serena Cosgrove, Audrey Hudgins, Ben Howe, and Dan Washburn for being exceptional colleagues, comrades, and friends. I couldn't have made it through with anybody else. Thanks also to my Seattle U colleagues Theresa Earenfight, Paulette Kidder, Hazel Hahn, Nova Robinson, and Franc Guerrero.

Thank you to Andrea Blatz, Elizabeth Ellingboe, Anne T. Strother, Charles B. Dibble, Amanda Seligman, Rae Ganci Hammers, kind and generous reviewers, and everyone at the University of Chicago Press. Double, triple, and quadruple thanks to Tim Mennel, who never gave up on this book or on me. I've appreciated your confidence more than I can ever say, especially when I did not share it. I couldn't have made it through *this* with anybody else, either.

Thanks to Erin Greb for my beautiful maps, David Luljak for my beautiful index, and Kiersten Marie for my beautiful author photos.

Thanks to everyone who has published (and read!) my other work on Baltimore: *Politico*, *CityLab*, *The Nation*, the *Journal of Urban History*, the Urban History Association's *Metropole* blog, Temple University Press, Rutgers University Press, *Planning Perspectives*, and the University of North Carolina Press's Center for the Study of the American South. Thanks to Jessica Elfenbein, Betsy Nix, Tom Hollowak, Nicole King, Kate Drabinski, and Joshua Clark Davis for putting together terrific anthologies about Baltimore and including me in them. A version of the Tyson Street story appeared on the Urban History Association's *The Metropole* as "Slum Clearance à la Mode: The Battle for Baltimore's Tyson Street" on November 26, 2018. (Thank you, Ryan Reft!) Other parts of this book are adapted from my essays "'Shove Those Black Clouds Away!' Jim Crow Schools and Jim Crow Neighborhoods Before *Brown*" in King, Drabinski, and Davis's *Baltimore Revisited: Stories of Inequality and Resistance in a U.S. City* (Rutgers University Press, 2019); "The 'Baltimore Idea' and the Cities It Built" in *Southern Cultures* 25, no. 2 (Summer 2019); and "'White Man's Lane': Hollowing Out the Highway Ghetto in Baltimore" in Elfenbein, Nix, and Hollowak's *Baltimore '68: Riots and Rebirth in an American City* (Temple University Press, 2011). Thank you to the Urban History Association, Rutgers University Press, the Center for the Study of the American South, and Temple University Press for permission to reprint this material.

Thanks to everyone who has read or listened to bits and pieces of this book over the years, especially Nerd Camper Chris Bonastia, Derfner Son Kevin Murphy and Former Derfner Son Kevin O'Rourke, Josh Wolff, Jessica Rosenberg, Kristina Washburn, and Dan Washburn.

Thank you to Kristina Washburn and Dan Washburn, Veronica Mayorga and Kip Gatto, tennis pals, and the good folks at the Madrona Arms for keeping me sane. Thank you to Jessica Rosenberg for being a terrific friend and traveling companion, for letting me spend a million nights on her couch in Washington, DC, and for spending the government shutdown of 2013 in the Baltimore City Archives photographing property-tax records on my behalf.

For better and (for him) worse, Jeremy Derfner has read almost every word I've ever written at least once, and I could not and would not have finished this book without him. He has also made it much, much better. I wrote in the acknowledgments to my dissertation that he is "a brilliant genius, an ace editor, and an extraordinary friend," and I stand by it.

Thank you to my family, whose patience with this project, and with me, has been inexhaustible. My parents, Charlie Lieb and Kathy Lieb, taught me what it means to work hard and persevere. My mom's company has improved many trips to, and meals in, Baltimore and Annapolis, and my dad has helped me with this project in more ways than I can count. My sister, Alison Lieb, has enviably managed to forget about the book entirely, except for the time I made her photocopy a thousand pages of HUD manuals at the University of Texas library, and her husband Josh Issermoyer has been a marvelous addition to the family. Thanks in particular to my nephew and niece Chase Issermoyer and Reese Issermoyer, who love Baltimore as much as I do and who have also proven to be marvelous traveling companions. I will see you all on the beach in Cape May!

Thank you to my husband, Luke Hizer, who has been living with this book for as long as he's been living with me. Now you are free to be as loud as you want.

Finally, thanks to first-rate canine muses Jake, Ellie, and Orvy. As Sam Eagle said, you are all weirdos. I love you.

Abbreviations

BCA   Baltimore City Archives, Baltimore, MD
EPFL   Enoch Pratt Free Library, Baltimore, MD
MCHC   Maryland Center for History and Culture, Baltimore, MD
MSA   Maryland State Archives, Annapolis, MD
TUA   Temple University Libraries Special Collections Research Center, Urban Archives Pamphlet Collection, Philadelphia, PA
UB   University of Baltimore Special Collections and Archives, Baltimore, MD

Notes

Introduction

1. Year: 1930, Census Place: Jacksonville, Duval, Florida, p. 10B, Enumeration District: 0019, FHL microfilm: 2340047.
2. Ennis Davis, "Lost History: Saving What's Left of Sugar Hill," *Modern Cities*, February 7, 2017, https://www.moderncities.com/article/2017-feb-lost-history-saving-whats-left-of-sugar-hill.
3. "Lost Jacksonville: Sugar Hill," *Metro Jacksonville*, March 2, 2009, https://www.metrojacksonville.com/article/2009-mar-lost-jacksonville-sugar-hill.
4. Ennis Davis, "Ashley Street: The Harlem of the South," *Metro Jacksonville*, May 13, 2009, https://www.metrojacksonville.com/article/2009-may-ashley-street-the-harlem-of-the-south; "Jacksonville's Legacy: African-American Heritage Trail," September 2013, https://www.jacksonville.gov/welcome/docs/cvb13-008848-1-afriamericanherittrail(m)lorez.aspx.
5. Jacksonville Public Library, "History of Jacksonville Public Library," n.d., https://jaxpubliclibrary.org/about/history.
6. Ennis Davis, "Lost Jacksonville: Wilder Park," *Metro Jacksonville*, October 4, 2011, https://www.metrojacksonville.com/article/2011-oct-lost-jacksonville-wilder-park.
7. Davis, "Saving What's Left of Sugar Hill."
8. Jacksonville Historical Society, "Streetcars," n.d., https://www.jaxhistory.org/portfolio-items/streetcars/.
9. Ennis Davis and Robert Mann, *Reclaiming Jacksonville: Stories Behind the River City's Historic Landmarks* (History Press, 2012), 28.
10. Davis and Mann, *Reclaiming Jacksonville*, 28; "Architects Honor Jacksonville," *Tampa Bay Times*, November 19, 1965, 16.
11. Sam Mase, "Florida's Interstates: The Word Now Is Speed," *Tampa Bay Times*, October 4, 1964, 51.
12. Jacques Kelly, "Mary Rosemond, Community Activist, Dies," *Baltimore Sun*, January 28, 2011.
13. "Hamptonians Wed on Campus," *Baltimore Afro-American*, June 30, 1951, 11; Olmsted Brothers, *Report upon the Development of Public Grounds for Greater Baltimore* (1904), 76.
14. "Let Your Rent Buy a Beautiful New Home," *Baltimore Sun*, May 29, 1932, 17; "Walbrook Section," *Baltimore Sun*, July 14, 1935, 28.

15. Bureau of the Census, *U.S. Census of Population: 1950*, volume III, *Census Tract Statistics*, chap. 4 (Government Printing Office, 1952).

16. "Population Move Stumps School Board," *Baltimore Sun*, September 19, 1952, 36, 22.

17. *Baltimore Sun*, April 20, 1951, 29; Mary M. Rosemond, "Our Neighborhood," June 2004, Rosemont Neighborhood Improvement Association Records, 2004, 9B, box 16, folder 4, Baltimore Heritage Records, R0010-BH, Baltimore Studies Archives, University of Baltimore Special Collections and Archives, Baltimore, MD (hereafter cited as UB).

18. N. D. B. Connolly, afterword to Arnold R. Hirsch, *Making the Second Ghetto: Race and Housing in Chicago, 1940–1960*, 2nd ed. (University of Chicago Press, 2021), 280.

19. Hirsch, *Making the Second Ghetto*, xvi.

20. Kevin M. Kruse and Thomas J. Sugrue, *The New Suburban History* (University of Chicago Press, 2006); David M. P. Freund, *Colored Property: State Policy and White Racial Politics in Suburban America* (University of Chicago Press, 2007); Emily E. Straus, *Death of a Suburban Dream: Race and Schools in Compton, California* (University of Pennsylvania Press, 2014); Andrew R. Highsmith, *Demolition Means Progress: Flint, Michigan, and the Fate of the American Metropolis* (University of Chicago Press, 2015); Ansley T. Erickson, *Making the Unequal Metropolis: School Desegregation and Its Limits* (University of Chicago Press, 2017); Richard Rothstein, *The Color of the Law: A Forgotten History of How Our Government Segregated America* (Liveright, 2017); Paige Glotzer, *How the Suburbs Were Segregated: Developers and the Business of Exclusionary Housing, 1890–1960* (Columbia University Press, 2020).

21. Kevin M. Kruse, *White Flight: Atlanta and the Making of Modern Conservatism* (Princeton University Press, 2005); Beryl Satter, *Family Properties: How the Struggle over Race and Real Estate Transformed Chicago and Urban America* (Picador, 2010); Mark H. Rose and Raymond A. Mohl, *Interstate: Highway Politics and Policy Since 1939*, 3rd ed. (University of Tennessee Press, 2012); N. D. B. Connolly, *A World More Concrete: Real Estate and the Remaking of Jim Crow South Florida* (University of Chicago Press, 2014); Andrew Kahrl, *The Land Was Ours: How Black Beaches Became White Wealth in the Coastal South* (University of North Carolina Press, 2016); Francesca Russello Ammon, *Bulldozer: Demolition and Clearance of the Postwar Landscape* (Yale University Press, 2016); Keeanga-Yamahtta Taylor, *Race for Profit: How Banks and the Real Estate Industry Undermined Black Homeownership* (University of North Carolina Press, 2019); Walter Johnson, *The Broken Heart of America: St. Louis and the Violent History of the United States* (Hachette, 2020); Mike Amezcua, *Making Mexican Chicago: From Postwar Settlement to the Age of Gentrification* (University of Chicago Press, 2023); Ryan Reft, Amanda K. Phillips de Lucas, and Rebecca C. Retzlaff, *Justice and the Interstates: The Racist Truth About Urban Highways* (Island Press, 2023); Nicholas Dagen Bloom, *The Great American Transit Disaster: A Century of Austerity, Auto-Centric Planning, and White Flight* (University of Chicago Press, 2023).

22. Noliwe Rooks, *Cutting School: Privatization, Segregation, and the End of Public Education* (New Press, 2017), 2.

23. Rooks, *Cutting School*, 5.

24. Rooks, *Cutting School*, 20.

25. Olúfẹ́mi O. Táíwò, "A Framework to Help Us Understand the World," *Hammer & Hope* 1 (Winter 2023); Justin Leroy and Destin Jenkins eds., *Histories of Racial Capitalism* (Columbia University Press, 2021).

26. Alan M. Voorhees and Associates, Inc., "The Measurement of Residential Blight in Baltimore," October 1964, Measurement of Residential Blight, 10, box 4, folder 14, Baltimore Urban Renewal and Housing Authority Records, R0019-BURHA, Baltimore Studies Archives, UB.

27. Wendell E. Pritchett, "The 'Public Menace' of Blight: Urban Renewal and the Private Uses of Eminent Domain," *Yale Law & Policy Review* 21, no. 1 (2003): 1–52.

28. James Dilts, "How Not to Run a Roadway," MAD Expressway Conference Committee Report "History, Facts, and Opinions on Expressway," August 1968, UB; General—Conference Committee, "History, Facts and Opinions on Expressway," 6, box 6, folder 31, Movement Against Destruction Records, R0062-MAD, Baltimore Studies Archives, UB.

29. "A Home for You in Rosemont!," Rosemont Sales Program (1972), BRG48-40, box 6, Land Development Division, Vacant House Program Real Estate Files, 1969–1975, Department of Housing and Community Development, Baltimore City Archives, Baltimore, MD (hereafter cited as BCA).

30. *Time*, February 8, 1971.

31. Mark Reutter, "Fix-Up Draws Mixed Reviews," *Baltimore Sun*, September 29, 1974, TR1.

32. Matthew A. Crenson, *Baltimore: A Political History* (Johns Hopkins University Press, 2017); P. Nicole King, Kate Drabinski, and Joshua Clark Davis, eds., *Baltimore Revisited: Stories of Inequality and Resistance in a U.S. City* (Rutgers University Press, 2019); Mary Rizzo, *Come and Be Shocked: Baltimore Beyond John Waters and the Wire* (Johns Hopkins University Press, 2020); Lawrence T. Brown, *The Black Butterfly: The Harmful Politics of Race and Space in America* (Johns Hopkins University Press, 2022).

33. Samuel Joseph Rice, "A Study of the Experiences of Fifty Negro Families Who Moved into White Neighborhoods of Baltimore, Maryland in 1945 and 1946" (1947), 4–5, ETC Collection for Atlanta University Center Robert W. Woodruff Library, Atlanta, GA, Paper 2344.

34. Ira De A. Reid, *The Negro Community of Baltimore* (National Urban League, 1935), 15.

35. Antero Pietila, *Not in My Neighborhood: How Bigotry Shaped a Great American City* (Ivan R. Dee, 2010), 96.

36. W. Edward Orser, *Blockbusting in Baltimore: The Edmondson Village Story* (University Press of Kentucky, 1994).

37. Dalton Conley, *Being Black, Living in the Red: Race, Wealth, and Social Policy in America* (University of California Press, 1999), 38.

38. Author conversation with Helena Hicks, Baltimore, September 2018.

39. C. W. Grier, "Preliminary Conclusions on Social Impact of the Official Interstate Expressway Route upon the Rosemont Area," Urban Design Concept Associates, *Rosemont Area Studies*, February 1968, Rosemont Area Studies, 13, box 76, folder 35, Greater Baltimore Committee Records, R0046-GBC, Baltimore Studies Archives, UB.

40. Jeffrey L. Meikle, *Twentieth Century Limited: Industrial Design in America, 1925–1939* (Temple University Press, 2001); Donald Albrecht, *Norman Bel Geddes Designs America* (Harry N. Abrams, 2012).

41. Norman Bel Geddes, *Magic Motorways* (Random House, 1940).

42. Robert Caro, *The Power Broker: Robert Moses and the Fall of New York* (Vintage Books, 1974); Joseph F. C. DiMento and Cliff Ellis, *Changing Lanes: Visions and Histories of Urban Freeways* (MIT Press, 2013); Rose and Mohl, *Interstate*; Eric Avila, *The Folklore of the Freeway: Race and Revolt in the Modernist City* (University of Minnesota Press, 2014); Nicholas Dagen Bloom, *The Great American Transit Disaster: A Century of Austerity, Auto-Centric Planning, and White Flight* (University of Chicago Press, 2023).

43. "How S.O.M. Took on the Baltimore Road Gang," *Architectural Forum*, March 1969, 43.

44. Douglas H. Hauber, *The Baltimore Expressway Controversy: A Study of the Political Decision-Making Process* (Johns Hopkins University Center for Metropolitan Planning and

Research, 1974); Mark Reutter, "Baltimore's Expressway Controversy" (ca. 1970s), Reuter, Mark—Expressway Paper, 7A, box 7, folder 110, Movement Against Destruction Records, R0062-MAD, Baltimore Studies Archives, UB; Raymond A. Mohl, "The Interstates and the Cities: Highways, Housing, and the Freeway Revolt," *PRRAC Civil Rights Research*, 2002, 1–73; Raymond A. Mohl, "Stop the Road: Freeway Revolts in American Cities," *Journal of Urban History* 30, no. 5 (July 2004): 674–706; Emily Lieb, "Row House City: Unbuilding Residential Baltimore, 1940–1980" (PhD diss., Columbia University, 2010); Emily Lieb, "White Man's Lane: Hollowing Out the Highway Ghetto in Baltimore," in *Baltimore '68: Riots and Rebirth in an American City* edited by Jessica Elfenbein, Thomas Hollowak, and Elizabeth Nix (Temple University Press, 2011); Earl Swift, *The Big Roads: The Untold Story of the Engineers, Visionaries, and Trailblazers Who Created the American Superhighways* (Harper Collins, 2012); Crenson, *Baltimore: A Political History*; E. Evans Paull, *Stop the Road: Stories from the Trenches of Baltimore's Road Wars* (Boyle & Dalton, 2022).

45. "Movement Against Destruction Statement of December 10, 1969," Promotional, 3, Movement Against Destruction Records, R0062-MAD, Baltimore Studies Archives, UB.

46. Taylor, *Race for Profit*, 5.

47. "A Home for You in Rosemont!"; Rosemont Neighborhood Improvement Association Records, 1970–1971, 9B, box 15, folder 3, Baltimore Heritage Records, R0010-BH, Baltimore Studies Archives, UB.

48. "A Home for You in Rosemont!"; "Rosemont," *The Settler: A Chronicle of Home Ownership in Baltimore*, March 1975, Rosemont Neighborhood Improvement Association Records, 1970–1971, 9B, box 15, folder 3, Baltimore Heritage Records, R0010-BH, Baltimore Studies Archives, UB.

49. "Residents Warned on Rosemont," *Baltimore Afro-American*, January 25, 1972.

50. "Residents Warned on Rosemont"; "*Afro* Victory: City Spends $744,000 more in Rosemont Area," *Baltimore Afro-American*, June 17, 1972.

51. HCD Rosemont Home Care Catalog, "Rosemont Is Now," BRG48-40, box 2, Land Development Division, Vacant House Program Real Estate Files, 1969–1975, Department of Housing and Community Development, BCA.

52. Mark Reutter, "Fix-Up Draws Mixed Reviews," *Baltimore Sun*, September 29, 1974, TR1.

53. Reginald Fields, "Rosemont May Find Hope in Coppin," *Baltimore Sun*, September 26, 2004.

54. James D. Dilts, "Being Avoided by 3-A Is Rosemont's Success Story," *Baltimore Sun*, March 29, 1976, C1.

55. "Rosemont Won I-170 Battle; War Continues," *Baltimore Sun*, June 1, 1980, D3.

56. "Rosemont Won I-170 Battle."

Chapter One

1. "Population Move Stumps School Board," *Baltimore Sun*, September 19, 1952, 36, 22.

2. Year: 1940, Census Place: Baltimore, Baltimore City, Maryland, roll m-t0627-01531, page 63B, Enumeration District 4-562.

3. Larry Carson, "Rosemont Protests Bring End of Beer-Wine License," *Baltimore Evening Sun*, June 3, 1977, 31.

4. "Population Move Stumps School Board," 36.

5. Emily Lieb, "The 'Baltimore Idea' and the Cities It Built," *Southern Cultures* 25, no. 2 (2019): 104–20; Emily Lieb, "'Shove Those Black Clouds Away!' Jim Crow Schools and Jim Crow Neighborhoods Before *Brown*," in *Baltimore Revisited: Stories of Inequality and Resistance in a U.S. City*, edited by Nicole King, Kate Drabinski, and Joshua Clark Davis (Rutgers University Press, 2019), 24–36.

6. Joseph L. Arnold, "Baltimore: Southern Culture and a Northern Economy," in *Snowbelt Cities: Metropolitan Politics in the Northeast and Midwest Since World War II*, edited by Richard M. Bernard (Indiana University Press, 1990), 25–39.

7. Joel Garreau, *The Nine Nations of North America* (Avon, 1981), 67.

8. Barbara Jeanne Fields, *Slavery and Freedom on the Middle Ground: Maryland During the Nineteenth Century* (Yale University Press, 1985), 6–7.

9. Fields, *Slavery and Freedom on the Middle Ground*, 62.

10. Alan D. Anderson, *The Origin and Resolution of an Urban Crisis: Baltimore, 1890–1930* (Johns Hopkins University Press 1977), 19.

11. Matthew A. Crenson, *Baltimore: A Political History* (Johns Hopkins University Press, 2017), 278.

12. Mary Ellen Hayward and Charles Belfoure, *The Baltimore Rowhouse* (Princeton Architectural Press, 2001).

13. Walter F. Willcox, "The Negro Population," in *Negroes in the United States*, edited by Willcox and W. E. B. Du Bois, (Bureau of the Census, 1904), 12.

14. Crenson, *Baltimore*, 205, 278.

15. Crenson, *Baltimore*, 279.

16. Mary Ellen Hayward, *Baltimore's Alley Houses: Homes for Working People Since the 1780s* (Johns Hopkins University Press, 2008).

17. Karen Olson, "Old West Baltimore: Segregation, African-American Culture, and the Struggle for Equality," in *The Baltimore Book: New Views of Local History*, edited by Elizabeth Fee, Linda Shopes, and Linda Zeidman (Temple University Press, 1991), 57.

18. Margaret Law Callcott, *The Negro in Maryland Politics, 1870–1912* (Johns Hopkins University Press, 1969); Crenson, *Baltimore*, 279–340.

19. Callcott, *The Negro in Maryland Politics*, 16.

20. Robert J. Brugger, *Maryland, A Middle Temperament: 1634–1980* (Johns Hopkins University Press, 1996), 385.

21. Crenson, *Baltimore*, 295.

22. Callcott, *The Negro in Maryland Politics*, 82.

23. Callcott, *The Negro in Maryland Politics*, 86.

24. Michael Perman, *Struggle for Mastery: Disfranchisement in the South, 1888–1908* (University of North Carolina Press, 2001), 254.

25. Lieb, "The 'Baltimore Idea' and the Cities It Built"; Lieb, "'Shove Those Black Clouds Away!'"

26. Crenson, *Baltimore*, 279–80. The Peale Museum, "History of Male and Female Colored School No. 1" (n.d.). https://www.thepeale.org/school-one/.

27. "To Remain White School," *Baltimore Sun*, August 8, 1903, 12; *Fifty-Third Annual Report of the Board of Commissioners of Public Schools to the Mayor and City Council of Baltimore for the Year Ending December 31, 1881* (John B. Piet & Co, 1882), xxxi, BRG31-14-1-12, Board of School Commissioner Records, 1863–1901, Department of Education, BCA.

28. Thomas W. Hanchett, *Sorting Out the New South City: Race, Class, and Urban Development in Charlotte, 1875-1975* (University of North Carolina Press 1998).

29. Olson, "Old West Baltimore," 57–59; City of Baltimore Commission for Architectural and Historical Preservation, "Old West Baltimore," December 24, 2004, https://chap.baltimorecity.gov/old-west-baltimore.

30. City of Baltimore Department of Planning, "Baltimore: 2000 to 2010 Changes," January 2012, https://planning.baltimorecity.gov/sites/default/files/CENSUSCHANGES.pdf.

31. Joseph L. Arnold, "Suburban Growth and Municipal Annexation in Baltimore, 1745–1918," *Maryland Historical Magazine* 73, no. 2 (1978): 109–28; Maryland Geological Survey, "Map of Baltimore and Vicinity Showing Proposed Enlargements of Baltimore City" (1916), Baltimore City Sheet Maps, Johns Hopkins Sheridan Library Map Collections; Baltimore City Department of Public Works, "Historical Growth Map, City of Baltimore" (1977), Maryland State Archives, Annapolis, MD (hereafter cited as MSA).

32. Paige Glotzer, *How the Suburbs Were Segregated: Developers and the Business of Exclusionary Housing, 1890-1960* (Columbia University Press, 2020).

33. W. Ashbie Hawkins, "A Year of Segregation in Baltimore," *The Crisis*, November 1911, 27.

34. Gretchen Boger, "The Meaning of Neighborhood in the Modern City: Baltimore's Residential Segregation Ordinances, 1910–1913," *Journal of Urban History* 35, no. 2 (2009): 238.

35. United States Bureau of the Census, *Twelfth Census of the United States*, Year: *1900*, Census Place: *Baltimore Ward 15, Baltimore City (Independent City), Maryland*, roll 614, page 11A, Enumeration District: *0198*, FHL microfilm: 1240614.

36. Hanchett, *Sorting Out the New South City*.

37. "History of Male and Female Colored School No. 1."

38. "Protest to Board," *Baltimore Sun*, June 20, 1901, 12.

39. Andrew R. Highsmith and Ansley T. Erickson, "Segregation as Splitting, Segregation as Joining: Schools, Housing, and the Many Modes of Jim Crow," *American Journal of Education* 121, no. 4 (2015): 563–95; David G. Garcia and Tara J. Yosso, "'Strictly in the Capacity of Servant': The Interconnection Between Residential and School Segregation in Oxnard, California, 1934–1954," *History of Education Quarterly* 53, no. 1 (2013): 64–89; Jack A. Dougherty, "Shopping for Schools: How Public Education and Private Housing Shaped Suburban Connecticut," *Journal of Urban History* 38, no. 2 (2012): 205–24; Ansley T. Erickson, *Making the Unequal Metropolis: School Desegregation and Its Limits* (University of Chicago Press, 2016).

40. "Proposed Fulton Avenue Negro School," *Baltimore Sun*, September 16, 1903; "Indignant at School Board," *Baltimore Sun*, July 15, 1903; "Object to Colored School," *Baltimore Sun*, September 10, 1903; "Against Negro School," *Baltimore Sun*, October 13, 1910.

41. "To Keep Out Negroes," *Baltimore Sun*, November 8, 1907, 9.

42. Carl H. Nightingale, "The Transnational Contexts of Early Twentieth-Century American Urban Segregation," *Journal of Social History* 39, no. 3 (2006): 673.

43. "Residents Are Aroused," *Baltimore Sun*, September 26, 1910, 4.

44. Ordinance No. 610, *Ordinances and Resolutions of the Mayor and City Council of Baltimore, Passed at the Annual Session, 1910–1911* (Meyer & Thalheimer, 1911), 204.

45. "West Plan Is Amended," *Baltimore Sun*, October 10, 1910, 14.

46. Ordinance No. 610, 205.

47. Garrett Power, "Apartheid Baltimore Style: The Residential Segregation Ordinances of 1910–1913," *Maryland Law Review* 42, no. 2 (1982): 289–328; Boger, "The Meaning of Neighborhood in the Modern City."

48. "To Modify West Plan," *Baltimore Sun*, December 30, 1910, 8.
49. "Mr. Dashiell Opposes It," *Baltimore Sun*, January 8, 1911, 7.
50. "Mr. Dashiell Opposes It," *Baltimore Sun*, January 8, 1911, 7.
51. "Solid for West Law as It Is," *Baltimore Sun*, January 21, 1911, 16.
52. W. Ashbie Hawkins, "A Year of Segregation in Baltimore," *Crisis*, November 1911, 30.
53. "Segregation A Boon to Real Estate Sharps," *Baltimore Afro-American*, January 23, 1915, 1.
54. "Negro House Attacked," *Baltimore Sun*, September 18, 1913, 14.
55. "Negro House Attacked"; "Negro Homes Stoned," *Baltimore Sun*, September 26, 1913, 14.
56. "One Shot; One Stabbed," *Baltimore Sun*, September 27, 1913, 16.

57. *Negro Year Book: An Annual Encyclopedia of the Negro, 1914–1915*, ed. Monroe N. Work (Negro Year Book Publishing, 1914), 31.

58. David E. Bernstein, *Rehabilitating Lochner: Defending Individual Rights Against Progressive Reform* (University of Chicago Press, 2011); Power, "Apartheid Baltimore Style."

59. *Buchanan v. Warley*, 245 U.S. 60 (1917).
60. "Resent Negro Invasion," *Baltimore Sun*, November 18, 1917, 9.
61. Glotzer, *How the Suburbs Were Segregated*.

62. Eli Pousson, National Register of Historic Places Nomination Form: Edmondson Avenue Historic District, (October 2010); *Baltimore Sun*, April 11, 1915, 13.

63. Garrett Power, "The Unwisdom of Allowing City Growth to Work Out Its Own Destiny," *Maryland Law Review* 47, no. 3 (1988); Christopher Silver, "The Racial Origins of Zoning: Southern Cities from 1910–1940," *Planning Perspectives* 6, no. 2 (1991): 189–205; Joshua Gordon, "A *Euclid*-Turn: *R. B. Construction Co. v. Jackson* and the Zoning of Baltimore," *Maryland Historian* 22 (Spring/Summer 1991); Richard Rothstein, *The Color of Law: A Forgotten History of How Our Government Segregated America* (W. W. Norton, 2017).

64. Colin Campbell, "Neighbors Disavow Racist Opposition to Morgan State, a Century After Trying to Keep College Out of Northeast Baltimore," *Baltimore Sun*, November 7, 2019; *Diggs v. Morgan College*, 105 A. 157 (Court of Appeals of Maryland. 1918).

65. City of Baltimore Planning Commission, "History of Baltimore." The City of Baltimore Comprehensive Master Plan (Final Draft) (n.d.), 25–47.

66. *Annual Report of the Board of Commissioners of Public Schools to the Mayor and City Council of Baltimore*, BRG31-14-2, BRG31-14-3, BCA; *R. L. Polk & Co's Baltimore City Directory*.

67. Samuel Joseph Rice, "A Study of the Experiences of Fifty Negro Families Who Moved into White Neighborhoods of Baltimore, Maryland in 1945 and 1946" (1947), ETC Collection for Atlanta University Center Robert W. Woodruff Library, Atlanta, GA, Paper 2344.

68. Rice, "A Study of the Experiences of Fifty Negro Families," 4–5.
69. Arnold, "Suburban Growth and Municipal Annexation in Baltimore," 112.

70. "City of Baltimore Topographical Survey" (1894) and "18th Ward Baltimore City" (1898), Baltimore City Sheet Maps, Johns Hopkins Sheridan Libraries Map Collection.

71. John McGrain, "Calverton Mills," *Baltimore County History Trails* 34 (2001): 3, 4.

72. City of Baltimore Topographical Survey (1914). Baltimore City Department of Public Works, Map of Baltimore: Showing Streets Paved with Improved Paving to December 31, 1926; Baltimore Bureau of Plans and Surveys, Map of Baltimore City (1935), Johns Hopkins Sheridan Libraries Map Collection; United Railways and Electric Company, Total Mileage of System 404 648/1000, Baltimore City Sheet Maps, Johns Hopkins Sheridan Libraries Map Collection.

73. "Lauretta Avenue at Edmondson Terraces," *Baltimore Sun*, September 21, 1915, 3; "You Should Examine the Dwellings on Edmondson Terraces," *Baltimore Sun*, September 11, 1915, 13.

74. "Boom at Dukeland Park," *Baltimore Sun*, July 21, 1908, 9.

75. Baltimore City Department of Education, Map of School System, Baltimore City (1932), Baltimore City Sheet Maps, Johns Hopkins Sheridan Libraries Map Collection.

76. Baltimore City Department of Education, Map of School System, Baltimore City (1944), Baltimore City Sheet Maps, Johns Hopkins Sheridan Libraries Map Collection.

77. United States Bureau of the Census, *1950 United States Census of Population: Baltimore, Maryland Census Tracts*, 11–12.

78. Campbell Gibson and Kay Jung, "Historical Census Statistics on Population Totals by Race, 1790 to 1990, and by Hispanic Origin, 1970 to 1990, for Large Cities and Other Urban Places in the United States," Population Division Working Paper no. 76 (US Census Bureau, February 2005), table 21, https://www.census.gov/population/www/documentation/twps0076/twps0076.pdf.

79. Fanny McConnell Buford, *Racial Problems in Housing* (National Urban League, 1944), quoted in Rice, "A Study of the Experiences of Fifty Negro Families," 3.

80. Quoted in Rice, "A Study of the Experiences of Fifty Negro Families," 7–8.

81. "Soap and Paint Shortage in Public Schools," *Baltimore Afro-American*, September 6, 1930, 6.

82. Howell S. Baum, *Brown in Baltimore: School Desegregation and the Limits of Liberalism* (Cornell University Press 2010), 36.

83. Alan Barreca, Karen Clay, and Joel Tarr, "Coal, Smoke, and Death: Bituminous Coal and American Home Heating," NBER Working Paper 19881 (February 2014).

84. See Baum, *Brown in Baltimore*.

85. "Negroes Will Attempt to Enroll in School," *Baltimore Sun*, January 4, 1946, 7.

86. "Western High May Become Coeducational Negro School," *Baltimore Sun*, March 20, 1953, 17.

87. "City Drops Talks on Carver School," *Baltimore Sun*, June 23, 1949, 11.

88. "Reed Stages Protest on Carver School," *Baltimore Sun*, May 19, 1950, 40; "School Stand Is Attacked," *Baltimore Sun*, October 24, 1950, 17; "City Drops Talks on Carver School," *Baltimore Sun*, June 23, 1949, 11.

89. "Reed Stages Protest on Carver School," *Baltimore Sun*, May 19, 1950, 40.

90. Map of School System, Department of Education, Baltimore, Maryland (1951), Baltimore City Sheet Maps, Johns Hopkins Sheridan Libraries Map Collection.

91. "2 Places Ruined by Vandals' Acts," *Baltimore Sun*, May 30, 1945, 18.

92. "Negro School Enrollment—1: The Shifting Ratio," *Baltimore Sun*, February 23, 1954, 14.

93. "Poplar Grove Street (810)," Passano-O'Neill file, POF, H. Furlong Baldwin Library, Maryland Center for History and Culture, Baltimore, MD (hereafter cited as MCHC).

94. Federal Housing Administration, "Report on the Housing Market, Baltimore, Maryland, Standard Metropolitan Area, as of September 1, 1953."

95. "Douglass Gets Western High in Sept., 1954," *Baltimore Sun*, June 5, 1953, 36.

96. "Douglass Gets Western High in Sept., 1954," *Baltimore Sun*, June 5, 1953, 36.

97. "Influx of Students Taxes Baltimore School Facilities," *Baltimore Sun*, September 9, 1953, 36.

98. City of Baltimore Department of Education Bureau of Research, *School Plant Directory* (1952), Maryland Department, Enoch Pratt Free Library, Baltimore, MD (hereafter cited as EPFL).

99. "3,000 New Pupils to Be Enrolled," *Baltimore Sun*, September 2, 1933, 10; "School's Open in Baltimore," *Baltimore Afro-American*, September 19, 1953, 14.

100. "School's Open in Baltimore," *Baltimore Afro-American*, September 19, 1953, 14.
101. "Poplar Grove Street (810)."

Chapter Two

1. "Mrs. Helen L. M. Bowers," *Baltimore Sun*, July 24, 1952, 13.
2. Baltimore City Superior Court (Land Records) 1931–1931, SCL 5225, p. 0182, MSA CE 168-523; Baltimore City Superior Court (Land Records) 1931–1931, SCL 5225, p. 0513, MSA CE 168-523.
3. "He Helped to Rout the Kaiser's Hordes," *Baltimore Evening Sun*, January 15, 1919, 6; "Bowers Rites are Tuesday," *Baltimore Sun*, May 31, 1970, 24.
4. "Mrs. Helen L.M. Bowers," *Baltimore Sun*, July 24, 1952, 13; National Archives, Seventeenth Census of the United States, 1950, Census Place: Baltimore, Baltimore, Maryland, roll: 6046, p. 7, Enumeration District: 4-1431.
5. "Three Baltimore Men Are Missing in Action," *Baltimore Evening Sun*, September 16, 1943, 36.
6. *Baltimore Evening Sun*, July 23, 1952, 54.
7. *Baltimore Sun*, October 4, 1953, 54.
8. *Baltimore Sun*, December 27, 1953, 34.
9. *Baltimore Sun*, June 15, 1952, 105.
10. *Baltimore Sun*, October 1, 1952, 26.
11. *Baltimore Sun*, October 1, 1952, 26.
12. National Archives, Seventeenth Census of the United States, 1950, Census Place: Baltimore, Maryland, roll 4574, p. 12; Enumeration District: 4-914; Minutes of Caroline County Roads Board, Book 1 (June 11, 1956–November 19, 1963), MSA; *Maryland Manual* 1951–52, MSA.
13. "Joseph Sinclair Wiles, 84, Vaccination Gun Inventor," *Baltimore Sun*, November 25, 1998, 117; Lula Sheffey, "Solid American Family: The Joseph Wileses Teach and Help Others," *Baltimore Afro-American*, September 7, 1968, 27.
14. Sheffey, "Solid American Family," 27.
15. "The Rosemont Home Improvement Association" (n.d.), Rosemont Neighborhood Improvement Association Records, 1969–1970, 9B, box 15, folder 2, Baltimore Heritage Records, R0010-BH, Baltimore Studies Archives, UB.
16. "Services Set for Holsey," *Baltimore Sun*, April 18, 1967, 13.
17. "Marian H. Barclift," *Baltimore Sun*, December 4, 2009, A24.
18. "Marian H. Barclift"; "201 Edgewood Street," *Baltimore Sun*, March 29, 1953, 54.
19. "Dallas J. Barclift, Sr.," *Baltimore Sun*, May 25, 1987, 46.
20. "Hamptonians Wed on Campus," *Baltimore Afro-American*, June 30, 1951, 11.
21. Maryland Commission on Interracial Problems and Relations, *An American City in Transition: The Baltimore Community Self-Survey of Inter-Group Relations* (1955), 31, 46.
22. Harold A. McDougall, *Black Baltimore: A New Theory of Community* (Temple University Press, 1993), 43. Baltimore City Commission for Historical and Architectural Preservation, "Harry O. Wilson House: Landmark Designation Report," July 11, 2017; Baltimore City Commission for Historical and Architectural Preservation, "Landmark Designation Report: W. E. B. DuBois House," January 16, 2007; Timmy Reid, "Hamilton-Lauraville: An Olmsted Neighborhood Becomes a Gardening Hotspot in Baltimore," *Baltimore Fishbowl*, May 6, 2022.
23. Jane Berger, *A New Working Class: The Legacies of Public-Sector Employment in the Civil*

Rights Movement (University of Pennsylvania Press, 2021), 13; Maryland Commission on Interracial Problems and Relations, *An American City in Transition*, 30.

24. Rhonda Y. Williams, *The Politics of Public Housing: Black Women's Struggles Against Urban Inequality* (Oxford University Press, 2004), 29. See also Andrew Wiese, *Places of Their Own: African American Suburbanization in the Twentieth Century* (University of Chicago Press, 2004); Mary E. Pattillo, *Black on the Block: The Politics of Race and Class in the City* (University of Chicago Press, 2007); Preston H. Smith II, *Racial Democracy and the Black Metropolis: Housing Policy in Postwar Chicago* (University of Minnesota Press, 2012); N. D. B. Connolly, *A World More Concrete: Real Estate and the Remaking of Jim Crow South Florida* (University of Chicago Press, 2014); Emily Lieb, "'Baltimore Does Not Condone Profiteering in Squalor': The Baltimore Plan and the Problem of Housing-Code Enforcement in an American City," *Planning Perspectives* 33, no. 1 (2017): 75–95.

25. "The Rosemont Home Improvement Association."

26. Baltimore Urban League, *Directory of Organizations*, May 1957, Maryland Department, EPFL.

27. Rosemont Neighborhood Improvement Association Records, 1952–1968, 9B, box 15, folder 1, Baltimore Heritage Records, R0010-BH, Baltimore Studies Archives, UB.

28. "Arthur Murray School and You . . . ," *Baltimore Afro-American*, April 16, 1955, 8; Jacques Kelly, "Gwendolyn E. Biddle," *Baltimore Sun*, April 9, 2015, 12.

29. "For Baltimore's Fern Scotland, It Was a Long Road to Bowling's Pinnacle," *Baltimore Afro-American*. November 15, 1986, 9; B. M. Phillips, "If You Ask Me," *Baltimore Afro-American*, November 12, 1955, 14.

30. "Poplar Grove Street (611–613)," Passano-O'Neill file, POF, H. Furlong Baldwin Library, MCHC; "New Walbrook Library Branch to be Dedicated on Monday," *Baltimore Evening Sun*, April 12, 1957, 34; "Walbrook Library Branch Slated To Open April 15," *Baltimore Evening Sun*, March 22, 1957, 26.

31. Louise Campbell, "In Baltimore, New Options Are Opened and New Alliances Formed," *City* 2 (September/October 1968): 31.

32. "Rosedale," Passano-O'Neill file, POF, H. Furlong Baldwin Library, MCHC; Joseph Legg, *The Burying Grounds of Baltimore* (self-published, n.d.); Earl Swift, *The Big Roads: The Untold Story of the Engineers, Trailblazers, Visionaries, and Trailblazers Who Created the American Superhighways* (Mariner Books, 2011), 234.

33. "We Workers" (n.d.), Rosemont Neighborhood Improvement Association Records, 1952–1968, 9B, box 15, folder 1, Baltimore Heritage Records, R0010-BH, Baltimore Studies Archives, UB.

34. Rosemont Neighborhood Improvement Association Records, 9B, box 15, folder 20, Baltimore Heritage Records, R0010-BH, Baltimore Studies Archives, UB.

35. Mary Rosemond/Rosemont Neighborhood Improvement Association, Inc., "Letter of Philosophy," Rosemont Neighborhood Improvement Association Records, 1952–1968, 9B, box 15, folder 1, Baltimore Heritage Records, R0010-BH, Baltimore Studies Archives, UB.

36. Carroll E. Williams, "The Drive Behind Block-Busting," *Baltimore Sun*, September 23, 1955, 20.

37. Antero Pietila, *Not in My Neighborhood: How Bigotry Shaped a Great American City* (Ivan R. Dee, 2010), 96.

38. Dalton Conley, *Being Black, Living in the Red: Race, Wealth, and Social Policy in America* (University of California Press, 1999), 38.

39. Kenneth T. Jackson, *Crabgrass Frontier: The Suburbanization of the United States* (Oxford

University Press, 1985); Richard Rothstein, *The Color of Law: A Forgotten History of How Our Government Segregated America* (Liveright, 2017); Mehrsa Baradaran, *The Color of Money: Black Banks and the Racial Wealth Gap* (Harvard University Press, 2017); Freund, *Colored Property*; Louis Hyman, *Debtor Nation: The History of America in Red Ink* (Princeton University Press, 2011).

40. Kenneth A. Snowden, "Research Institute for Housing America Special Report: Mortgage Banking in the United States, 1870–1940" (RIHA, 2013), 64.

41. Hyman, *Debtor Nation*, 47. Amanda Tillotson, "Race, Risk and Real Estate: The Federal Housing Administration and Black Homeownership in the Post World War II Home Ownership State," *DePaul Journal for Social Justice* 8, no. 1 (2014): 25–52.

42. Hyman, *Debtor Nation*, 48.

43. Jackson, *Crabgrass Frontier*, 193.

44. Alyssa Katz, *Our Lot: How Real Estate Came to Own Us* (Bloomsbury, 2010).

45. Calvin Bradford, "Financing Home Ownership: The Federal Role in Neighborhood Decline," *Urban Affairs Quarterly*, March 1979, 320.

46. Amy E. Hillier, "Residential Security Maps and Neighborhood Appraisals: The Home Owners' Loan Corporation and the Case of Philadelphia," *Social Science History* 29, no. 2 (2005): 207; Amy E. Hillier, "Redlining and the Home Owners' Loan Corporation," *Journal of Urban History* 29, no. 4 (2003): 394–420; LaDale C Winling and Todd M Michney, "The Roots of Redlining: Academic, Governmental, and Professional Networks in the Making of the New Deal Lending Regime," *Journal of American History* 108, no. 1 (2021): 42–69; Price V. Fishback, Jonathan Rose, Kenneth A. Snowden, and Thomas Storrs, "New Evidence on Redlining by Federal Housing Programs in the 1930s," NBER Working Paper 29244 (September 2021).

47. Dan Immergluck, *Foreclosed: High-Risk Lending, Deregulation, and the Undermining of America's Mortgage Market* (Cornell University Press, 2009), 31.

48. Immergluck, *Foreclosed*, 32.

49. US Census Bureau, "Historical Census of Housing Tables: Homeownership" (2000), https://www.census.gov/data/tables/time-series/dec/coh-owner.html.

50. *The Banking Reform Act of 1971: Hearings before the Committee on Banking and Currency, House of Representatives, Ninety-Second Congress, First Session* (April 20, 21, 22 23, 26, 27, 1971), 325–26.

51. Lizabeth Cohen, *A Consumers' Republic: The Politics of Mass Consumption in Postwar America* (Vintage, 2003), 214.

52. Hyman, *Debtor Nation*, 65; Lizabeth Cohen, *A Consumers' Republic*, 205.

53. Fishback, Rose, Snowden, and Storrs, "New Evidence on Redlining by Federal Housing Programs in the 1930s."

54. "Residential Security Map of Baltimore Md." (1937), Baltimore City Sheet Maps, Johns Hopkins Sheridan Library Map Collections.

55. *Annual Report of the Voluntary Home Mortgage Credit Program* 3 (1956), 30.

56. Freund, *Colored Property*, 129.

57. Freund, *Colored Property*, 133.

58. Baradaran, *The Color of Money*, 92.

59. Hyman, *Debtor Nation*, 142.

60. Hyman, *Debtor Nation*, 142.

61. *Annual Report of the Voluntary Home Mortgage Credit Program* 3 (1956), 30. See also Keeanga-Yamahtta Taylor, *Race for Profit: How Banks and the Real Estate Industry Undermined Black Homeownership* (University of North Carolina Press, 2019), 45.

62. Baradaran, *The Color of Money*, 108.

63. Hyman, *Debtor Nation*, 143.

64. Urban Institute Housing Finance Policy Center, "Black-White Homeownership Gap: A Closer Look Across MSAs," June 2019.

65. Pietila, *Not in My Neighborhood*, 110.

66. Maryland Commission on Interracial Problems and Relations, *An American City in Transition: The Baltimore Community Self-Survey of Inter-Group Relations* (1955), 30.

67. Norris Vitchek to Alfred Balk, "Confessions of a Block-Buster," *Saturday Evening Post*, July 14–21, 1962, 15; Beryl Satter, *Family Properties: How the Struggle over Race and Real Estate Transformed Chicago and Urban America* (Picador, 2010).

68. Horace Ayers, "Mortgage-Form Signature Repudiated," *Baltimore Evening Sun*, January 25, 1972, 24.

69. James D. Dilts, "Landlord's Lament: 'Don't Blame Goldseker,'" *Baltimore Sun*, March 9, 1971, C20, C12.

70. Dilts, "Landlord's Lament."

71. W. Edward Orser, *Blockbusting in Baltimore: The Edmondson Village Story* (University Press of Kentucky, 1994).

72. Andrew Wiese, *Places of Their Own: African American Suburbanization in the Twentieth Century* (University of Chicago Press, 2004), 161.

73. Baltimore City Superior Court (Land Records) 1954–1954, MLP 9408, p. 0120, MSA CE 168-9416.

74. Baltimore City Superior Court (Land Records) 1954–1954, MLP 9408, p. 0121, MSA CE 168-9416.

75. Baltimore City Superior Court (Land Records) 1953–1953, MLP 9289, p. 0332, MSA CE 168-9297.

76. Baltimore City Superior Court (Land Records) 1955–1955, MLP 9925, p. 0089, MSA CE 168-9933; Federal Reserve Bank of St. Louis, "Residential Mortgage Market Changes: 1955–1957," *Monthly Review* 39, no. 6 (1957), 77; Saul B. Klaman, "The Postwar Pattern of Mortgage Interest Rates" (NBER, 1961), 74–98.

77. Baltimore City Superior Court (Land Records) 1955–1955, MLP 9925, p. 0080, MSA CE 168-9933.

78. Steven I. Batoff, "Maryland's Savings and Loan Crisis of 1985: The Resulting Legislative Reform," *University of Baltimore Law Review* 16, no. 3 (1987): 406–8.

79. Activists, Inc., "A Conspiracy to Defraud and Exploit Homebuyers: The Story of Jefferson Federal Savings and Loan" (n.d.), 5, sub-series 10F, box 16, folder 12, Citizens Planning and Housing Association Records, R0032-CPHA, Baltimore Studies Archives, UB.

80. Activists, Inc., "A Conspiracy to Defraud and Exploit Homebuyers," 7.

81. Activists, Inc., "A Conspiracy to Defraud and Exploit Homebuyers," 7.

82. Activists, Inc., "A Conspiracy to Defraud and Exploit Homebuyers," iv.

83. Eric Siegel, "The Riddle of Morris Goldseker's Legacy," *Baltimore Sun Magazine*, February 5, 1978, 12.

84. "Housing Exploitation Charged," *Baltimore Sun*, March 5, 1971, C33, C20; "The Lusk Reports: No House Sale Here Goes Unreported," *Washington Post*, June 6, 1980.

85. Activists, Inc., "A Conspiracy to Defraud and Exploit Homebuyers," iii.

86. Baltimore City Superior Court (Land Records) 1958–1958, JFC 392, p. 0523, MSA CE 168-10710.

87. Baltimore City Superior Court (Land Records) 1952–1952, MLP 8890, p. 0245, MSA CE 168-8898.

88. Baltimore City Superior Court (Land Records) 1953–1953, MLP 9061, p. 0245, MSA CE 168-9069.

89. Maryland Commission on Interracial Problems and Relations, *An American City in Transition*, 31.

90. East–West Expressway Land Acquisition Files, folder 2410 Lauretta, BRG60, Department of Planning, BCA.

91. Samuel DuBois Cook Center on Social Equity at Duke University, "The Plunder of Black Wealth in Chicago: New Findings on the Lasting Toll of Predatory Housing Contracts," May 2019, ii, https://socialequity.duke.edu/wp-content/uploads/2019/10/Plunder-of-Black-Wealth-in-Chicago.pdf.

92. Pietila, *Not in My Neighborhood*, 104.

93. Martin Millspaugh and Gurney Breckenfeld, *The Human Side of Urban Renewal: A Study of the Attitude Changes Produced by Neighborhood Rehabilitation* (Ives Washburn, 1960); Emily Lieb, "'Baltimore Does Not Condone Profiteering in Squalor': The Baltimore Plan and the Problem of Code Enforcement in an American City," *Planning Perspectives* 33, no. 1 (2018): 75–95.

94. Samuel DuBois Cook Center on Social Equity at Duke University, "The Plunder of Black Wealth in Chicago," 2–3.

95. Orser, *Blockbusting in Baltimore*, 86.

96. Orser, *Blockbusting in Baltimore*, 137.

97. Activists, Inc., "A Conspiracy to Defraud and Exploit Homebuyers."

Chapter Three

1. John Feinstein, "'Soft Shoes': Colleagues Ask What He's Up To," *Washington Post*, March 15, 1982.

2. John Feinstein, "Harry McGuirk," *Washington Post*, June 29, 1982.

3. "McGuirk Provokes a Mixture of Fear and Awe," *Baltimore Sun*, April 3, 1977, 34.

4. "Councilmen Pessimistic on Factory," *Baltimore Afro-American*, April 13, 1957; "City Council Actions Taken," *Baltimore Sun*, February 4, 1969, C8.

5. "Rosemont Unit Fights New Factory," *Baltimore Afro-American*, April 9, 1957.

6. Amanda I. Seligman, *Block by Block: Neighborhoods and Public Policy on Chicago's West Side* (University of Chicago Press, 2005).

7. Jonathan Lethem, "A Neighborhood, Authored," *The New Yorker*, August 28, 2023, 49.

8. Mary Rosemond/Rosemont Neighborhood Improvement Association, Inc., "Letter of Philosophy" (n.d.), Rosemont Neighborhood Improvement Association Records, 1952–1968, 9B, box 15, folder 1, Baltimore Heritage Records, R0010-BH, Baltimore Studies Archives, UB.

9. Paige Glotzer, *How the Suburbs Were Segregated: Developers and the Business of Exclusionary Housing, 1890–1960* (Columbia University Press, 2020); Elizabeth Evitts Dickinson, "Roland Park: One of America's First Garden Suburbs and Built for Whites Only," *Johns Hopkins Magazine*, Fall 2014.

10. Joshua Gordon, "A Euclid-Turn: *R. B. Construction Co. v. Jackson* and the Zoning of Baltimore," *Maryland Historian* 22 (Spring/Summer 1991).

11. Maryland Geological Society and Maryland Harbor Board, "Map of Baltimore and Vicinity Showing Proposed Enlargements of Baltimore City also Main Lines of the Various Railroads"

(1917); Northern Central Railway, "Map Showing Tracks and Stations in Baltimore" (1909); "City of Baltimore Reproduction of the Use District Map, Part of the Zoning Ordinance (ordinance No. 1247, approved March 30, 1931): as Amended to December 31, 1948/the Board of Municipal and Zoning Appeals, William C. Bloom, chairman, Hon. Thomas d'Alesandro, Jr., Mayor," Baltimore City Sheet Maps, Johns Hopkins Sheridan Library Map Collections; "To Start Campaign for Zoning Scheme," *Baltimore Evening Sun*, March 6, 1923, 11.

12. Baltimore City Superior Court (Land Records) 1972–1972, RHB 2975, pp. 0489–0491, MSA CE 168-13293; Baltimore City Superior Court (Land Records) 1957–1957, JFC 32, p. 0372, MSA CE 168-10350.

13. Baltimore City Superior Court (Land Records) 1957–1957, JFC 32, p. 0367, MSA CE 168-10350.

14. Baltimore City Superior Court (Land Records) 1972–1972, RHB 2975, pp. 0489–0491, MSA CE 168-13293; Baltimore City Superior Court (Land Records) 1957–1957, JFC 32, p. 0372, MSA CE 168-10350.

15. Mary M. Rosemond, "Our Neighborhood," March 28, 2004, Rosemont Neighborhood Improvement Association Records, 2004, 9B, box 16, folder 4, Baltimore Heritage Records, R0010-BH, Baltimore Studies Archives, UB.

16. Olmsted Brothers, *Report upon the Development of Public Grounds for Greater Baltimore* (Municipal Art Society, 1904); Michael P. McCarthy, "Park Visions in Conflict: Baltimore's Debate over the Leakin Bequest," *Maryland Historical Magazine* 98, no. 2 (2003): 187–203.

17. Barry Kessler and David Zang, "The Play Life of a City: Baltimore's Recreation and Parks, 1900–1955" (Baltimore City Life Museums and Baltimore City Department of Recreation and Parks, 1989), 44; "Swimming in the City," *Baltimore Style*, June 17, 2008; Carroll E. Williams, "Negroes Lose on Play Ratio, Director Says," *Baltimore Sun*, April 20, 1946, 20; "Kelly Says Park Facilities Meet Needs for Most Sports," *Baltimore Sun*, April 18, 1943, 26.

18. Williams, "Negroes Lose on Play Ratio"; "Kelly Says Park Facilities Meet Needs."

19. Buddy Lonesome, "Fighting Sailors Resent Ban on Mixed Sports," *Baltimore Afro-American*, June 23, 1951, 7; "Citizens Rap Beach Project," *Baltimore Afro-American*, February 9, 1952, 17.

20. "Segregation on Four Golf Courses Ends," *Baltimore Sun*, July 10, 1951, 28.

21. "Swimming in the City."

22. "Board to Ponder Policy for Beach," *Baltimore Afro-American*, March 17, 1951, 6.

23. "Segregation on Four Golf Courses Ends."

24. Rosemont Neighborhood Improvement Association Records, 1952–1968, 9B, Baltimore Heritage Records, R0010-BH, Baltimore Studies Archives, UB.

25. James Carey Martien, "The Zoning Problem," *Baltimore Sun*, February 23, 1949, 10.

26. "Radcliffe Given City Zoning Post," *Baltimore Sun*, June 1, 1957, 30.

27. "Councilmen Pessimistic on Factory," *Baltimore Afro-American*, April 13, 1957; "City Council Actions Taken," *Baltimore Sun*, February 4, 1969, C8.

28. "Rosemont Unit Fights New Factory"; Board of Supervisors of Elections of Baltimore City, "Map of Baltimore City 1954 Showing Boundaries of Precincts, Wards and Legislative Districts, " Baltimore City Sheet Maps, Johns Hopkins Sheridan Library Map Collections.

29. "Rosemont Box Factory Plan Protested," *Baltimore Evening Sun*, April 10, 1957, 62.

30. "Rosemont Unit Fights New Factory"; "Thieves Loot Box Factory," *Baltimore Evening Sun*, June 19, 1964, 27; "Absolute Public Auction Sale: Building to Be Demolished," *Baltimore Sun*, October 22, 1967.

31. "Change Asked in School Site," *Baltimore Sun*, May 17, 1957, 42; *Seven Years of Desegregation in the Baltimore Public Schools: A Report*, March 1963, 14, EPFL; Donald Bremner, "Residents Hit W. Baltimore School Site," *Baltimore Evening Sun*, May 29, 1957.

32. Department of Education, "Map of School System, Baltimore, Maryland," 1956, Baltimore City Sheet Maps, Johns Hopkins Sheridan Library Map Collections.

33. Howell S. Baum, *"Brown" in Baltimore: School Desegregation and the Limits of Liberalism* (Cornell University Press, 2010); *One Hundred Twenty-First Report of the Board of School Commissioners of Baltimore City to the Mayor and City Council* (July 1, 1952–June 30, 1954), BRG31-1-2-7-6, Instructional Division Records, 1945–1956, Department of Education, BCA; League of Women Voters, *Desegregation Baltimore Public Schools: History Problems Solutions*, September 20, 196, Desegregation Baltimore Public Schools, 1963, 10, box 28, folder 42, League of Women Voters of Baltimore City Records, R0061-LWV, Baltimore Studies Archives, UB.

34. *Equality of Educational Opportunity: A Progress Report for the Baltimore City Public Schools* (March 19, 1964), 56, EPFL; "Desegregation in the Baltimore City Schools: Study Sponsored by the Maryland Commission on Interracial Problems and the Baltimore Commission on Human Relations" (July 1955), 10; League of Women Voters, *Desegregation Baltimore Public Schools*, 1; Elinor Pancoast et al., "The Report of a Study on Desegregation in the Baltimore City Schools by the Maryland Commission on Interracial Problems and the Baltimore Commission on Human Relations" (1956), 17; "School Board Adopts Policy Erasing Racial Basis for Registration," *Baltimore Sun*, June 11, 1954, 38.

35. *Equality of Educational Opportunity*, 56. *Seven Years of Desegregation*, 3.

36. *Equality of Educational Opportunity*, 56, 58. *Seven Years of Desegregation*, 3.

37. Baltimore City Superior Court (Block Book), 1954–1959, 2448–2484, p. 0095–96, MSA CE 9-99; "Change Asked in School Site."

38. Wendell E. Pritchett, "The 'Public Menace' of Blight: Urban Renewal and the Private Uses of Eminent Domain," *Yale Law & Policy Review* 21, no. 1 (2003): 3.

39. Amy Lavine, "Urban Renewal and the Story of *Berman v. Parker*," *The Urban Lawyer* 42, no. 2 (2010): 453.

40. Lavine, "Urban Renewal and the Story of *Berman v. Parker*."

41. Pritchett, "The 'Public Menace' of Blight," 1–52.

42. Francesca Russello Ammon, *Bulldozer: Demolition and Clearance of the Postwar Landscape* (Yale University Press, 2016), 238.

43. Donald Bremner, "Residents Hit W. Baltimore School Site," *Baltimore Evening Sun*, May 29, 1957.

44. Bremner, "Residents Hit W. Baltimore School Site."

45. Baltimore City Superior Court (Land Records, Grantee Index) 1959–1959, M–R p. 0040, MSA CE 166-459; Baltimore City Superior Court (Land Records, Grantee Index) 1960–1960, M–R, p. 0032, MSA CE 166-467; Baltimore City Superior Court (Land Records) 1960–1960, JFC 862, p. 0413, MSA CE 168-11180; Baltimore City Superior Court (Land Records) 1959–1959, JFC 732, p. 0425, MSA CE 168-11050.

46. Minutes of the Board of School Commissioners, January 16, 1958, 6, BRG31-14-9-8, Published Materials, 1951–1960, Department of Education, BCA.

47. City of Baltimore Topographical Survey, 1914; Baltimore City Department of Public Works, Map of Baltimore: Showing Streets Paved with Improved Paving to December 31, 1926, Baltimore City Sheet Maps, Johns Hopkins Sheridan Library Map Collections; "Making Their Suburb a Beauty Spot," *Baltimore Sun*, March 20, 1910, 15.

48. "Rosedale," Passano-O'Neill file, POF, H. Furlong Baldwin Library, MCHC.

49. Legg, *The Burying Grounds of Baltimore*.

50. Koritha Mitchell, *From Slave Cabins to the White House: Homemade Citizenship in African American Culture* (University of Illinois Press, 2020).

51. Minutes of the Board of School Commissioners of Baltimore City, May 16, 1957, 85, BRG31-14-9-7, Published Materials, 1951–1960, Department of Education, BCA.

52. Minutes of the Board of School Commissioners, May 16, 1957, 85.

53. "Change Asked in School Site."

54. Minutes of the Board of School Commissioners, May 16, 1957, 85.

55. "Change Asked in School Site."

56. "Change Asked In School Site"; "Residents Hit W. Baltimore School Site."

57. Minutes of the Board of School Commissioners of Baltimore City, January 16, 1958, 9.

58. Stephen F. Nordlinger, "Nine Schools Are Planned," *Baltimore Morning Sun*, April 24, 1959, 11; *One Hundred and Twenty-Fourth Annual Report of the Board of School Commissioners of Baltimore* (1960), BRG31-14-4-11, Individual School Records, 1943–1966, Department of Education, 53, BCA; "New Schools Are Planned," *Baltimore Morning Sun*, December 9, 1959, 17; "New Belmont School Construction Slated," *Baltimore Morning Sun*, March 12, 1961, 22; "Walbrook Due New School," *Baltimore Sun*, March 17, 1961, 28; Baltimore City Superior Court (Land Records, Grantee Index) 1959–1959, M–R p. 0040, MSA CE 166-459; Baltimore City Superior Court (Land Records, Grantee Index) 1960–1960, M–R, p. 0032, MSA CE 166-467; Baltimore City Superior Court (Land Records) 1960–1960, JFC 862, p. 0413, MSA CE 168-11180; Baltimore City Superior Court (Land Records) 1959–1959, JFC 732, p. 0425, MSA CE 168-11050.

59. "The Rosemont Home Improvement Association," Rosemont Neighborhood Improvement Association Records, 1969–1970, 9B, box 15, folder 2, Baltimore Heritage Records, R0010-BH, Baltimore Studies Archives, UB.

60. "New Belmont School Construction Slated," *Baltimore Sun*, March 12, 1961, 22.

61. Belmont Elementary P.T.S.A, Collection of Edward M. Rosemond Jr.

62. "The Rosemont Home Improvement Association."

Chapter Four

1. "Frustrated Fables," *Baltimore Evening Sun*, September 8, 1959; Martha J. Vill, "Building Enterprise in Late Nineteenth-Century Baltimore," *Journal of Historical Geography* 12, no. 2 (1986): 162–81.

2. Maryland Historical Trust, "National Register of Historic Places Registration: Mt. Vernon Place Historic District," February 1972; Virginia Paty, "Picasso, Cats and Gay Facades—That's Arty Tyson Street Now," *Baltimore Evening Sun*, May 17, 1948.

3. "Artist Colony-To-Be Seen For Tyson Street," *Baltimore Evening Sun*, January 13, 1947.

4. "Picasso, Cats and Gay Facades."

5. "Picasso, Cats and Gay Facades."

6. National Archives, Washington, DC, Seventeenth Census of the United States, 1950, Census Place: Baltimore, Maryland, roll 2114, p. 4, Enumeration District: 4-516.

7. Shelley L. Murphy, "Slum Clearance à La Mode," *Baltimore Magazine*, October 1949.

8. "Picasso, Cats and Gay Facades."

9. Emily Lieb, "'Slum Clearance à la Mode': The Battle For Baltimore's Tyson Street," *The Metropole*. November 26, 2018, https://themetropole.blog/2018/11/26/slum-clearance-a-la-mode1-the-battle-for-baltimores-tyson-street/.

10. Shelley Murphy, "On Tyson Street," *Baltimore Sun*, January 29, 1989, 6E.

11. Charles T. LeViness, "Baltimore's Harbor Tunnel—Breaking the Traffic Barrier," *American Highways*, July 1956, 8, Highways, 1956–1971, 4, box 3, folder 12, Greater Baltimore Committee Records, R0046-GBC, Baltimore Studies Archives, UB.

12. "Our Traffic Problem and Its Solution," Radio Report to the People by Joseph S. Clark, Jr., Mayor of Philadelphia, June 4, 1954, 121–31, Temple University Libraries Special Collections Research Center, Urban Archives Pamphlet Collection, Philadelphia, PA (hereafter cited as TUA); Automotive Club of Maryland, "Road Map of Greater Baltimore" (1929), Baltimore City Sheet Maps, Johns Hopkins Sheridan Library Map Collections.

13. Federal Highway Administration, "Motor Vehicle Registrations, by States, 1900–1995," April 1997, 6. https://www.fhwa.dot.gov/ohim/summary95/mv201.pdf.

14. LeViness, "Baltimore's Harbor Tunnel."

15. LeViness, "Baltimore's Harbor Tunnel."

16. "Backers of Baltimore," *Baltimore Sun*, January 6, 1955. "Highways Sub-Committee Report," 9, Highways, 1956–1971, 4, box 3, folder 12, Greater Baltimore Committee Records, R0046-GBC, Baltimore Studies Archives, UB.

17. *Baltimore City Directory* (1956), Maryland Department, EPFL.

18. Highways, 1956–1971, 4, box 3, folder 12, Greater Baltimore Committee Records, R0046-GBC, Baltimore Studies Archives, UB. *Baltimore City Directory* (1956).

19. William Leach, *Land of Desire: Merchants, Power, and the Rise of a New American Culture* (Vintage Books, 1993).

20. Lizabeth Cohen, "Buying into Downtown Revival: The Centrality of Retail to Postwar Urban Renewal in American Cities," *Annals of the American Academy of Political and Social Science* 611 (May 2007), 83; Alison Isenberg, *Downtown America: A History of the Place and the People Who Made It* (University of Chicago Press, 2004), 87–88, 84.

21. "Old Baltimore Department Stores (Pictures)," *Baltimore Sun*, April 14, 2014, https://www.baltimoresun.com/2014/04/14/old-baltimore-department-stores-pictures/#; K. Meghan Gross, "Chronology: Baltimore's Downtown Department Stores," *Generations*, Winter 2001; Michael J. Lisicky, *Baltimore's Bygone Department Stores: Many Happy Returns* (History Press, 2012).

22. D. A. Wallace, interview with Mr. Albert Hutzler, Jr., July 15, 1957, 8, Library, 10, Greater Baltimore Committee Records, R0046-GBC, Baltimore Studies Archives, UB.

23. Jon C. Teaford, *Rough Road to Renaissance: Urban Revitalization in America, 1940–1985* (Johns Hopkins University Press, 1990), 19.

24. "Edmondson Village Set For Opening," *Baltimore Evening Sun*, April 30, 1947, 33.

25. "Baltimore: Stewart's Department Store." *Baltimore Style*, August 17, 2010.

26. *Baltimore Style*, August 17, 2010.

27. A Survey of Shopping with Department Store, 10, box 19, folder 43, Greater Baltimore Committee Records, R0046-GBC, Baltimore Studies Archives, UB.

28. Isenberg, *Downtown America*, 174.

29. Moss, "The Downtown Problem."

30. Joel Garreau, *The Nine Nations of North America* (Avon, 1981), 67; Paul A. Kramer, "White Sales: The Racial Politics of Baltimore's Jewish-Owned Department Stores, 1935–1965," in *Enterprising Emporiums: The Jewish Department Stores of Downtown Baltimore* (Jewish Museum of Maryland, 2001), 37–65.

31. Grace Elizabeth Hale, *Making Whiteness: The Culture of Segregation in the South, 1890–1940* (Vintage, 1998), 185.

32. "Stewart's, Newest Dept. Store to Close Doors to Race," *Baltimore Afro-American*, August 10, 1929, 1.

33. Harry Cooper, "Interview with Mr. Paul Sowell, President, Brager-Eisenberg Department Store," July 15, 1957, 4, Cooper, Harry B—Interviews: Local & Others, 13, box 38, folder 44, Greater Baltimore Committee Records, R0046-GBC, Baltimore Studies Archives, UB; "Stewart's, Newest Dept. Store to Close Doors to Race." *Baltimore Afro-American*, August 10, 1929, 1.

34. "Department Stores in 8 Dixie Cities Welcome Trade of All," *Baltimore Afro-American*, October 10, 1936, 19.

35. Harry Cooper, "Mr. Leonard Novogrod, General Manager, The May Company, Vice-President, The May Company—Nationally," July 19, 1957, 5–6, Cooper, Harry B—Interviews: Local & Others, 13, box 38, folder 44, Greater Baltimore Committee Records, R0046-GBC, Baltimore Studies Archives, UB.

36. Hale, *Making Whiteness*, 188.

37. "14 Stores Added to Orchid List, Bringing Total to 44," *Baltimore Afro-American*, February 10, 1945, 20; "List of 'Orchid' Stores Now 26," *Baltimore Afro-American*, January 27, 1945, 20.

38. "They Can't Tell!," *Baltimore Afro-American*, May 24, 1947, M8.

39. B. M. Phillips, "If You Ask Me," *Baltimore Afro-American*, March 22, 1952, 22J.

40. Cooper, "Mr. Leonard Novogrod."

41. Kramer, "White Sales"; "Old Baltimore Department Stores."

42. David A. Wallace, "Interview with Mr. Julius Westheimer, President, Gutman's Department Store," July 9, 1957, Greater Baltimore Committee Records, R0046-GBC, Baltimore Studies Archives, UB.

43. H. B. Cooper, Transcript of interview with Mr. Isaac Lycett, Jr. (July 2, 1957), Greater Baltimore Committee Records, R0046-GBC, Baltimore Studies Archives, UB.

44. "Backers of Baltimore," *Baltimore Sun*, January 6, 1955.

45. "The First Vital Step Toward the Greater Downtown Baltimore of Tomorrow," 10, box 19, folder 22, Greater Baltimore Committee Records, R0046-GBC, Baltimore Studies Archives, UB.

46. Martin Millspaugh, "Baltimore's Charles Center," in *Baltimore's Charles Center: A Case Study of Downtown Renewal*, edited by Martin Millspaugh (Urban Land Institute Technical Bulletin 51, November 1964), 15, box 13, folder UAP 071-1, TUA.

47. Emily Lieb, "'Baltimore Does Not Condone Profiteering in Squalor': The Baltimore Plan and the Problem of Housing-Code Enforcement in an American City," *Planning Perspectives* 33, no. 1 (2017); Alexander von Hoffman, "A Study in Contradictions: The Origins and Legacy of the Housing Act of 1949," *Housing Policy Debate* 11, no. 2 (2000); Alexander von Hoffman, "Enter the Housing Industry, Stage Right: A Working Paper on the History of Housing Policy" (Harvard University Joint Center for Housing Studies, February 2008).

48. Robert M. Fogelson, *Downtown: Its Rise and Fall* (Yale University Press 2003), 375–76.

49. Quoted in in Michael P. McCarthy, *The Living City: Baltimore's Charles Center & Inner Harbor Development* (Maryland Historical Society, 2002), 19–20.

50. Quoted in Isenberg, *Downtown America*, 188.

51. Quoted in Francesca Russello Ammon, *Bulldozer: Demolition and Clearance of the Postwar Landscape* (Yale University Press 2016), 146.

52. Wendell E. Pritchett, "The 'Public Menace' of Blight: Urban Renewal and the Private Uses of Eminent Domain," *Yale Law & Policy Review* 21, no. 1 (2003); Amy Lavine, "Urban Renewal and the Story of Berman v. Parker," *The Urban Lawyer* 42, no. 2 (Spring 2010); *Berman v. Parker*, 348 U.S. 26 (1954).

53. Lewis Mumford, "The Responsibilities of the Business Community: Address Presented at New Home Office Building, the Baltimore Life Insurance Co., Baltimore, Maryland," April 24, 1961, 14, box 9, folder 052-8, TUA.

54. Archibald Coleman Rogers, AIA, "The Charles Center Project," *Journal of the AIA*, March 1959, 30.

55. "The First Vital Step Toward the Greater Downtown Baltimore of Tomorrow."

56. William J. Boucher III to Leonard Novogrod, August 3, 1956, Highways, 1956–1971, 4, box 3, folder 12, Greater Baltimore Committee Records, R0046-GBC, Baltimore Studies Archives, UB.

57. LeViness, "Baltimore's Harbor Tunnel."

58. City of Baltimore Planning Commission, *Study for East–West Expressway* (1960).

59. "The Politics of Highway Finance, 1945–1950," in Mark H. Rose and Raymond A. Mohl, *Interstate: Highway Politics and Policy Since 1939*, 3rd ed. (University of Tennessee Press, 2012), 29–40.

60. Richard F. Weingroff, "Federal-Aid Highway Act of 1956: Creating The Interstate System," *Public Roads* 60, no. 1 (Summer 1996).

61. National Archives and Records Administration, "Milestone Documents: National Interstate and Defense Highways Act (1956)."

62. Lewis, *Divided Highways*, 86.

63. Lewis, *Divided Highways*, 88.

64. Lewis, *Divided Highways*, 88.

65. "Highways Subcommittee Report to the Members of the Greater Baltimore Committee," August 15, 1957, 3, Highways, 1956–1971, 4, box 3, folder 12, Greater Baltimore Committee Records, R0046-GBC, Baltimore Studies Archives, UB.

66. Mark Reutter, "Before the City Council" (ca. 1970s), 13, Reuter, Mark—Thesis—Chapter I: Before the City Council, 7A, box 7, folder 112, Movement Against Destruction Records, R0062-MAD, Baltimore Studies Archives, UB.

67. Expressway Conference Committee, "History, Facts, and Opinions on Expressway," August 1968, 6–7, General—Conference Committee, "History, Facts and Opinions on Expressway," 6, box 6, folder 31, Movement Against Destruction Records, R0062-MAD, Baltimore Studies Archives, UB.

68. "History, Facts, and Opinions on Expressway."

69. *Study for East–West Expressway*, vol. 2, sheet 6, Baltimore City Sheet Maps, Johns Hopkins Sheridan Library Map Collections.

70. "There's No Joy In Tyson Street," *Baltimore American*, September 30, 1956.

71. Louis Azrael, "Death Sentence on Tyson Street," *Baltimore News-Post*, July 16, 1957.

72. Robert Moses et al., *Baltimore Arterial Report*, October 9, 1944, 7; Raymond A. Mohl, "The Interstates and the Cities: Highways, Housing and the Freeway Revolt" (Poverty and Race Research Action Council, 2002), 27.

73. "Robert C. Davidson (1850–1924)," Archives of Maryland Biographical Series, Maryland State Archives; "Baltimore Men in New York," *Electric Railway Journal* 49, no. 17 (1917): 793.

74. Douglas H. Hauber, *The Baltimore Expressway Controversy: A Study of the Political Decision-Making Process* (Johns Hopkins University Center for Metropolitan Planning and Research, 1974), 5.

75. Robert K. Nelson et al., *Mapping Inequality: Redlining in New Deal America*, edited by Robert K. Nelson and Edward L. Ayers. [Richmond, Va.]: University of Richmond. Digital Scholarship Lab, [2015].

76. Moses, *Baltimore Arterial Report*, 9.
77. "Expressway Would Raze 200 Blocks," *Baltimore Morning Sun*, October 16, 1944, 20.
78. "Expressway Would Raze 200 Blocks."
79. Richard Rothstein, *The Color of Law: A Forgotten History of How Our Government Segregated America* (Liveright, 2017), 128.
80. "Picasso, Cats and Gay Facades."
81. "Tyson Street."
82. "Tyson Street Skips a Century," *Living for Young Homemakers*, September/October 1949, 53.
83. "Tyson Streeters Tell Mayor They Plan Fight to Finish," *Baltimore Sun*, August 21, 1957, 23.
84. "Tyson Street's Pastel Block."
85. "Tyson Street Backers to See D'Alesandro, Aides Today," *Baltimore Sun*, October 3, 1956, 27.
86. "Planners Ease Tyson St. Blues," *Baltimore Sun* (October 11, 1956), 42.
87. Richard M. Flanagan, "The Housing Act of 1954: A Sea Change in National Urban Policy," *Urban Affairs Review*, November 1, 1997; Von Hoffman, "Enter the Housing Industry, Stage Right"; Lieb, "Baltimore Does Not Condone Profiteering in Squalor."
88. "Tyson Street Discussion Held," *Baltimore Sun*, September 10, 1957, 36.
89. "There's No Joy In Tyson Street."
90. John Goodspeed, "Tyson Street's Pastel Block," *Baltimore Sun*, October 20, 1957, SM15.
91. Eileen Canzian, "None Spoke for Blacks Uprooted by Highway," *Baltimore Sun*, June 2, 1980, A1.
92. *Study for East-West Expressway*, vol. 1, 1.
93. "Planners Ease Tyson St. Blues."
94. Gabrielle Wise, "Tyson Street Tour Extended," *Baltimore Sun*, June 2, 1964.
95. *Study for East-West Expressway*, vol. 2, sheets 1–5.
96. City of Baltimore Planning Commission, *Study for East-West Expressway* (1960), 10, Baltimore City Sheet Maps, Johns Hopkins Sheridan Library Map Collections.
97. *Study for East-West Expressway*, vol. 2, sheet 6.
98. Louise Campbell, "Transport: A Concept Team for Baltimore," *CITY*, November 1967, 15.
99. Douglas H. Hauber, *The Baltimore Expressway Controversy: A Study of the Political Decision-Making Process* (Johns Hopkins University Center for Metropolitan Planning and Research, 1974), 5.
100. Walter Johnson, *The Broken Heart of America: St. Louis and the Violent History of the United States* (Basic Books, 2020), 298.
101. Samuel Joseph Rice, "A Study of the Experiences of Fifty Negro Families Who Moved into White Neighborhoods of Baltimore, Maryland in 1945 and 1946" (1947), 7–8, Atlanta University Center, Robert W. Woodruff Library, Paper 2344.
102. Letter from Robert D. Meyers, Mahool Advertising, to H. Warren Buckler Jr. and Frances Morton, Citizens Planning and Housing Association (n.d. [1957]), Highways, 1956–1971, 4, box 3, folder 12, Greater Baltimore Committee Records, R0046-GBC, Baltimore Studies Archives, UB.
103. *Study for East-West Expressway*, vol. 2, sheet 1.
104. *Study for East-West Expressway*, vol. 2, sheet 2.
105. *Study for East-West Expressway*, vol. 2, sheets 3–5.

106. "The Rosemont Home Improvement Association," Rosemont Neighborhood Improvement Association Records, 1969–1970, 9B, box 15, folder 2, Baltimore Heritage Records, R0010-BH, Baltimore Studies Archives, UB.

107. *Study for East-West Expressway*, vol. 1, 1.

108. Hauber, "The Baltimore Expressway Controversy"; Mark Reutter, "Baltimore's Expressway Controversy" (ca. 1970s), 24, Reuter, Mark—Expressway Paper, 7A, box 7, folder 110, Movement Against Destruction Records, R0062-MAD, Baltimore Studies Archives, UB; Emily Lieb, "Row House City: Unbuilding Residential Baltimore, 1940–1980" (PhD diss., Columbia University, 2010); Earl Swift, *The Big Roads: The Untold Story of the Engineers, Visionaries, and Trailblazers Who Created the American Superhighways* (Harper Collins, 2012); Matthew A. Crenson, *Baltimore: A Political History* (Johns Hopkins University Press, 2017). E. Evans Paull, *Stop the Road: Stories from the Trenches of Baltimore's Road Wars* (Boyle & Dalton, 2022).

109. "Mayor Asks Restudy of Road Route," *Baltimore Sun*, September 27, 1958, 26; *Study for East-West Expressway*; Jerry Adler, "East-West Expressway Mapped: Planners Ask 8-Lane Route," *Baltimore American*, January 31, 1960.

110. Hauber, "The Baltimore Expressway Controversy," 8.

111. Hauber, "The Baltimore Expressway Controversy," 8.

112. Department of Planning, "Staff Report on Expressway Consultants' Route," December 5, 1961, 7, vertical files, EPFL.

113. "An Oral History of Barbara Mikulski, Conducted by Mildred Rahn," April 30, 1974, East-West Expressway Collection, H. Furlong Baldwin Library, Maryland Center for History and Culture, OH 8057; J. Anthony Lukas, "Irate Crowd Hits Planned Expressway," *Baltimore Sun*, January 31, 1962, 34.

114. "Excuse to Postpone?," *Baltimore Sun*, October 13, 1961, 10.

115. *Movement Against Destruction v. Volpe*, 361 F. Supp. 1360 (D. Md. 1973).

116. "Irate Crowd Hits Planned Expressway."

117. Reutter, "Baltimore's Expressway Controversy," 24.

118. "Irate Crowd Hits Planned Expressway"; "Building a Papier Mache Bridge from the Refuse of Citizen Crossfire on the East-West Expressway," *Baltimore Sun*, April 26, 1972, C6.

119. "Expressway Chronicle: News Stories Since 1958 Show Deadlock on Routes," *Baltimore Sun*, April 17, 1967, C7.

120. "Expressway Chronicle."

121. "Expressway Chronicle."

122. "East-West Plan Stymied," *Baltimore Sun*, April 17, 1967, C7.

123. David Allison, "The Battle Lines of Baltimore," *Innovation Magazine*, July 1969, Battle Lines of Baltimore, 1969, sub-series 10J, box 11, folder 18, Citizens Planning and Housing Association Records, R0032-CPHA, Baltimore Studies Archives, UB.

Chapter Five

1. Horace Ayers, "Action Slated on Expressway Ordinance," *Baltimore Sun*, June 2, 1967, B6; Urban Design Concept Associates, "Recommendations—Draft," February 27, 1970, GBC Unprocessed Materials Series 2, box 5, Baltimore Studies Archives, UB; Maryland State Roads Commission, *Location Study Report: I-170 Rosemont Bypass*, August 12, 1970, Rosemont Bypass Study, 13, box 76, folder 36, Greater Baltimore Committee Records, R0046-GBC, Baltimore Studies Archives, UB.

2. "Leakin Park Road Plan Opposed," *Baltimore Sun*, June 2, 1967, C24.

3. Matthew A. Crenson, *Baltimore: A Political History* (Johns Hopkins University Press, 2017), 484.

4. "Leakin Park Road Plan Opposed."

5. "West Baltimoreans Protest Expressway Route in Area," *Baltimore Sun*, June 2, 1967, C6.

6. "West Baltimoreans Protest Expressway Route."

7. James D. Dilts, "Who Wants the Expressway?," *Baltimore Sun*, June 6, 1971, D3; "On the Road and the Parks," *Baltimore Sun*, December 24, 1972, K1.

8. "Action Slated on Expressway Ordinance."

9. Steve Anderson, "Jones Falls Expressway: Historical Overview" (n.d.), http://www.dcroads.net/roads/jones-falls/.

10. Edgar L. Jones, "Six Inner-City Problems," *Baltimore Sun*, May 19, 1963, 12.

11. Case Number 73-2136, *Movement Against Destruction, et al., Appellants, v. John Volpe et al., Appellees*, 4, box 2, folder 26, Movement Against Destruction Records, R0062-MAD, Baltimore Studies Archives, UB.

12. "Expressway Leg Okayed," *Baltimore Sun*, February 22, 1966, C6; Douglas H. Hauber, *The Baltimore Expressway Controversy: A Study of the Political Decision-Making Process* (Johns Hopkins University Center for Metropolitan Planning and Research, 1974); Mark Reutter, "Baltimore's Expressway Controversy" (ca. 1970s); Reuter, Mark—Expressway Paper, 7A, box 7, folder 110, Movement Against Destruction Records, R0062-MAD, Baltimore Studies Archives, UB; Emily Lieb, "Row House City: Unbuilding Residential Baltimore, 1940–1980" (PhD diss., Columbia University, 2010); Earl Swift, *The Big Roads: The Untold Story of the Engineers, Visionaries, and Trailblazers Who Created the American Superhighways* (Harper Collins, 2012); Matthew A. Crenson, *Baltimore: A Political History* (Johns Hopkins University Press, 2017); E. Evans Paull, *Stop the Road: Stories from the Trenches of Baltimore's Road Wars* (Boyle & Dalton, 2022).

13. "Expressway Leg Okayed"; Mark Reutter, "Baltimore's Expressway Controversy: The History," 2; *Movement Against Destruction v. Volpe*, 500 F.2d 29 (4th Cir. 1974).

14. Mary Rizzo, *Come and Be Shocked: Baltimore Beyond John Waters and the Wire* (Johns Hopkins University Press, 2020).

15. *Berman v. Parker*, 348 U.S. 26 (1954).

16. Letter from Interstate Division for Baltimore City to Mr. and Mrs. John H. Wells, September 19, 1967, Department of Legislative Reference, Department Public Works, Bureau Interstate Division B.C., R/W Files, Schedule No. 561, container R/W 8, folder 030015, BCA.

17. James D. Dilts, "Haunted Village," *Baltimore Sun*, October 13, 1968, D1.

18. Baltimore City Superior Court (Land Records) 1955–1955, MLP 9692, p. 0059, MSA CE 168-9700; "Haunted Village."

19. "Haunted Village."

20. Letter from Interstate Division to Mr. and Mrs. John H. Wells, BCA.

21. Letter from Eugene Feinblatt, BURHA Chair, to Hon. Robert C. Weaver, Secretary, Department of Housing and Urban Development, November 1, 1966, 1964-12–1968-03, 2, box 2, folder 1. Baltimore Urban Renewal and Housing Authority Records, R0019-BURHA, Baltimore Studies Archives, UB.

22. "Land Buying Method Hit," *Baltimore Sun*, February 17, 1966, 29.

23. "Land Buying Method Hit."

24. Department of Legislative Reference Records Management, Department Public Works,

Bureau Interstate Division B.C., R/W Files, schedule no. 561, container R/W 26, folder 38065 R&S Construction Co. 2716 Edmondson Ave, BCA.

25. Department of Legislative Reference, Department Public Works, Bureau Interstate Division B.C., R/W Files, Schedule No. 561, container R/W 8, folder 030015, BCA.

26. Department of Legislative Reference, Department Public Works, Bureau Interstate Division B.C., R/W Files, Schedule No. 561, container R/W 8, folder 030015, BCA.

27. "Homeowners Took a Loss from City for Road That Goes Nowhere," *Baltimore Sun*, June 1, 1980, A1, A3.

28. "A History of the Relocation Action Movement," 07A, box 7, folder 105, Movement Against Destruction Records, R0062-MAD, Baltimore Studies Archives, UB; James D. Dilts, "Expressway 'Victims' Fight Back." *Baltimore Morning Sun*, March 17, 1968.

29. "A History of the Relocation Action Movement."

30. "Homeowners Took a Loss from City."

31. "Tommy Promises Attempt to Aid Displaced Persons," *Baltimore Evening Sun*, August 30, 1967, D3.

32. "Homeowners Took a Loss from City."

33. Douglas H. Hauber, "The Baltimore Expressway Controversy: A Study of the Political Decision-Making Process" (Johns Hopkins University Center for Metropolitan Planning and Research, May 15, 1974), 70.

34. Crenson, *Baltimore*, 444.

35. George P. Matysek Jr., "Baltimore Cardinal Booed, Heckled at '66 Hearing for Backing Fair Housing," *National Catholic Reporter*, April 11, 2018; Kenneth D. Durr, *Behind the Backlash: White Working-Class Politics in Baltimore, 1940–1980* (University of North Carolina Press, 2003), 126–27.

36. Durr, *Behind the Backlash*,127.

37. Letter from Edgar M. Ewing, Acting Director of BURHA, to Honorable Joseph Allen, City Solicitor, on "Replacement of Homes Purchased for Public Purposes" (November 1, 1967), Correspondence, 2, Baltimore Urban Renewal and Housing Authority Records, R0019-BURHA, Baltimore Studies Archives, UB.

38. "Haunted Village."

39. "A History of the Relocation Action Movement."

40. Thomas Edsall, "Downhill for 12 Years: Family Won't Visit Woman in Slum," *Baltimore Evening Sun*, April 24, 1967, B1.

41. "Haunted Village."

42. "Expressway 'Victims' Fight Back."

43. Letter from Danny Gant, CORE Target City Project Director (November 4, 1967); Ben A. Franklin, "CORE's 'Target City' Program in Baltimore Now Hailed for Its Moderation," *New York Times*, April 16, 1967; Rhonda Y. Williams, "The Pursuit of Audacious Power: Rebel Reformers and Neighborhood Politics in Baltimore, 1966–1968," in *Neighborhood Rebels: Black Power at the Local Level*, edited by Peniel Joseph (Palgrave Macmillan 2010), 215–41.

44. Richard H. Levine, "Five-Year Rights Campaign Contemplated By C.O.R.E.," *Baltimore Sun*, October 7, 1966, C28, C15; Crenson, *Baltimore*, 446–51; Williams, "The Pursuit of Audacious Power."

45. Williams, "The Pursuit of Audacious Power," 219.

46. Expressway Conference Committee, "History, Facts, and Opinions on Expressway"

(August 1968), 8, General—Conference Committee, "History, Facts and Opinions on Expressway," 6, box 6, folder 31, Movement Against Destruction Records, R0062-MAD, Baltimore Studies Archives, UB.

47. Adam Spiegel, "Mayor Vows Fight to Aid Relocated Home Owners," *Baltimore Evening Sun*, September 21, 1967, C3.

48. "Home Prices Spur Drive," *Baltimore Sun*, October 4, 1967, C12.

49. "Mayor Vows Fight to Aid Relocated Home Owners"; "Home Prices Spur Drive."

50. Department of Legislative Reference, Department Public Works, Bureau Interstate Division B.C., R/W Files, Schedule No. 561, container R/W 8, folder 030015, BCA.

51. Annotated Code of Maryland, Art. 89B S504, Department of Legislative Reference Records Management, Department of Public Works, R/W Files, Schedule No. 561, container R/W 33, folder Chapman, Oscar and Mary 929 Rosedale Street, BCA; *National Cooperative Highway Research Program Report 107: New Approaches to Compensation for Residential Takings* (Highway Research Board, 1970), 11.

52. Annotated Code of Maryland (1968 Supplement), Section 6A of Article 33A, Department of Legislative Reference Records Management, Department of Public Works, R/W Files, Schedule No. 561, container R/W 33, folder Chapman, Oscar and Mary 929 Rosedale Street, BCA.

53. Annotated Code of Maryland, Art. 89B S504, Department of Legislative Reference Records Management, Department of Public Works, R/W Files, Schedule No. 561, container R/W 33, folder Chapman, Oscar and Mary 929 Rosedale Street, BCA.

54. Department of Legislative Reference, Department Public Works, Bureau Interstate Division B.C., R/W Files, schedule no. 561, container R/W 8, folder 030015, BCA.

55. "Haunted Village."

56. Baltimore County Circuit Court (Land Records) 1968–1974, OTG 4931, pp. 0174–0177, MSA CE 62-4786.

57. "Relocation Action Movement" (June 19, 1968), Relocation Action Movement (RAM), 7A, box 7, folder 105, Movement Against Destruction Records, R0062-MAD, Baltimore Studies Archives. UB.

58. "Haunted Village."

59. "Haunted Village."

60. Activists, Inc., "A Conspiracy to Defraud and Exploit Homebuyers: The Story of Jefferson Federal Saving and Loan" (1971), Resources—"A Conspiracy to Defraud and Exploit Homebuyers: The Story of Jefferson Federal Saving and Loan" Activists, Inc., 1971, 10F, box 16, folder 12, Citizens Planning and Housing Association Records, R0032-CPHA, Baltimore Studies Archives, UB; Activists, Inc., "Baltimore Under Siege: The Impact of Financing on the Baltimore Home Buyer (1960–1970)" (September 1971), ii, Baltimore Under Siege, 1971, 6, box 1, folder 13, Baltimore Neighborhoods, Incorporated Records, R0015-BNI, Baltimore Studies Archives, UB.

61. Activists, "Baltimore Under Siege"; James D. Dilts, "Some Savings Firms Finance Speculators," *Baltimore Sun*, September 20, 1971, C20.

62. James D. Dilts, "2 Neighborhoods: Speculators Take a Cut," *Baltimore Sun*, September 19, 1971, A20.

63. Activists, "A Conspiracy to Defraud and Exploit Homebuyers."

64. "Council Gets Coordinator of Programs," *Cumberland Evening Times*, December 16, 1974, 9.

65. Maryland State Roads Commission's Interstate Division for Baltimore City, "Interim Brochure: Relocation Assistance Section" (June 10, 1969), 16–17, Relocation—Maryland State

Roads Commission's Interstate Division for Baltimore City Interim Brochure—Relocation Assistance Section, 1969-06-10–1971-08-01, 5, box 5, folder 18, Movement Against Destruction Records, R0062-MAD, Baltimore Studies Archives, UB.

66. *R.A.M. Observer* vol. 5 (July 26, 1968), 2, box 1, folder 43, Southeast Council Against the Road Records, R0108-SCAR, Baltimore Studies Archives, UB.

67. Department of Housing and Community Development, Land Development Division, Vacant House Program Real Estate Files 1969–1975, BRG48-40, BCA.

68. Department of Housing and Community Development, Land Development Division, Vacant House Program Real Estate Files 1969–1975, BRG48-40, BCA.

69. Department of Legislative Reference Records Management, Department Public Works, Bureau Interstate Division B.C., R/W files, schedule no. 561, container no. R/W 26, folder 038056, BCA.

70. Department of Legislative Reference Records Management, Department Public Works, Bureau Interstate Division B.C., R/W files, schedule no. 561, container no. R/W 26, folder 38069, BCA.

71. Department of Legislative Reference Records Management, Department Public Works, Bureau Interstate Division B.C., R/W files, schedule no. 561, container no. R/W 26, folder 38069, BCA.

72. Department of Legislative Reference Records Management, Department Public Works, Bureau Interstate Division B.C., R/W files, schedule no. 561, container no. R/W 26, folder 38107, BCA.

73. Department of Legislative Reference Records Management, Department of Public Works, R/W Files, schedule no. 561, container no. R/W 33, folder 047043 John Hammock-Ada (wife) 937 Ellicott Drive, BCA.

74. Department of Legislative Reference Records Management, Department of Public Works, R/W Files, schedule no. 561, container no. R/W 33, folder 047048 947 Ellicott Driveway, BCA.

75. Department of Legislative Reference Records Management, Department Public Works, Bureau Interstate Division B.C., R/W Files, schedule no. 561, container no. R/W 26, folder 038058, BCA.

76. Department of Legislative Reference Records Management, Department Public Works, Bureau Interstate Division B.C., R/W Files, schedule no. 561, container no. R/W 26, folder 38073, BCA.

77. Department of Legislative Reference Records Management, Department Public Works, Bureau Interstate Division B.C., R/W Files, schedule no. 561, container no. R/W 26, folder 038058, BCA.

78. Department of Legislative Reference Records Management, Department Public Works, Bureau Interstate Division B.C., R/W Files, schedule No. 561, container no. R/W 26, folder 38061 Dora Schabb 2708 Edmondson Ave, BCA.

79. Department of Legislative Reference Records Management, Department of Public Works, R/W Files, schedule no. 561, container no. R/W 33, folder 047040, BCA; Department of Legislative Reference Records Management, Department Public Works, Bureau Interstate Division B.C., R/W Files, schedule no. 561, container no. R/W 26, folder 38075, BCA; Department of Legislative Reference Records Management, Department Public Works, Bureau Interstate Division B.C., R/W Files, schedule no. 561, container no. R/W 26, folder 38077, BCA.

80. Department of Legislative Reference Records Management, Department of Public

Works, R/W Files, schedule no. 561, container no. R/W 33, folder Chapman, Oscar and Mary 929 Rosedale Street, BCA.

81. Folder Chapman, Oscar and Mary; Department of Legislative Reference Records Management, Department of Public Works, R/W Files, schedule no. 561, container no. R/W 33, folder 047021, BCA.

82. Folder Chapman, Oscar and Mary, BCA; folder 047021, BCA.

83. "State Ban on Causing Neighborhood Panic," *Baltimore Sun*, June 17, 1972, Blockbusting, vertical files, EPFL.

84. Activists, "Baltimore Under Siege," i.

85. W. Edward Orser, *Blockbusting in Baltimore: The Edmondson Village Story* (University Press of Kentucky, 1997). Gregory Smithsimon, *Liberty Road: Black Middle-Class Suburbs and the Battle Between Civil Rights and Neoliberalism* (NYU Press, 2022).

86. "Rosemont Schedule of Properties," BRG48-40, box 3; "Rosemont FHA 235 Settlement Receipts," BRG48-40, box 8, Department of Housing and Community Development, Land Development Division, Vacant House Program Real Estate Files 1969–1975, BCA.

87. *Baltimore Sun*, July 2, 1965, 30; *Baltimore Sun*, June 29, 1958, C10.

88. "Foes Describe Road's Effects," *Baltimore Sun*, August 8, 1969, C13.

89. "Foes Describe Road's Effects."

Chapter Six

1. Minutes, 1969-01–1969-12, 1, box 1, folder 6, Movement Against Destruction Records, R0062-MAD, Baltimore Studies Archives, UB.

2. Movement Against Destruction statement (January 1968), S03B, box 5, 1969–71, Movement Against Destruction Records, R0062-MAD, Baltimore Studies Archives, UB.

3. General—Conference Committee, "History, Facts and Opinions on Expressway," 6, box 6, folder 31, Movement Against Destruction Records, R0062-MAD, Baltimore Studies Archives, UB.

4. "History, Facts, and Opinions," 7–8.

5. "History, Facts, and Opinions," 1.

6. "History, Facts, and Opinions," 8.

7. R.N.I.A. (July 1966), Parks and Playgrounds—Alexander Odum Playground, 1966–1972, 9B, box 17, folder 1, Baltimore Heritage Records, R0010-BH, Baltimore Studies Archives, UB.

8. R.N.I.A. (July 1966).

9. ACLU of Maryland, "Public Housing and Areas of Minority Concentration, 1960" (2003), https://www.aclu-md.org/sites/default/files/field_documents/map3_1960.pdf.

10. D. Bradford Hunt, *Blueprint for Disaster: The Unraveling of Chicago Public Housing* (University of Chicago Press, 2009); Lawrence J. Vale, *Purging the Poorest: Public Housing and the Design Politics of Twice-Cleared Communities* (University of Chicago Press, 2013); Nicholas Dagen Bloom, Fritz Umbach, and Lawrence J. Vale, eds., *Public Housing Myths: Perception, Reality, and Social Policy* (Cornell University Press, 2015).

11. Rhonda Y. Williams, *The Politics of Public Housing: Black Women's Struggles Against Urban Inequality* (Oxford University Press, 2005), 129.

12. Williams, *The Politics of Public Housing*, 135.

13. Letter from Larry Reich, Director, Baltimore Planning Commission Department of Planning, to Joseph S. Wiles (August 2, 1966), Parks and Playgrounds—Alexander Odum Play-

ground, 1966–1972, 9B, box 17, folder 1, Baltimore Heritage Records, R0010-BH, Baltimore Studies Archives, UB.

14. Meeting minutes (1966), Parks and Playgrounds—Alexander Odum Playground, 1966–1972, 9B, box 17, folder 1, Baltimore Heritage Records, R0010-BH, Baltimore Studies Archives, UB.

15. Local Defendant's Exhibits—LX-287: Letter to the *Morning Sun* Paper from Rose J. Gallop and Joseph S. Wiles, 3B, box 2, folder 204, American Civil Liberties Union of Maryland Records, R0002-ACLU, Baltimore Studies Archives, UB.

16. R.N.I.A. Meeting Minutes (August 1966), Parks and Playgrounds—Alexander Odum Playground, 1966–1972, 9B, box 17, folder 1, Baltimore Heritage Records, R0010-BH, Baltimore Studies Archives, UB.

17. R.N.I.A. Meeting Minutes (August 1966).

18. Mary Rosemond/Rosemont Neighborhood Improvement Association, Inc., "Letter of Philosophy," Rosemont Neighborhood Improvement Association Records, 1952–1968, 9B, box 15, folder 1, Baltimore Heritage Records, R0010-BH, Baltimore Studies Archives, UB.

19. N. D. B. Connolly, *A World More Concrete: Real Estate and the Remaking of Jim Crow South Florida* (University of Chicago Press, 2014), 270–71.

20. R.N.I.A. Meeting Minutes (August 1966).

21. R.N.I.A. Meeting Minutes (August 1966).

22. James D. Dilts, "Rosemont Group Gains Delay of Housing Site Ruling," *Baltimore Sun*, March 13, 1971, B6.

23. Connolly, *A World More Concrete*, 269–70, 241.

24. Rosemont Neighborhood Improvement Association Records, 1952–1968, 9B, box 15, folder 1, Baltimore Heritage Records, R0010-BH, Baltimore Studies Archives, UB.

25. R.N.I.A. Meeting Minutes (July 1966), Parks and Playgrounds—Alexander Odum Playground, 1966–1972, 9B, box 17, folder 1, Baltimore Heritage Records, R0010-BH, Baltimore Studies Archives, UB.

26. Raymond A. Mohl, "The Interstates and the Cities: Highways, Housing, and the Freeway Revolt," *PRRAC Civil Rights Research*, 2002, 46.

27. Axelrod, Joseph Presentation—Engineers Club, 1969-10-29, 7A, box 7, folder 20, Movement Against Destruction Records, R0062-MAD, Baltimore Studies Archives, UB.

28. Douglas H. Hauber, *The Baltimore Expressway Controversy: A Study of the Political Decision-Making Process* (Johns Hopkins University Center for Metropolitan Planning and Research, 1974); Mark Reutter, "Baltimore's Expressway Controversy" (ca. 1970s), Reuter, Mark—Expressway Paper, 7A, box 7, folder 110, Movement Against Destruction Records, R0062-MAD, Baltimore Studies Archives, UB; Raymond A. Mohl, "The Interstates and the Cities: Highways, Housing, and the Freeway Revolt," *PRRAC Civil Rights Research*, 2002, 1–73; Raymond A. Mohl, "Stop the Road: Freeway Revolts in American Cities," *Journal of Urban History* 30, no. 5 (July 2004): 674–706; Emily Lieb, "Row House City: Unbuilding Residential Baltimore, 1940–1980" (PhD diss., Columbia University, 2010); Emily Lieb, "White Man's Lane: Hollowing Out the Highway Ghetto in Baltimore," in *'68: Riots and Rebirth in an American City*, edited by Jessica I. Elfenbein, Thomas L. Hollowak, and Elizabeth M. Nix, *Baltimore* (Temple University Press, 2011), 51–69; Earl Swift, *The Big Roads: The Untold Story of the Engineers, Visionaries, and Trailblazers Who Created the American Superhighways* (Harper Collins, 2012); Sidney Wong, "Architects and Planners in the Middle of a Road War: The Urban Design Concept Team in Baltimore, 1966–71," *Journal of Planning History* 12, no. 2 (May 2013): 179–202; Matthew A. Crenson,

Baltimore: A Political History (Johns Hopkins University Press, 2017). E. Evans Paull, *Stop the Road: Stories from the Trenches of Baltimore's Road Wars* (Boyle & Dalton, 2022).

29. Norman Klein, "Baltimore Urban Design Concept Team," *Highway Research Record*, 1968.

30. Nathaniel Owings, "Baltimore—Its Concept Team and Environment," *The American Aesthetic* (Harper & Row, 1969), 2; James D. Dilts, "We Must Destroy You To Save You," *Baltimore Sun*, August 4, 1968, D3; Mohl, "Stop the Road," 693.

31. Wong, 185; Dilts, "We Must Destroy You."

32. Urban Design Concept Associates, *Rosemont Area Studies*, 13, box 76, folder 35, Greater Baltimore Committee Records, R0046-GBC, Baltimore Studies Archives, UB.

33. *Rosemont Area Studies*.

34. "Community Opinion," *Rosemont Area Studies*.

35. *Rosemont Area Studies*.

36. Michael Yockel, "100 Years: The Riots of 1968," *Baltimore Magazine*, May 2007; Peter B. Levy, "The Dream Deferred: The Assassination of Martin Luther King, Jr. and the Holy Week Uprisings of 1968," in *Baltimore '68: Riots and Rebirth in an American City*, edited by Jessica I. Elfenbein, Thomas L. Hollowak, and Elizabeth M. Nix\ (Temple University Press, 2011), 3–25.

37. "Guard Called Out In Baltimore Riot," *Baltimore Sun*, April 7, 1968, 10.

38. "West Baltimore Is an Ugly No-Man's Land," *Baltimore Sun*, April 9, 1968.

39. "City Seen 'Returning to Normal,' " *Baltimore Sun*, April 9, 1968, 2.

40. "1,900 Infantrymen Join Riot Force," *Baltimore Sun*, April 9, 1968, 9.

41. Interview with Barbara Gaines, ca. 2006–8, 1, Baltimore Sixty-Eight Riots Collection, R0142-BSR, Baltimore Studies Archive, UB.

42. Jane Motz, "Report on Baltimore Civil Disorders, April, 1968" (American Friends Service Committee, 1968), 1, Baltimore Sixty-Eight Riots Collection, R0142-BSR, Baltimore Studies Archive, UB.

43. Barbara Samuels, "The 1968 Riots and the History of Public Housing Segregation in Baltimore," April 4, 2008, Baltimore Sixty-Eight Riots Collection, R0142-BSR, Baltimore Studies Archive, UB.

44. Motz, "Report on Baltimore Civil Disorders, April, 1968," 26.

45. National Advisory Commission on Civil Disorders. *Report of the National Advisory Commission on Civil Disorders*. (Government Printing Office, 1968), 39, 38.

46. Peter B. Levy and Katherine Kulbicki, "Mapping the Baltimore '68 Riots" (April 2008), Baltimore Sixty-Eight Riots Collection, R0142-BSR, Baltimore Studies Archive, UB.

47. Maryland Crime Investigating Commission, "The April, 1968 Civil Disturbances," *Maryland Crime Report* 68, no. 2 (July 1968), 4, Baltimore Sixty-Eight Riots Collection, R0142-BSR, Baltimore Studies Archive, UB; Lieb, "White Man's Lane."

48. Louise Campbell, "In Baltimore, New Options Are Opened and New Alliances Formed," *City*, 1968-09–1968-10, 7A, box 7, folder 35, Movement Against Destruction Records, R0062-MAD, Baltimore Studies Archives, UB.

49. 3-A Expressway System, 9, box 7, folder 82, Southeast Council Against the Road Records, R0108-SCAR, Baltimore Studies Archives, UB.

50. Dilts, "We Must Destroy You."

51. "Western Cemetery," *Baltimore Sun*, March 2, 1850, 2.

52. Charles R. Curtis Jr., "Our Readers Say: Like It Is," *Baltimore Afro-American*, December 21, 1969, 4.

53. *Rosemont Area Studies*.

NOTES TO PAGES 101–105

54. R.N.I.A. Annual Report (June 1968), 2–3, Rosemont Neighborhood Improvement Association Records, 1969–1970, 9B, box 15, folder 2, Baltimore Heritage Records, R0010-BH, Baltimore Studies Archives, UB; Dilts, "We Must Destroy You."

55. "Elusive Expressway," *Baltimore Morning Sun*, December 14, 1968.

56. David Runkel, "Stark Attacks Highway Route in Rosemont," *Baltimore Sun*, October 25, 1968.

57. "Parley Ends Secrecy on Road Route," *Baltimore Sun*, October 30, 1968, C28.

58. Jane L. Keidel, "Route Options Open, Aide Says," *Baltimore Sun*, November 2, 1968, B6.

59. "How S.O.M. Took on the Baltimore Road Gang," *Architectural Forum*, March 1969, 45.

60. "Rosemont," Department of Legislative Reference Records Management, Department of Public Works, R/W Files, schedule no. 561, container no. R/W 33, BCA.

61. "Rosemont," BCA.

62. "Condemnation Law Delay Sought," *Baltimore Sun*, January 2, 1969, 12.

63. "Rosemont," BCA.

64. *Rosemont Area Studies*.

65. UDCA, *Baltimore's Interstate Expressway Newsletter* 1 (December 10, 1968), 3–4, 3A, box 2, Movement Against Destruction Records, R0062-MAD, Baltimore Studies Archives, UB.

66. "When Should a Home Owner in a Condemnation Area Sell His Home????????," 7A, box 1, Movement Against Destruction Records, R0062-MAD, Baltimore Studies Archives, UB.

67. "Elusive Expressway," *Baltimore Morning Sun*, December 14, 1968.

68. "Community Opinion." *Rosemont Area Studies*.

69. Local Defendant's Exhibits—LX-287 letter to the *Morning Sun* Paper from Rose J. Gallop and Joseph S. Wiles, 3B, box 2, folder 204, American Civil Liberties Union of Maryland Records, R0002-ACLU, Baltimore Studies Archives, UB.

70. "Condemnation Law Delay Sought," *Baltimore Sun*, January 2, 1969, 12.

71. Department of Legislative Reference Records Management, Department Public Works, Bureau Interstate Division B.C., R/W Files, schedule no. 561, container no. R/W 26, folder 38068 James E. Greene Jr. 2722 Edmondson Ave, BCA.

72. Department of Legislative Reference Records Management, Department Public Works, Bureau Interstate Division B.C., R/W Files, schedule no. 561, container no. R/W 26, folder 38066, BCA.

73. Department of Legislative Reference Records Management, Department Public Works, Bureau Interstate Division B.C., R/W Files, schedule no. 561, container no. R/W 26, folder 38069, BCA.

74. Department of Legislative Reference Records Management, Department of Public Works, R/W Files, schedule no. 561, container no. R/W 33, folder 047025, Walter C. Oliver +, 942-Rosedale St, BCA.

75. Department of Legislative Reference Records Management, Department Public Works, Bureau Interstate Division B.C., R/W Files, schedule no. 561, container no. R/W 26, folder 38103, BCA.

76. Department of Legislative Reference Records Management, Department Public Works, Bureau Interstate Division B.C., R/W Files, schedule no. 561, container no. R/W 26, folder 38103, BCA.

77. "Enjoin City, Court Asked," *Baltimore Sun*, April 25, 1969, C8.

78. Department of Legislative Reference Records Management, Department Public Works, Bureau Interstate Division B.C., R/W Files, schedule no. 561, container no. R/W 26, BCA.

79. "Enjoin City."

80. Joseph M. Axelrod to Stephen M. Bojanowski (March 29, 1969), Rosemont, Department of Legislative Reference Records Management, Department of Public Works, R/W Files, schedule no. 561, container no. R/W 33, BCA.

81. Axelrod, Engineers Club.

82. Janelee Keidel, "Most Rosemont Owners Selling," *Baltimore Sun*, March 13, 1969, C20, C10.

83. Rose Gallop to Thomas D'Alesandro, May 16, 1969, Rosemont Neighborhood Improvement Association Records, 1969–1970, 9B, box 15, folder 2, Baltimore Heritage Records, R0010-BH, Baltimore Studies Archives, UB.

84. Minutes, 1969-01–1969-12, 1, box 1, folder 6, Movement Against Destruction Records, R0062-MAD, Baltimore Studies Archives, UB.

85. Letter from Mary Rosemond to Thomas D'Alesandro, May 1969, Movement Against Destruction Records, R0062-MAD, Baltimore Studies Archives, UB.

86. Letter from Thomas D'Alesandro to Mary Rosemond, May 1969, Movement Against Destruction Records, R0062-MAD, Baltimore Studies Archives, UB.

87. Statement of Delegate Walter S. Orlinsky Presented at the Rosemont Corridor Hearing, August 6, 1969, Public Hearings, 6, Movement Against Destruction Records, R0062-MAD, Baltimore Studies Archives, UB.

88. US Department of Transportation, *Federal Laws, Regulations, and Material Relating to the Federal Highway Administration* (1970).

89. Minutes, 1969-01–1969-12, 1, box 1, folder 6, Movement Against Destruction Records, R0062-MAD, Baltimore Studies Archives, UB.

90. May 26, 1969, Minutes, 1969-01–1969-12, 1, box 1, folder 6, Movement Against Destruction Records, R0062-MAD, Baltimore Studies Archives, UB.

91. July 7, 1969, Minutes, 1969-01–1969-12, 1, box 1, folder 6, Movement Against Destruction Records, R0062-MAD, Baltimore Studies Archives, UB.

92. July 20, 1969, Minutes, 1969-01–1969-12, 1, box 1, folder 6, Movement Against Destruction Records, R0062-MAD, Baltimore Studies Archives, UB.

93. "Foes Describe Road's Effects," *Baltimore Sun*, August 8, 1969, C13.

94. Meeting minutes, Movement Against Destruction, S07A, box 7, folder 105, Movement Against Destruction Records, R0062-MAD, Baltimore Studies Archives, UB.

95. "Axelrod to Quit in June as Deputy Works Chief," *Baltimore Sun*, April 15, 1976, C7.

96. "Expressway Opponents Vilify Officials," *Baltimore Sun*, August 7, 1969, A10.

97. Janelee Keidel, "An Expressway Bridges a Gulf Between People," *Baltimore Sun*, August 17, 1969, K2.

98. Letter from J. Bond to Joseph Wiles et al., January 28, 1970, 7A, box 6, folder 52, Movement Against Destruction Records, R0062-MAD, Baltimore Studies Archives, UB.

99. James D. Dilts, "Who Wants the Expressway?," *Baltimore Sun*, June 6, 1971.

100. "Expressway Opponents Vilify Officials," *Baltimore Sun*, August 7, 1969, A10.

101. "Expressway Opponents Vilify Officials."

102. Rosemont Public Hearings—Orlinsky, Walter S.—Statement, 1969-08-09, 6, box 6, folder 53, Movement Against Destruction Records, R0062-MAD, Baltimore Studies Archives, UB.

103. City Council Ordinance no. 1072, 1969.

104. Hauber, "The Baltimore Expressway Controversy," 70.

105. General—Citizens Meeting with John A. Volpe, 6, box 5, folder 35, Movement Against Destruction Records, R0062-MAD, Baltimore Studies Archives, UB.

106. "Order to Reconsider Road Through Rosemont Assailed," *Baltimore Sun*, December 11, 1969, C8.

107. "Mayor to Reveal Road Choice," *Baltimore Sun*, June 14, 1970, 20.

108. "Council Votes Zoning 3 Sought," *Baltimore Sun*, November 3, 1970, C5.

109. "Road Bypass Is Opposed," *Baltimore Sun*, December 18, 1970, C15.

110. Stu Weschler, August 8, 1969, Rosemont Public Hearings, 6, box 6, folder 52, Movement Against Destruction Records, R0062-MAD, Baltimore Studies Archives, UB.

111. Stu Weschler, August 8, 1969.

Chapter Seven

1. Carolyn Tyson/Save Our American Environment, "The Road: Beating a Path through the City" (n.d.), Society For The Preservation of Federal Hill, Montgomery St., & Fells Point, 7A, box 7, folder 113, Movement Against Destruction Records, R0062-MAD, Baltimore Studies Archives, UB.

2. "Picketing Limit Is Set By Judge," *Baltimore Sun*, March 26, 1960, 20, 30. William F. Zorzi, "Baltimore's Northwood: Remembrance of Desegregation Past," *Maryland Matters*, July 9, 2020, https://marylandmatters.org/2020/07/09/baltimores-northwood-remembrance-of-desegregation-past/.

3. "Jobs Assured 16 Teen-Agers," *Baltimore Sun*, June 28, 1969, A10.

4. "Talent Show Is Held in West Baltimore Clearing," *Baltimore Sun*, August 28, 1969, A12.

5. "Talent Show Is Held in West Baltimore Clearing."

6. Jane L. Keidel, "Embry Will Need the Patience of Job," *Baltimore Sun*, July 14, 1968, K2.

7. Esther W. Redd to Commissioner Robert C. Embry, Department of Housing and Community Development (October 15, 1969), Relocation Action Movement (RAM), 7A, box 7, folder 105, Movement Against Destruction Records, R0062-MAD, Baltimore Studies Archives, UB.

8. A. G. Christensen, "Potential Buyers–Rosemont," September 30, 1970; A. G. Christensen to Ottavio Grande, December 14, 1971, BRG48-40, box 6, Rosemont Prospective Purchasers 1970–71, BCA.

9. "Foes Describe Road's Effects," *Baltimore Sun*, August 8, 1969, C13.

10. "Rosemont Schedule of Properties," BRG48-40, box 3; "Rosemont FHA 235 Settlement Receipts," BRG48-40, box 8, Department of Housing and Community Development, Land Development Division, Vacant House Program Real Estate Files 1969–1975, BCA.

11. "Residents of Rosemont Surprised On Rowhouse Renovation Loans."

12. Urban Design Concept Associates, *Rosemont Area Studies* (February 1968). Rosemont Area Studies, 13, box 76, folder 35, Greater Baltimore Committee Records, R0046-GBC, Baltimore Studies Archives, UB.

13. "Hi! Neighbors, It's Clean Up Time" (February 17, 1970), Rosemont Neighborhood Improvement Association Records, 1969–1970, 9B, box 15, folder 2, Baltimore Heritage Records, R0010-BH, Baltimore Studies Archives, UB.

14. *The Settler: A Chronicle of Home Ownership in Baltimore* 2, no. 2 (1975): 1–2.

15. Letter from R.N.I.A. to City Council, January 24, 1972, Rosemont Neighborhood Improvement Association Records, 1971–1972, 9B, box 15, folder 4, Baltimore Heritage Records,

R0010-BH, Baltimore Studies Archives, UB; "Enjoin City, Court Asked," *Baltimore Sun*, April 25, 1969, C8.

16. Paul D. Samuel, "$5 Million Approved To Help Rosemont," *Baltimore Sun*, June 7, 1971, vertical files, EPFL.

17. Script, Mrs. Mary M. Rosemond (n.d.), Rosemont Neighborhood Improvement Association Records, 1969–1970, 9B, box 15, folder 2, Baltimore Heritage Records, R0010-BH, Baltimore Studies Archives, UB.

18. "Movement Against Destruction Statement of December 10, 1969," Promotional, 3, Movement Against Destruction Records, R0062-MAD, Baltimore Studies Archives, UB.

19. "The Rosemont Dilemma!!!," Rosemont Neighborhood Improvement Association Newsletter, 1971, 2, Rosemont Neighborhood Improvement Association Records, 1971–1972, 9B, box 15, folder 4, Baltimore Heritage Records, R0010-BH, Baltimore Studies Archives, UB.

20. National Advisory Commission on Civil Disorders, *Report of the National Advisory Commission on Civil Disorders* (Government Printing Office, 1968), 4.

21. Alison Isenberg, *Downtown America: A History of the Place and the People Who Made It* (University of Chicago Press, 2004), 231; Lizabeth Cohen, *A Consumers' Republic: The Politics of Mass Consumption in Postwar America* (Vintage Books, 2003), 373.

22. Rebecca K. Marchiel, *After Redlining: The Urban Reinvestment Movement in the Era of Financial Deregulation* (University of Chicago Press, 2020), 56.

23. "FHA Mortgage Insurance Programs During the 1960s: An Inquiry Into the Relative Emphasis of Program Policies on Housing Needs in the Suburbs and in Older, Declining Areas" (Department of Housing and Urban Development, October 1974).

24. John McClaughry, "The Troubled Dream: The Life and Times of Section 235 of the National Housing Act," *Loyola University Law Journal* 6, no. 1 (Winter 1975): 11; Paul George Lewis, "Housing and American Privatism: The Origins and Evolution of Subsidized Home-Ownership Policy," *Journal of Policy History* 5, no. 1 (1993): 37; Lewis Hyman, *Borrow: The American Way of Debt* (Vintage Books, 2012), 187.

25. Housing and Urban Development Act of 1968, Public Law 90-448, 82 Stat. 476, codified at 12 U.S.C. §1701U.

26. HUD Commissioner's Letter, August 2, 1968; Karen M. Hult, *Agency Merger and Bureaucratic Redesign* (University of Pittsburgh Press, 1987), 132.

27. Fred McGhee, "The Most Important Housing Law Passed in 1968 Wasn't the Fair Housing Act," *Shelterforce*, September 5, 2018, https://shelterforce.org/2018/09/05/the-most-important-housing-law-passed-in-1968-wasnt-the-fair-housing-act/.

28. *Journal of the Senate of the United States of America: Second Session of the Ninetieth Congress* (1968), 110–11.

29. Keeanga-Yamahtta Taylor, *Race for Profit: How Banks and the Real Estate Industry Undermined Black Homeownership* (University of North Carolina Press, 2019), 4.

30. Jung Hyun Choi et al., 2019. "Explaining the Black-White Homeownership Gap: A Closer Look at Disparities across Local Markets" (Urban Institute, 2019), 11.

31. Elise Gould and Jessica Schieder, "Poverty Persists 50 Years After the Poor People's Campaign," May 17, 2018, Economic Policy Institute, https://www.epi.org/publication/poverty-persists-50-years-after-the-poor-peoples-campaign-black-poverty-rates-are-more-than-twice-as-high-as-white-poverty-rates.

32. Marchiel, *After Redlining*, 58.

33. Robert Schafer and Charles G. Field, "Section 235 of the National Housing Act:

Homeownership for Low-Income Families?"; Jon Pynoos, Robert Schafer, and Chester Hartman, *Housing Urban America*, 2nd ed. (Aldine Publishing, 1980), 485; Hult, *Agency Merger*, 132; Department of Housing and Urban Development, "Family Income Limits for FHA Sections 235 and 236 Housing Based on 135% of Approved or Permissible Public Housing Admission Limits," April 1, 1971, BRG48-40-1, folder Rosemont "As-Is" Purchase, BCA.

34. US Department of Housing and Urban Development Office of Policy Development and Research, "U.S. Housing Market Conditions: Historical Data," Spring 1997.

35. "Format for 235 and 236 Program(s)," BRG48-40-1, folder Rosemont "As-Is" Purchase, BCA.

36. Lyndon B. Johnson, "Remarks at the Dedication of the Department of Housing and Urban Development Building" (September 9, 1968), https://www.presidency.ucsb.edu/documents/remarks-the-dedication-the-department-housing-and-urban-development-building.

37. James D. Dilts, "Homebuyers Say FHA Slows Program," *Baltimore Sun*, June 15, 1971, C22.

38. Marchiel, *After Redlining*, 57.

39. Calvin Bradford, "Financing Home Ownership: The Federal Role in Neighborhood Decline," *Urban Affairs Quarterly*, March 1979, 327.

40. Marchiel, *After Redlining*, 58.

41. Taylor, *Race for Profit*, 4–6.

42. Marchiel, *After Redlining*, 59.

43. John Herbers, "U.S. Report Finds Fraud in Housing: Cites Wide Abuse in Federal Home Ownership Plan," *New York Times*, January 6, 1971, 1.

44. Herbers, "U.S. Now Big Landlord."

45. Schafer and Field, "Section 235 of the National Housing Act," 495.

46. James B. Steele, "An Anatomy of Failure: The Poor as Homeowners," *Washington Post*, February 27, 1972.

47. Ronald Kessler, "Patman: FHA Aids Profiteers," *Washington Post*, July 31, 1970, A1.

48. Hays, *The Federal Government and Urban Housing*, 115.

49. Schafer and Field, "Section 235 of the National Housing Act," 495.

50. Brian D. Boyer, *Cities Destroyed for Cash: The FHA Scandal at HUD* (Follett, 1973), 111.

51. "'235' Low-Income Housing Due Back Without the Bugs," *Baltimore Afro-American*, April 3, 1971, 6.

52. "1,500 Vacant Homes in 'Operation Rescue,'" *Baltimore Sun*, December 15, 1968, 6F.

53. Philadelphia Housing Association/Citizens' Council on City Planning, *A Working Paper, Proposed Recommendations Relating to Site Selection for the Used-House Program of the Philadelphia Housing Authority*, January 11, 1963, 3; Committee on Public Housing Development Policy, Philadelphia Housing Association/Citizens' Council on City Planning, *Recommended Criteria for Selecting Neighborhoods and Structures for the Used-House Program of the Philadelphia Housing Authority*, July 1959, 2–3, TUA.

54. Thomas Marudas, "Baltimore City's Vacant House Program" (1972), 2, BRG48-40, box 12, folder Vacant House Program—History, BCA; "Vacant Houses," *Baltimore Sun*, May 10, 1969.

55. "The Vacant House Program," BRG48-40, box 12, folder Vacant House Program, BCA.

56. Baltimore Neighborhoods, Inc., "A Real Estate Industry Interpretation of Title VIII (Open Housing Provisions) of the Federal Civil Rights Bill," *History Exhibits from the Baltimore Studies Archives*, https://ubarchives.omeka.net/items/show/15541.

57. "1,500 Vacant Homes in 'Operation Rescue,'" *Baltimore Sun*, December 15, 1968, 6F.

58. Andrew R. Highsmith, "Prelude to the Subprime Crash: Beecher, Michigan, and the Origins of the Subprime Crisis," *Journal of Policy History* 24, no. 4 (2012): 585.

59. Robert Embry to George Terry and George Kimbrow, August 2, 1971, BRG48-40-1, folder Rosemont "As-Is" Purchase, BCA.

60. R.N.I.A. Meeting Minutes, August 1966.

61. Rosemont Neighborhood Improvement Association Newsletter, November–December 1969, Rosemont Neighborhood Improvement Association Records, 1969–1970, 9B, box 15, folder 2, Baltimore Heritage Records, R0010-BH, Baltimore Studies Archives, UB.

62. Joseph Wiles to Robert Embry, March 6, 1970, Rosemont Neighborhood Improvement Association Records, 1969–1970, 9B, box 15, folder 2, Baltimore Heritage Records, R0010-BH, Baltimore Studies Archives, UB.

63. Letter from R.N.I.A. Executive Committee, July 27, 1970, Rosemont Neighborhood Improvement Association Records, 1969–1970, 9B, box 15, folder 2, Baltimore Heritage Records, R0010-BH, Baltimore Studies Archives, UB.

64. Ed Croom, "HCD Meeting in Rosemont Area," April 22, 1971, BRG48-40, folder Rosemont Coalition, BCA.

65. Robert Hubbard to Mark Joseph, "Planning Meeting for Informational Meeting and Survey Work in Rosemont Corridor" (April 13, 1971), BRG48-40; Robert C. Embry to George Terry (President, Rosemont Coalition) (May 19, 1971), BRG48-40, box 6 "Rosemont Coalition" 1971–72, Department of Housing and Community Development, Land Development Division, Vacant House Program Real Estate Files 1969–1975, BCA.

66. A. G. Christensen to Mark K. Joseph, "Rosemont" (April 21, 1971), BRG48-40, folder Rosemont Coalition, BCA.

67. "Residents of Rosemont Surprised On Rowhouse Renovation Loans."

68. Thomas N. Marudas, "Baltimore City's Vacant House Program" (1974), 11.

69. George E. Terry to Walter Orlinsky (November 19, 1971), BRG48-40, box 6, "Rosemont Coalition" 1971–72, BCA.

70. Terry to Orlinsky, November 19, 1971, Rosemont Coalition Complaints, December 2, 1971, BRG48-40, folder Rosemont Coalition, BCA.

71. Paul D. Samuel, "Rosemont Area Set for Code Compliance," *Baltimore Sun*, April 30, 1970.

72. Meeting minutes, November 9, 1971, Rosemont Neighborhood Improvement Association Records, 1971–1972, 9B, box 15, folder 4, Baltimore Heritage Records, R0010-BH, Baltimore Studies Archives, UB.

73. Meeting minutes, October 5, 1971, Rosemont Neighborhood Improvement Association Records, 1971–1972, 9B, box 15, folder 4, Baltimore Heritage Records, R0010-BH, Baltimore Studies Archives, UB.

74. "Del. Brailey Criticizes Housing Inspectors: Housing Inspections Too Severe," *Baltimore Afro-American*, May 9, 1972, 14.

75. "Del. Brailey Criticizes Housing Inspectors."

76. BRG48-40-1, folder Rosemont code enforcement, BCA.

77. Christensen to Joseph, April 21, 1971, BCA.

78. Croom, "HCD Meeting in Rosemont Area," BCA.

79. A. G. Christensen, "Potential Buyers-Rosemont," September 30, 1970; A. G. Christensen to Ottavio Grande, December 14, 1971, BRG48-40, box 6, Rosemont Prospective Purchasers 1970–71, BCA.

80. Christensen, "Potential Buyers-Rosemont."

81. "Priority Items for Discussion with FHA," May 10, 1972, BRG48-40, folder Rosemont

NOTES TO PAGES 127-130

Coalition, BCA; Department of Housing and Community Development Rosemont Fact Sheet, December 7, 1971, Rosemont Neighborhood Improvement Association Records, 1971–1972, 9B, box 15, folder 4, Baltimore Heritage Records, R0010-BH, Baltimore Studies Archives, UB.

82. Mark K. Joseph to A. G. Christensen, "Rosemont Rehabilitation," October 1, 1970, BRG48-40, folder Rosemont Coalition, BCA.

83. Croom, "HCD Meeting in Rosemont Area," BCA.

84. Ruby Maclin to Cornelius A. Tinsley, May 1971, BRG48-40-1, folder 1971 Rosemont chron, BCA.

85. Baltimore City Superior Court (Land Records) 1954–1954, MLP 9408, p. 0131, MSA CE 168-9416.

86. Department of Housing and Community Development, Land Development Division, Vacant House Program Real Estate Files 1969–1975, BRG48-40, BCA.

87. Department of Housing and Community Development, Land Development Division, Vacant House Program Real Estate Files 1969–1975, BRG48-40, BCA.

88. Department of Housing and Community Development, Land Development Division, Vacant House Program Real Estate Files 1969–1975, BRG48-40, BCA.

89. Baltimore County Circuit Court (Land Records) 1969–1974, OTG 5025, pp. 0713–0715, MSA CE 62-4880.

90. Ruby Maclin to Cornelius A. Tinsley, May 1971, BRG48-40-1, folder 1971 Rosemont chron, BCA.

91. George Terry to Robert Embry, April 28, 1971, BRG48-40, folder 1971 Rosemont chron, BCA.

92. Robert Embry to George Terry and George Kimbrow, August 2, 1971; Bob Maddox to Mark Joseph, September 20, 1971, BRG48-40-1, folder Rosemont "As-Is" Purchase, BCA.

93. A. G. Christensen to Mark K. Joseph, "Memorandum: As Is Purchase of Rosemont Properties," July 8, 1971, BRG48-40-1, folder Rosemont "As-Is" Purchase, BCA.

94. Christensen to Joseph, July 8, 1971, BCA.

95. BRG48-40-1, folder Rosemont "As-Is" Purchase, BCA.

96. Appraisal Report, Housing Authority of Baltimore City Vacant House Program (MD2-40), BRG48-40-1, folder Rosemont "As Is" 901 Rosedale; Bob Maddox to Mark Joseph, September 21, 1971, BRG48-40-1, folder Rosemont "As-Is" Purchase, BCA.

97. Robert Embry to George Terry and George Kimbrow, March 8, 1972, BRG48-40-1, folder Rosemont "As-Is" Purchase, BCA.

98. James D. Dilts, "Changing City—We Must Destroy You to Save You," *Baltimore Sun*, August 4, 1968, D3.

99. "The Rosemont Dilemma!!!," Rosemont Neighborhood Improvement Association Newsletter, 1971, 2, Rosemont Neighborhood Improvement Association Records, 1971–1972, 9B, box 15, folder 4, Baltimore Heritage Records, R0010-BH, Baltimore Studies Archives, UB.

100. "East–West Expressway," Rosemont Neighborhood Improvement Association Newsletter, November 1970, 3–4, Rosemont Neighborhood Improvement Association Records, 1970–1971, 9B, box 15, folder 3, Baltimore Heritage Records, R0010-BH, Baltimore Studies Archives, UB.

101. Millie Rahn, Maryland Historical Society Oral History Office, interview with Mr. William Boucher, Executive Director, Greater Baltimore Committee, April 3, 1974, OH 5071, Cassette 071, MCHC.

102. "Tyson Street Discussion Held," *Baltimore Sun*, September 10, 1957, 36.

Chapter Eight

1. Malcolm Jones, "James Rouse Sparked New Life in Old Cities," *Newsweek*, April 21, 1996; Ann Forsyth, *Reforming Suburbia: The Planned Communities of Irvine, Columbia, and the Woodlands* (University of California Press, 2005).
2. Jack Rosenthal, "A Tale of One City," *New York Times*, December 26, 1971, SM4.
3. "A Tale of One City."
4. Emily Lieb, "'Baltimore Does Not Condone Profiteering in Squalor': The Baltimore Plan and the Problem of Housing-Code Enforcement in an American City," *Planning Perspectives* 33, no. 1 (2018): 75–95.
5. Nicholas Dagen Bloom, *Merchant of Illusion: James Rouse, America's Salesman of the Businessman's Utopia* (Ohio State University Press, 2004); Joshua Olsen, *Better Places, Better Lives: A Biography of James Rouse* (Urban Land Institute, 2003).
6. "A Tale of One City."
7. "A Tale of One City."
8. Libby Solomon, "This Week in Columbia History: Overnight Campouts Became Common in Scramble for Housing," *Baltimore Sun*, August 10, 2017.
9. "A Tale of One City."
10. "A Tale of One City."
11. Michael Chabon, "Maps and Legends," in *Maps and Legends: Reading and Writing along the Borderlands* (Harper Perennial, 2008), 15–16.
12. Chabon, "Maps and Legends."
13. "A Tale of One City."
14. Chabon, "Maps and Legends."
15. "A Tale of One City."
16. "Rosemont Development," *Baltimore Afro-American*, January 22, 1972, B-6.
17. "Rosemont Development."
18. *Baltimore Afro-American*, April 23, 1977, 20.
19. "Own a Home of Your Own in Rosemont," *Baltimore Afro-American*, February 12, 1972, 14.
20. Department of Housing and Urban Development, "Family Income Limits for FHA Sections 235 and 236 Housing Based on 135% Of Approved or Permissible Public Housing Admission Limits," April 1, 1971, BRG48-40-1, folder Rosemont "As-Is" Purchase, BCA.
21. "Rosemont Schedule of Properties," BRG48-40, box 3; "Rosemont FHA 235 Settlement Receipts," BRG48-40, box 8; BRG48-40-1, folder Rosemont Applicants, BCA.
22. James B. Steele, "An Anatomy of Failure: The Poor as Homeowners," *Washington Post*, February 27, 1972.
23. Brian D. Boyer, *Cities Destroyed for Cash: The FHA Scandal at HUD* (Follett, 1973), 106.
24. Activists, Inc., "Baltimore Under Siege: The Impact of Financing on the Baltimore Home Buyer (1960–1970)" (September 1971), I, Baltimore Under Siege, 1971, 6, box 1, folder 13, Baltimore Neighborhoods, Incorporated Records, R0015-BNI, Baltimore Studies Archives, UB.
25. James D. Dilts, "Goldseker Tells 26: Buy or Face Eviction," *Baltimore Sun*, July 9, 1971, C20.
26. "Goldseker Tells 26," C20.
27. Memorandum from A G. Christensen, "Rosemont Sales," January 20, 1972, BRG48-40, box 6, Rosemont Sales Program 1972, BCA.

28. S. Lee Martin & Co., "A Home for You in Rosemont!," BRG48-40, box 6, Rosemont Sales Program 1972, BCA.

29. "Vacant Home Program Gets $5 Million," *Baltimore Afro-American*, July 22, 1972, B-16, B-9.

30. Breana Pitts, "Remembering Lee Martin, Morgan State Track Star of the Early 1960s," *Baltimore Afro-American*, May 25, 2014.

31. George Terry and George Kimbrow to Mark Joseph, August 14, 1971, BRG48-40-1, folder Rosemont broker correspondence, BCA.

32. S. Lee Martin to A. G. Christensen, July 19, 1971, BRG48-40-1, folder Rosemont broker correspondence, BCA.

33. "How We Plan to Help Develop the Rosemont Area," BRG48-40-1, folder Rosemont broker correspondence, BCA.

34. Jerry R. Engelman to A. G. Christensen, January 5, 1972; Jerry R. Engelman to A. G. Christensen, January 25, 1972, BRG48-40-1, folder Rosemont broker correspondence 1972 January, BCA.

35. Jerry R. Engelman to A. G. Christensen, January 25, 1972, BRG48-40-1, folder Rosemont broker correspondence, BCA.

36. Roger M. Windsor to R. C. Embry, "Rosemont—S. Lee Martin & Co.," May 9, 1972, BRG48-40-1, folder Rosemont broker correspondence, BCA.

37. Windsor to Embry, "Rosemont—S. Lee Martin & Co.," BCA.

38. Roger Windsor to S. Lee Martin, October 16, 1972, BRG48-40-1, folder Rosemont broker correspondence 1972 August–December, BCA.

39. Jerry R. Engelman to A. G. Christensen, January 14, 1972, BRG48-40-1, folder Rosemont broker correspondence 1972 January, BCA.

40. Memo from A. G. Christensen, subject "2412 Lauretta Avenue," September 22, 1971, BRG48-40-1, folder Rosemont broker correspondence 1971 October–December, BCA.

41. Department of Housing and Community Development, Land Development Division, Vacant House Program Real Estate Files 1969–1975, BRG48-40, BCA.

42. Department of Housing and Community Development, Land Development Division, Vacant House Program Real Estate Files 1969–1975, BRG48-40, BCA.

43. Nancy J. Schwerzler, "HUD Taking Over $2 Million Slum in Annapolis After Owners Default," *Baltimore Sun*, September 23, 1975, C1.

44. "Sidney H. Tinley, 62; Headed Mortgage Firm," *Baltimore Sun*, December 15, 1976, A6.

45. Emily Lieb, "'Baltimore Does Not Condone Profiteering in Squalor': The Baltimore Plan and the Problem of Housing-Code Enforcement in an American City," *Planning Perspectives* 33, no. 1 (2017): 75–95.

46. Martin Millspaugh and Gurney Breckenfeld, *The Human Side of Urban Renewal: A Study of the Attitude Changes Produced by Neighborhood Rehabilitation* (Ives Washburn, 1960), 14; "Brotherhood Pilot House: The Baltimore Plan Pilot Program" (July 19, 1951); Dorothy Shipley Granger Papers box 11, folder 15, Schlesinger Library, Harvard University; Baltimore Urban Renewal and Housing Agency, *It's Happening in Baltimore! Annual Report for 1957* (Housing Authority of Baltimore City, 1957). See also Alexander von Hoffman, "Enter the Housing Industry, Stage Right: A Working Paper on the History of Housing Policy" (Harvard Joint Center for Housing Studies, 2008), 26.

47. "Steady, Legal Pressure Against Slum Profiteering," *Baltimore Sun*, November 18, 1947, 12.

48. Ann Forsyth, *Reforming Suburbia: The Planned Communities of Irvine, Columbia, and the Woodlands* (University of California Press, 2005).

49. Department of Housing and Community Development, Land Development Division, Vacant House Program Real Estate Files 1969–1975, BRG48-40, BCA.

50. Paul D. Samuel, "Solicitor Is Urged to Reconsider Rosemont Housing Project O.K.," *Baltimore Evening Sun* May 15, 1971, 18.

51. Marchiel, *After Redlining*, 61.

52. Marchiel, *After Redlining*, 61.

53. Mark Joseph to James Rouse, April 7, 1971, BRG48-40-2, folder 1971–72 Rosemont Correspondence: Rouse Co., BCA; Harry B. Wilson Jr., "Exploiting the Home-Buying Poor: A Case Study of Abuse of the National Housing Act," *Saint Louis University Law Journal* 17, no. 4 (1973).

54. "Exploiting the Home-Buying Poor," 548.

55. A. G. Christensen to Mark K. Joseph, "Rosemont Rehabilitation," September 1, 1971, BRG48-40, box 6, folder Rosemont: Rehabilitation 1970–1972, BCA.

56. Martin Gottlieb, "Builder Probed on Loans Chosen for U.S. Slum Job," *New York Daily News*, June 28, 1977, 21.

57. James D. Dilts, "Sale of Houses Begins; Developer Faces Charges," *Baltimore Sun*, January 21, 1972, C22, C9.

58. "Tax Fraud Charged to Father and Son," *New York Times*, March 12, 1966, 56.

59. "Weintraub Attorney Sees Hope in Ruling," *Yonkers Herald Statesman*, January 21, 1986, 3; "Developer Gets Year in Jail, Fine," *Hartford Courant*, May 12, 2000.

60. "Developer Gets Year in Jail."

61. "Sale of Houses Begins."

62. "Residents Warned on Rosemont," *Baltimore Afro-American*, January 25, 1972, 1–2.

63. "Rep. Mitchell Investigates: Shoddy Work Found in Rosemont Homes," *Baltimore Afro-American*, January 29, 1972, A1, A2.

64. Scott Ponemone and Paul Evans, "Mitchell, Embry Return—Rosemont Gets Okay," *Baltimore Afro-American*, February 12, 1972, A1, A3.

65. "Rep. Mitchell Investigates."

66. "Mitchell, Embry Return."

67. "Rep. Mitchell Investigates."

68. "Mitchell, Embry Return."

69. "Mitchell, Embry Return."

70. R. Allen Hays, *The Federal Government and Urban Housing*, 2nd ed. (SUNY Press, 1995), 114.

71. Marchiel, *After Redlining*, 64.

72. Boyer, *Cities Destroyed for Cash*, 98.

73. Hays, *The Federal Government and Urban Housing*, 116.

74. "*Afro* Victory: City Spends $744,000 more in Rosemont Area," *Baltimore Afro-American*, June 17, 1972.

75. Frank DelGrosso to Ottavio F. Grande, "Rosemont FHA-235, Morelite Construction Company, Progress Meeting Minutes," August 10, 1972, BRG48-40, box 6, folder Rosemont Meetings 1972 February–August, BCA.

76. Mark Reutter, "U.S. and City Investigate Records from Vacant House Program," *Baltimore Sun*, December 8, 1974, Trend 1.

77. Memorandum from John A. Donaho to Mayor William Donald Schaefer, "Progress

NOTES TO PAGES 142-146

Report—Rosemont," January 21, 1975, BRG48-40, box 5, Highway Acquisition, BCA; Mark Reutter, "Fix-Up Draws Mixed Reviews," *Baltimore Sun*, September 29, 1974, TR10.

78. "Grande Defense Rests; No Defendants Testify," *Baltimore Evening Sun*, October 20, 1977, 2.

79. "Brown Linked to Goldstein Death," *Baltimore Sun*, April 20, 1974, B4; "Missed Point," *Baltimore Evening Sun*, December 11, 1974, A22.

80. Mark Reutter, "U.S. and City Investigate Records from Vacant House Program," *Baltimore Sun*, December 8, 1974, Trend 1.

81. Robert C. Embry, "Letters," *Baltimore Sun*, October 13, 1974, Trend 2.

82. Dan Rodricks, "Ottavio Grande's Criminal Case Goes On and On, a la Mandel," *Baltimore Evening Sun*, March 4, 1980, D1.

83. "Ottavio Grande's Criminal Case Goes On and On."

84. "Grande Case Defense Rests Without Calling Any of 6 Defendants," *Baltimore Evening Sun*, October 20, 1977, 1; "Grande Guilty: Jury Says Contractors Rigged Bids and Gave City Official Pay-Offs," *Baltimore Evening Sun* (October 28, 1977), 1; "Mayor Silent on Conviction of Grande," *Baltimore Evening Sun*, October 29, 1977, 1.

85. "Grande's Abilities Were Not Disputed," *Baltimore Sun*, October 29, 1977, A5.

86. "Grande's Abilities Were Not Disputed."

87. "Grande's Abilities Were Not Disputed."

88. Baltimore City Superior Court (Land Records) 1973–1973, RHB 3009, pp. 0317–0319, MSA CE 168-13327.

89. Thomas & Ruby Maclin, n.d., BRG48-40-2, folder 1973 Rosemont Correspondence: Rouse Co., BCA.

90. HUD to Rouse Co, May 7, 1973, BRG48-40-2, folder 1973 Rosemont Correspondence: Rouse Co., BCA.

91. Thomas & Ruby Maclin, n.d., BRG48-40-2, folder 1973 Rosemont Correspondence: Rouse Co., BCA.

92. Roger Windsor to Ottavio Grande, "Rosemont Carpet Installations," January 9, 1974, box MSA SC 5511 BC/27/4/34, folder 1974 Rosemont Home Ownership Development—Roger Windsor, BCA.

93. "Rosemont Carpet Installations."

94. Roger Windsor to Ottavio Grande, "Rosemont Carpet Installations," January 24, 1974, box MSA SC 5511 BC/27/4/34, folder 1974 Rosemont Home Ownership Development—Roger Windsor, BCA.

95. Hays, *The Federal Government and Urban Housing*, 117.

96. Rosemont Sales Program, "Financial Counselor Script," 1972, BRG48-40, box 6, Rosemont Sales Program 1972 January–May, BCA.

97. "Financial Counselor Script."

98. Marudas, "Baltimore City's Vacant House Program," 10.

99. Resident Family Services Division, "Home Care Services Program" (draft, n.d.), BRG48-40, box 2, Rosemont Counselling: Home Care Services, BCA.

100. "Domestic Science," *Baltimore Sun*, December 14, 1970.

101. Department of Housing and Community Development, "The Rosemont Home Care Catalog: Rosemont Is Now" (draft, n.d.), BRG48-40, box 6, folder Rosemont Counselling, BCA.

102. "Rosemont Is Now."

103. "Rosemont Schedule of Properties," BRG48-40, box 3; "Rosemont FHA 235 Settlement

Receipts," BRG48-40, box 8, BCA; Baltimore City Superior Court (Land Records) 1972–1972, RHB 2931, pp. 0741–0744, MSA CE 168-13249.

104. Baltimore City Superior Court (Land Records) 1976–1976, RHB 3326, pp. 0304–0305, MSA CE 168-13646; *Baltimore Sun*, February 22, 1976, 10MX.

105. "Rosemont Schedule of Properties," BCA; "Rosemont FHA 235 Settlement Receipts," BCA; Baltimore City Superior Court (Land Records) 1978–1978, RHB 3568, pp. 0474–0475, MSA CE 168-13888.

106. "Rosemont Schedule of Properties"; "Rosemont FHA 235 Settlement Receipts," BCA.

107. "Rosemont Schedule of Properties," BCA; "Rosemont FHA 235 Settlement Receipts," BCA; Baltimore City Superior Court (Land Records) 1973–1973, RHB 3023, pp. 0287–0290, MSA CE 168-13343; Baltimore City Superior Court (Land Records) 1979–1979, WA 3822, pp. 0852–0853, MSA CE 168-14142.

108. Letter from Belva Scott, Homeownership Counselor, "Report on Delinquent Mortgages—Rosemont," November 20, 1974, 48-47, box 6, folder 2737 Edmondson, BCA.

109. Baltimore City Circuit Court (Land Records) 2020–2020, MB 21970, pp. 0271–0273, MSA CE 164-31127.

110. "HFC Lends Illegally, U.S. Says," *Baltimore Sun*, July 8, 1978, A13; "Rosemont Schedule of Properties"; "Rosemont FHA 235 Settlement Receipts," BCA.

111. "Rosemont Schedule of Properties"; "Rosemont FHA 235 Settlement Receipts," BCA.

112. "Unhappy Owners of 16 Rosemont Homes."

113. Marchiel, *After Redlining*, 64.

114. Complaint, *Thompson v. HUD*, Civil Action No. MJG-95-309 (D. Md. January 29, 2004).

115. R.N.I.A. to Robert C. Embry Jr., July 17, 1972, Rosemont Neighborhood Improvement Association Records, 1971–1972, 9B, box 15, folder 4, Baltimore Heritage Records, R0010-BH, Baltimore Studies Archives, UB.

116. Complaint, *Thompson v. HUD*, 1995-01-31, FD 4875, box S3D-B71, folder 42, American Civil Liberties Union of Maryland Records, R0002-ACLU, Baltimore Studies Archives, UB.

117. T. Lee Hughes, "Rosemont Fears Housing Development," *Baltimore News-American*.

118. Letter from Roger M. Windsor, Director, Home Ownership Development Program, to Hugh F. Coyle, Vice President, James W. Rouse & Company, Inc., February 20, 1974, BRG48-40, box 2, folder Rosemont Counseling, BCA.

119. John McClaughry, "The Troubled Dream: The Life and Times of Section 235 of the National Housing Act," *Loyola University Law Journal* 6, no. 1 (1975): 1–45.

120. "Rosemont Schedule of Properties"; "Rosemont FHA 235 Settlement Receipts," BCA.

121. "Federal Compensation for Victims of the 'Homeownership for the Poor' Program," *Yale Law Journal* 84, no. 2 (1974): 294–323.

122. Brian D. Boyer, *Cities Destroyed for Cash: The FHA Scandal at HUD* (Follett, 1973), 111.

123. Boyer, *Cities Destroyed for Cash*, 4.

124. Baltimore City Superior Court (Land Records) 1974–1974, RHB 3168, pp. 0864–0867, MSA CE 168-13488; author conversation with Drusilla Bunch (Rosemont, Baltimore, 2019).

125. Baltimore City Superior Court (Land Records) 1974–1974, RHB 3110, pp. 0264–0267, MSA CE 168-13430; author conversation with Leslie Carl Howard (Rosemont, Baltimore, 2019).

126. Peter Coviello, "Memos of Blood and Fire." *n+1*, March 7, 2025.

127. James Dilts, "Unhappy Owners of 16 Rosemont Homes Feel the City Sold Them Short," *Baltimore Sun*, July 20, 1977.

128. Baltimore City Superior Court (Land Records) 1973-1973, RHB 2992, pp. 0089-0093, MSA CE 168-13310.
129. "Unhappy Owners of 16 Rosemont Homes."
130. "Unhappy Owners of 16 Rosemont Homes."
131. See Rosemont Neighborhood Improvement Association, Inc., "Let's Talk About Our Neighborhood," June 2004, Rosemont Neighborhood Improvement Association Records, 2004, 9B, box 16, folder 4, Baltimore Heritage Records, R0010-BH, Baltimore Studies Archives, UB.
132. "Rosemont Won I-170 Battle; War Continues," *Baltimore Sun*, June 1, 1980, D3.

Conclusion

1. "Nature Walk and Rally for Leakin Park" flyer, October 1975; Robert P. Wade, "Park Lovers Span Road-Periled Leakin," *Baltimore Sun* (October 6, 1975), Parks-Baltimore-Leakin 1, vertical files, EPFL.
2. George L. Scheper, "Leakin Park, a Disputed Highway Route," *Baltimore Sun*, February 7, 1976, 12.
3. Lily Geismer, *Don't Blame Us: Suburban Liberals and the Transformation of the Democratic Party* (Princeton University Press, 2015); Chad Montrie, *The Myth of Silent Spring: Rethinking the Origins of American Environmentalism* (University of California Press, 2018); Adam Rome, *The Bulldozer in the Countryside: Suburban Sprawl and the Rise of American Environmentalism* (Cambridge University Press, 2001); Douglas Brinkley, *Silent Spring Revolution: John F. Kennedy, Rachel Carson, Lyndon Johnson, Richard Nixon, and the Great Environmental Awakening* (HarperCollins, 2022).
4. *Silent Spring Revolution*.
5. Joseph F.C. DiMento and Cliff Ellis, *Changing Lanes: Visions and Histories of Urban Freeways* (MIT Press, 2012).
6. *Changing Lanes*, 116.
7. *Changing Lanes*, 126.
8. Mildred Rahn, "An Oral History of Barbara Mikulski for the East-West Expressway Collection," April 30, 1974, 4, Maryland Historical Society, OH 8057, MCHC.
9. *Changing Lanes*, 123.
10. Douglas H. Hauber, *The Baltimore Expressway Controversy: A Study of the Political Decision-Making Process* (Johns Hopkins University Center for Metropolitan Planning and Research, 1974); Mark Reutter, "Baltimore's Expressway Controversy" (ca. 1970s), Reuter, Mark—Expressway Paper, 7A, box 7, folder 110, Movement Against Destruction Records, R0062-MAD, Baltimore Studies Archives, UB; Raymond A. Mohl, "The Interstates and the Cities: Highways, Housing, and the Freeway Revolt," *PRRAC Civil Rights Research*, 2002, 1-73. Raymond A. Mohl, "Stop the Road: Freeway Revolts in American Cities," *Journal of Urban History* 30, no. 5 (July 2004), 674-706. Emily Lieb, "Row House City: Unbuilding Residential Baltimore, 1940-1980" (PhD diss., Columbia University, 2010); Lieb, "White Man's Lane"; Earl Swift, *The Big Roads: The Untold Story of the Engineers, Visionaries, and Trailblazers Who Created the American Superhighways* (New York: Harper Collins, 2012); Matthew A. Crenson, *Baltimore: A Political History* (Johns Hopkins University Press, 2017); E. Evans Paull, *Stop the Road: Stories from the Trenches of Baltimore's Road Wars* (Boyle & Dalton, 2022).
11. *Silent Spring Revolution*, xix.

12. Kevin M. Kruse and Julian E. Zelizer, *Fault Lines: A History of the United States Since 1974* (W. W. Norton, 2019), 29.

13. Adam Rome, *The Genius of Earth Day: How a 1970 Teach-In Unexpectedly Made the First Green Generation* (Hill and Wang, 2013).

14. National Historic Preservation Act, Public Law. 89-665, 80 Stat. 915; Barry Mackintosh, "The National Historic Preservation Act and the National Park Service: A History" (History Division, National Park Service, Department of the Interior, 1986).

15. Federal Highway Administration Environmental Review Toolkit, "Legislation, Regulations, and Guidance: Section 4(f)," https://www.environment.fhwa.dot.gov/legislation/section4f.aspx.

16. Statement by the President Upon Signing the Federal-Aid Highway Act of 1968, August 24, 1968. https://www.presidency.ucsb.edu/documents/statement-the-president-upon-signing-the-federal-aid-highway-act-1968; John A. Swanson, Associate Director, Right-of-Way and Location, Bureau of Public Roads, "New Provisions of the Federal Aid Highway Act of 1968." https://uknowledge.uky.edu/cgi/viewcontent.cgi?article=1243&context=ktc_proceedings.

17. A.Q. Mowbray, *Road to Ruin: A Critical View of the Federal Highway Program* (J. B. Lippincott, 1968).

18. "Addressing the Quiet Crisis."

19. "Addressing the Quiet Crisis"; United States Environmental Protection Agency, "What Is the National Environmental Policy Act?," https://www.epa.gov/nepa/what-national-environmental-policy-act; National Environmental Policy Act of 1969, Public Law 91-190, 83 Stat. 852; Lily Geismer, *Don't Blame Us: Suburban Liberals and the Transformation of the Democratic Party* (Princeton University Press, 2015), 111.

20. *Changing Lanes*, 130–31.

21. Yale Rabin, "Federal Urban Transportation Policy and the Highway Planning Process in Metropolitan Areas," *Annals of the American Academy of Political and Social Science* 451 (1980): 28; Leland J. White, "Dividing Highway: Citizen Activism and Interstate 66 in Arlington, Virginia," *Washington History* 13, no. 1 (2001): 58; Francesca Rusello Ammon, *Bulldozer: Demolition and Clearance of the Postwar Landscape* (Yale University Press, 2016), 300–301; Mark H. Rose and Raymond A. Mohl, *Interstate*, 135–58; Robert D. Bullard, "Environmental Justice in the 21st Century: Race Still Matters," *Phylon* 49, nos. 3/4 (2001): 151–71.

22. Joan Wright and Jeff Stansbury, "The Planned Disruption of Baltimore—Part I," *Conservation News & Comment* 4:12 (March 23, 1973), 3; Brief for the Appellants, Case Number 73-2136, *Movement Against Destruction et al., Appellants, v. John Volpe et al., Appellees*, Appeal from the United States District Court for the District of Maryland (1973); *Movement Against Destruction v. Volpe*, 361 F. Supp. 1360 (D. Md. 1973), Summary of Suit, US District Court for Maryland, 4, box 2, folder 31, Movement Against Destruction Records, R0062-MAD, Baltimore Studies Archives, UB.

23. Carolyn Tyson/Save Our American Environment, "The Road: Beating A Path Through the City: Save Our American Environment Society For The Preservation of Federal Hill, Montgomery St., & Fells Point," 7A, box 7, folder 113, Movement Against Destruction Records, R0062-MAD, Baltimore Studies Archives, UB; *Eleanor Marie Lukowski et al. v. John A Volpe*, Affidavits—Eleanor Lukowski, 3, box 2, folder 73, Southeast Council Against the Road Records, R0108-SCAR, Baltimore Studies Archives, UB.

24. "Data Sheet: Plaintiffs: M-A-D vs DOT-FHWA," November 7, 1972; MAD et al. v. John Volpe et al.—Plaintiffs Data Sheet, 1972, 4, box 2, folder 27, Movement Against Destruction Records, R0062-MAD, Baltimore Studies Archives, UB.

NOTES TO PAGES 154–157   221

25. John A. Volpe Papers, Northeastern University. https://archivesspace.library.northeastern.edu/repositories/2/resources/851.

26. *Citizens to Preserve Overton Park v. Volpe*, 401 U.S. 402 (1971); Raymond A. Mohl, "Citizen Activism and Freeway Revolts in Memphis and Nashville: The Road to Litigation." *Journal of Urban History* 40, no. 5 (2014): 870–93.

27. Richard Weingroff, "The Dwight D. Eisenhower System of Interstate and Defense Highways Part V—Interstate Withdrawal-Substitution Program—Interstate Withdrawal-Substitution Program Legislative History and Related Information" (2017), https://www.fhwa.dot.gov/highwayhistory/data/page05.cfm.

28. "Information on the ALTERNATE Routes for I-170" (1969), R0007 BCP S13 B7, BCA.

29. Statement by Barbara Holdridge for the Board of Trustees of Volunteers Opposing Leakin Park Expressway, Inc. (V.O.L.P.E.) (January 27, 1972), 2, Volunteers Opposing Leakin Park Expressway, Inc. (V.O.L.P.E.), 1972–1973, 2, box 1, folder 94, Movement Against Destruction Records, R0062-MAD, Baltimore Studies Archives, UB.

30. US Department of Transportation Federal Highway Administration and Interstate Division for Baltimore City, State Highway Administration, Department of Transportation, State of Maryland, "Draft Environmental Impact Statement/Section 4(f) Statement: Administrative Action for I-70N" (November 10, 1972), 24.

31. Robert H. Giles Jr., "A Study of the Effects of a Highway on the Ecology of Leakin Park," September 1969, 10, FHWA-MD-EIS-72-D, A Study of the Effects of a Highway on the Ecology of Leakin Park, 13, box 77, folder 17, Greater Baltimore Committee Records, R0046-GBC, Baltimore Studies Archives, UB.

32. Statement by Barbara Holdridge.

33. Tyson, "The Road."

34. Transcript, "East-West Expressway, First Day's Proceedings Before City Council of Baltimore, Enoch Pratt Free Library, January 25, 1972," 3, BCA.

35. Tyson, "The Road."

36. Douglas H. Hauber, "The Baltimore Expressway Controversy: A Study of the Political Decision-Making Process" (Johns Hopkins University Center for Metropolitan Planning and Research, May 15, 1974), 38, 40; "Walter Orlinsky, Colorful City Politician, Dies at 63," *Baltimore Sun*, February 10, 2002.

37. "No Way to Repeal a Destroyed House," *Baltimore Sun*, June 9, 1972, A14.

38. Testimony of Larry Reich, Baltimore City Director of Planning, Transcript, "East-West Expressway, First Day's Proceedings Before City Council of Baltimore, Enoch Pratt Free Library, January 25, 1972," 14, BCA.

39. Remarks of Charles L. Benton, Baltimore City Director of Finance, Transcript, "East-West Expressway, First Day's Proceedings before City Council of Baltimore, Enoch Pratt Free Library, January 25, 1972," 89, 92, BCA.

40. Remarks of Robert C. Embry, Baltimore City Housing Commissioner, Transcript, "East-West Expressway, First Day's Proceedings before City Council of Baltimore, Enoch Pratt Free Library, January 25, 1972," 65, BCA; George L. Jude, "3-A—A Boon to Blacks," *Baltimore Sun*, January 31, 1973, A18.

41. Patricia J. Tamburo, "So City Can Compete," *Baltimore Sun*, February 19, 1973, A12.

42. Harold A. Crone to Joseph M. Axelrod, January 19, 1973, Expressway—Leakin Park/Gwynns Falls Park Segment, 13, box 76, folder 14, Greater Baltimore Committee Records, R0046-GBC, Baltimore Studies Archives, UB.

43. J. W. Colbert to Joseph M. Axelrod, January 18, 1973, Expressway—Leakin Park/Gwynns Falls Park Segment, 13, box 76, folder 14, Greater Baltimore Committee Records, R0046-GBC, Baltimore Studies Archives, UB.

44. James D. Dilts, "Mayor Urged to Send Aides to Explain Highway Policies," *Baltimore Sun*, May 5, 1971, A12.

45. Case Number 73-2136, Movement Against Destruction et al., Appellants, v. John Volpe et al., Appellees.

46. Mildred Rahn, "An Oral History of Carolyn Tyson for the East–West Expressway Collection," April 3, 1974, 10, Maryland Historical Society, OH 8056, MCHC.

47. "An Oral History of Carolyn Tyson."

48. 3-A Expressway—Benefits to Blacks, 7A, box 7, folder 119, Movement Against Destruction Records, R0062-MAD, Baltimore Studies Archives, UB.

49. Tyson, "The Road."

50. Tyson, "The Road."

51. Richard Weingroff, "Interstate Withdrawal-Substitution Program Legislative History and Related Information," https://www.fhwa.dot.gov/highwayhistory/data/page05.cfm.

52. Mike Klingaman, "In the 1970s, It Wasn't a Pandemic That Brought Baltimore to a Standstill," *Baltimore Sun*, May 27, 2020.

53. "It Wasn't a Pandemic."

54. *Movement Against Destruction v. Volpe* (D. Md. 1973), June 22, 1973, https://www.casemine.com/judgement/us/5914c6e3add7b049347de6f4. Decision of the Court, United States Court of Appeals for the Fourth Circuit, *Movement Against Destruction et al., Appellants, v. John A. Volpe et al., Appellees*, decided March 19, 1974; Decision of the Court, United States District Court for the District of Maryland, *MAD et al. v. Trainor et al.* (March 19, 1975); *MAD et al. v. Trainor, Richard H., et al.*—Civil Court No. M-74-666—Opinion, 1975-03-17, 4, box 2, folder 37, Movement Against Destruction Records, R0062-MAD, Baltimore Studies Archives, UB.

55. *Movement Against Destruction v. Volpe*.

56. "Highway Plans Changed Often over the Years," *Baltimore Sun*, June 2, 1980, A1, A4.

57. Carolyn Tyson/Save Our American Environment, "The Road: Beating a Path Through the City" (n.d.), Society for the Preservation of Federal Hill, Montgomery St., & Fells Point, 7A, box 7, folder 113, Movement Against Destruction Records, R0062-MAD, Baltimore Studies Archives, UB.

58. *Movement Against Destruction v. Volpe*.

59. *Movement Against Destruction v. Volpe*.

60. "Highway Plans Changed Often over the Years."

61. "Highway Plans Changed Often over the Years."

62. "Highway Plans Changed Often over the Years"; Tyson, "The Road."

63. "U.S. 40 East: Baltimore," July 14, 2012, https://www.aaroads.com/guides/us-040-east-baltimore-md/; "Franklin-Mulberry Expressway: Historical Overview" (n.d.). *DC Roads*. http://www.dcroads.net/roads/franklin-mulberry/; "US 40, former I-170" (n.d.). https://www.alpsroads.net/roads/md/us_40/170.html.

64. John C. Armor to Chester L. Brooks, Regional Director, Mid-Atlantic Region, National Park Service, March 13, 1975, John C. Armor, Esquire—Correspondence—Federal Government, 1975–1977, 4, box 2, folder 21, Movement Against Destruction Records, R0062-MAD, Baltimore Studies Archives, UB.

65. John C. Armor to Robert Henri Binder, Assistant Secretary, Department of Transpor-

NOTES TO PAGES 161–163   223

tation, November 10, 1975, John C. Armor, Esquire—Correspondence—Federal Government, 1975–1977, 4, box 2, folder 21, Movement Against Destruction Records, R0062-MAD, Baltimore Studies Archives, UB.

66. Jeffrey R. Brown, Eric A. Morris, and Brian D. Taylor, "Planning for Cars in Cities: Planners, Engineers, and Freeways in the 20th Century," *Journal of the American Planning Association* 75, no. 2 (2009): 173.

67. Pietro S. Nivola, "Apocalypse Now? Whither the Urban Fiscal Crisis," *Polity* 14, no. 3 (1982), 371–94; Jane Berger, *A New Working Class: The Legacies of Public-Sector Employment in the Civil Rights Movement* (University of Pennsylvania Press, 2021).

68. Remarks of Larry Reich, Director of Planning, Transcript, "East-West Expressway, First Day's Proceedings Before City Council of Baltimore, Enoch Pratt Free Library, January 25, 1972," 14–15, BCA.

69. Remarks of Larry Reich.

70. Remarks of Larry Reich.

71. Meg Jacobs, *Panic at the Pump: The Energy Crisis and the Transformation of American Politics in the 1970s* (Hill and Wang, 2016), 125.

72. Brown, Morris, and Taylor, "Planning for Cars in Cities."

73. Brian D. Taylor, "Public Perceptions, Fiscal Realities, and Freeway Planning: The California Case," *Journal of the American Planning Association* 61, no. 1 (1995): 43–56.

74. Taylor, "Public Perceptions, Fiscal Realities, and Freeway Planning," 54.

75. Taylor, "Public Perceptions, Fiscal Realities, and Freeway Planning," 51.

76. Taylor, "Public Perceptions, Fiscal Realities, and Freeway Planning," 51; Remarks of Robert C. Embry, Baltimore City Housing Commissioner, Transcript, "East-West Expressway, First Day's Proceedings Before City Council of Baltimore, Enoch Pratt Free Library, January 25, 1972," 65, BCA.

77. "Report on Bill No. 23—Concerning the Interstate Highway System for Baltimore City," June 26, 1980, 2, box 1, folder 67, Movement Against Destruction Records, R0062-MAD, Baltimore Studies Archives, UB.

78. "Report on Bill No. 23."

79. Michael Wentzel and Kelly Gilbert, "Mayor Eyes I-70 Funds to Repair Bridges," *Baltimore Evening Sun*, March 19, 1981, 1.

80. "Report on Bill No. 23."

81. "Report on Bill No. 23."

82. Scott M. Kozel, "Baltimore City Interstates—Cancellations," http://www.roadstothefuture.com/Balt-City-Interstate-Cancel.html; Matthew A. Crenson, *Baltimore: A Political History* (Johns Hopkins University Press, 2017).

83. "Neighborhood Busters," *Baltimore Evening Sun*, December 24, 1969.

84. Ryan Reft, Amanda K. Phillips de Lucas, and Rebecca C. Retzlaff, *Justice and the Interstates: The Racist Truth About Urban Highways* (Island Press, 2023).

85. Joe Weber, "Route Change on the American Freeway System," *Journal of Transport Geography* 67 (2018):12–23; Joe Weber, "Continuity and Change in American Freeway Networks," *Journal of Transport Geography* 58 (2017): 31–39.

86. Richard Weingroff, "Interstate Withdrawal-Substitution Program Legislative History and Related Information," https://www.fhwa.dot.gov/highwayhistory/data/page05.cfm.

87. Weingroff, "Interstate Withdrawal-Substitution Program."

88. Federal Highway Administration, Office of Highway Policy Information, "Highway Finance Data Collection: Our Nation's Highways, 2011," https://www.fhwa.dot.gov/policyinformation/pubs/hf/pl11028/chapter1.cfm#.

89. Richard O. Baumbach Jr. and William E. Borah, *The Second Battle of New Orleans: A History of the Vieux Carré Riverfront Expressway Controversy* (University of Louisiana Press, 1981); Andrew Chamings, "'A Monstrous Mistake': Remembering the Ugliest Thing San Francisco Ever Built," *SFGate*, July 26, 2021.

90. Seattle Municipal Archives, "R. H. Thomson Expressway" (n.d.), https://www.seattle.gov/cityarchives/exhibits-and-education/seattle-voices/rh-thomson-expressway; "A Neighborhood Saved: History of Thomson Expressway," *Central District News* (Seattle), May 5, 2009.

91. Walt Crowley and Kit Oldham, "Seattle Voters Scrap Proposed Bay Freeway and R. H. Thomson Expressway on February 8, 1972," HistoryLink, February 17, 2012, https://historylink.org/File/3114.

92. Seattle Public Library, "Seattle's Freeway Revolt: A Directory of Historical Resources," 2017, https://spl.contentdm.oclc.org/digital/collection/p15015coll6/id/8732/.

93. Richard W. Cutler, *Greater Milwaukee's Growing Pains, 1950–2000: An Insider's View* (Milwaukee County Historical Society, 2001), 76–80.

94. Interview with Roy Evans, June 2017, https://climatesofinequality.org/project/roy-evans-explaining-how-the-park-west-freeway-project-destroyed-milwaukees-black-community/.

95. *Greater Milwaukee's Growing Pains*, 83.

96. *Greater Milwaukee's Growing Pains*, 87.

97. *Greater Milwaukee's Growing Pains*, 94.

98. Interview with Roy Evans.

99. John Gurda, "Racist Planning Decisions Led Milwaukee's Freeway System Along a Path of Least Resistance, with Great Damage to Communities of Color," *Milwaukee Journal-Sentinel*, August 9, 2022.

100. Christopher J. Bessert, "Milwaukee Freeways: Park Freeway," *Wisconsin Highways*, 2014, https://www.wisconsinhighways.org/milwaukee/park.html.

101. Rob Gurwitt, "Death of a Neighborhood," *Mother Jones*, September 2000; Lizabeth Cohen, *Saving America's Cities: Ed Logue and the Struggle to Renew Urban America in the Suburban Age* (FSG, 2019).

102. Quoted in Jeremy Leonard/Oak Street Historical Society, "Ghost Towns," spring 2016, https://jcleonard.co/oak-street-historical-society.

103. Francesca Russello Ammon, *Bulldozer: Demolition and Clearance of the Postwar Landscape* (Yale University Press, 2016), 164.

104. Dereen Shirnekhi, "Demolishing Oak Street," *The New Journal*, March 15, 2022, https://thenewjournalatyale.com/2022/03/demolishing-oak-street/; Harrison Silver, "Renewal to Wreckage: Redevelopment in New Haven and the Oak Street Project" (senior thesis, Trinity College, Hartford, CT, 2022), Trinity College Digital Repository, https://digitalrepository.trincoll.edu/theses/953.

105. "Downtown Crossing, New Haven: History," n.d., https://downtowncrossingnewhaven.com/history/.

106. Douglas W. Rae, *City: Urbanism and Its End* (Yale University Press, 2003), 337.

107. "Ghost Towns."

108. Murray Trachten quoted in Francesca Russello Ammon, *Bulldozer: Demolition and Clearance of the Postwar Landscape* (Yale University Press 2016), 175.

109. Isaac Yu, "'Stitching the City Back Together': Changes Coming to Downtown Streets Address York, South Frontage," *Yale Daily News*, April 4, 2022.

110. Liam Dillon, "Even Freeways That Don't Get Built Leave a Scar," *Los Angeles Times*, February 21, 2022, 1; Sherman Lewis, *The Rise and Fall of Hayward's Route 238 Bypass* (Hayward Area Planning Association, 2022).

111. Sarah Plake, "History of U.S. 71: How It Continues to Divide Neighborhoods Today," KSHB, August 15, 2022, https://www.kshb.com/news/local-news/investigations/history-of-u-s-71-how-it-continues-to-divide-neighborhoods-today; Celisa Calacal, "Kansas City Will Study How to Reconnect Neighborhoods Segregated by Highway 71," KCUR, August 15, 2022, https://www.kcur.org/news/2022-08-15/kansas-city-will-study-how-to-reconnect-neighborhoods-segregated-by-highway-71; Suzanne Hogan, "Highway 71 and the Road to Compromise," KCUR, June 3, 2014, https://www.kcur.org/community/2014-06-03/highway-71-and-the-road-to-compromise.

112. Brendan Wittstruck, "The Life and Death of the American Urban Interstate as Told by St. Louis' I-755," *NEXTSTL*, May 8, 2015; Eric Slotboom, "La Porte Freeway, SH 225," *Houston Freeways: A Historical and Visual Journey* (2003); "Boston's Cancelled Highways," n.d., http://www.bostonstreetcars.com/bostons-cancelled-highways.html.

113. Harry Jaffe, "The Insane Highway Plan That Would Have Bulldozed Washington D.C.'s Most Charming Neighborhoods," *Washingtonian*, October 21, 2015; Zachary M. Schrag, "The Freeway Fight in Washington, D.C.: The Three Sisters Bridge in Three Administrations," *Journal of Urban History* 30, no. 5 (2004): 648–73.

114. Benedict Anderson, *Imagined Communities: Reflections on the Origins of Nationalism* (Verso, 1983), 163–64.

115. *Imagined Communities*, 173.

116. James Dilts, "How Not to Run a Roadway," August 1968, General—Conference Committee, "History, Facts and Opinions on Expressway," 6, box 6, folder 31, Movement Against Destruction Records, R0062-MAD, Baltimore Studies Archives, UB.

117. Carolyn Tyson/Save Our American Environment, "The Road: Beating a Path Through the City," n.d., 2, box 7, Movement Against Destruction Records, R0062-MAD, Baltimore Studies Archives, UB.

118. Statement by Barbara Holdridge.

119. James D. Dilts, "Ads Dub Baltimore 'Charm City,'" *Baltimore Sun*, July 11, 1974, C1.

120. National Urban Coalition, *Urban Homesteading: Process and Potential* (January 1974), Maryland Department, EPFL.

121. Jacques Kelly, "Barre St. Site for $1 Homesteads," *Baltimore News-American*, December 21, 1975.

122. James D. Dilts, "The Blush Is Off the Rose of Homesteading," *Baltimore Sun*, August 19, 1979.

123. "The Blush Is Off the Rose."

124. Jacques Kelly, "Dollar Houses Click in First Year," *Baltimore News-American*, April 16, 1975.

125. Tracie Rozhon, "Split-Level Family Tries Homesteading," *Baltimore Sun*, December 12, 1976.

126. "First Year's Homesteaders Were Young, Middle Class," *Baltimore Evening Sun*, March 16, 1976.

127. *Otterbein Homestead Area Guidelines for Exterior Restoration* (Baltimore: Office of the Mayor, 1975).

128. "Redesigned House Suits Personalities," *Baltimore Evening Sun*, March 15, 1976.

129. "The Blush Is Off the Rose."

130. Michael Sumichrast and Lew Sichelman, "Baltimore Keeps Housing Relics from Junk Pile," *Hartford Courant*, May 20, 1979, 3D.

131. Virginia Inman, "Hey, That Gargoyle That You Got Rid of Has Found a Home: Restoration Fad Touches Off Boom for Salvage Outlets," *Wall Street Journal*, August 20, 1981, 20.

132. Ordinance No. 960. "Bldg. Vandals Costing City $10 Million," *Baltimore News-American*, March 25, 1971.

133. "Baltimore Keeps Housing Relics from Junk Pile."

134. Jill Jonnes, "Baltimore Recycles Building Salvage," *New York Times*, July 5, 1984, C3; "Baltimore Keeps Housing Relics from Junk Pile."

135. "Baltimore Keeps Housing Relics from Junk Pile."

136. Louise Sweeney, "French Pastry on the Baltimore Docks," *Christian Science Monitor*, August 28, 1980, B18.

137. Dale Russakoff, "Baltimore's Showplace Harborplace Opens Today," *Washington Post*, July 2, 1980, B1.

138. "French Pastry on the Baltimore Docks."

139. Jake Slagle Jr., "Inner Harbor: A New View from Baltimore." Lenora Heilig Nast, Laurence N. Krause, and R. C. Monk, *Baltimore: A Living Renaissance* (Historic Baltimore Society, 1982), 49.

140. Michael Demarest, "He Digs Downtown." *Time*, August 24, 1981.

141. Ward Morehouse III, "Cities Find Gold along the Waterfront," *Christian Science Monitor*, April 16, 1981, 8.

142. Emily Lieb, "Row House City: Unbuilding Residential Baltimore, 1940–1980" (PhD diss., Columbia University, 2010).

143. Jane Berger, *A New Working Class: The Legacies of Public-Sector Employment in the Civil Rights Movement* (University of Pennsylvania Press, 2021), 53.

144. Tom Kenworthy, "Two-Edged Sword," *Washington Post*, September 2, 1986.

145. Berger, *A New Working Class*, 238.

146. Jerry Bembry, "Drug Trade, Fear Challenge a Neighborhood's Stability," *Baltimore Sun*, September 25, 1988, 1A, 18A.

147. "Drug Trade, Fear."

148. Lawrence T. Brown, *The Black Butterfly: The Harmful Politics of Race and Space in America* (Johns Hopkins University Press, 2021).

149. Luke Broadwater, "Hogan Transportation Map Cuts Baltimore Out of Maryland," *Baltimore Sun*, June 25, 2015.

150. Baltimore Neighborhood Indicators Alliance, "Median Household Income," https://bniajfi.org/indicators/Census%20Demographics/mhhi.

151. Baltimore Neighborhood Indicators Alliance, "Unemployment Rate" (2021), https://bniajfi.org/indicators/Workforce%20And%20Economic%20Development/unempr/2021.

152. Baltimore Neighborhood Indicators Alliance, "Unemployment Rate" (2021), https://bniajfi.org/indicators/Workforce%20And%20Economic%20Development/unempr/2021; Baltimore Neighborhood Indicators Alliance, "Percent Residential Properties That Do Not Receive Mail" (2021), https://bniajfi.org/indicators/Housing%20And%20Community%20Development/nomail/2021.

153. Baltimore Neighborhood Indicators Alliance, "Rate of Street Light Outages per 1,000 Residents" (2021), https://bniajfi.org/indicators/Crime%20And%20Safety/lights/2021.

154. Complaint, *Baltimore Regional Initiative Developing Genuine Equality, Inc. v. State of Maryland*.

155. Alec MacGillis, "The Third Rail," *Places*, March 2016.

156. WBAL-TV, "'This Is Going to Happen': Moore Relaunches East–West Redline Transit Project in Baltimore," June 15, 2023, https://www.wbaltv.com/article/east-west-transit-investment-baltimore-governor-wes-moore/44203081.

Index

Note: Page numbers in italics refer to maps or illustrations.

3-A expressway plan, 101–10, 130, 151, 153, 156, 159–60, 162, 167
6-A expressway plan, 110
10-D expressway plan, 71–76, 81, 95–96, *98*, *99*, 100–106, 110, 116–17, 123, 125, 129–30, 132, 147, 154, 156, 160, 163
238 Freeway (Hayward, CA), 165
710 Freeway (San Gabriel Valley, CA), 165

Abbott, Sammie, 109
Abell, Arunah, 25
Abrams, Charles, 35
ACLU (American Civil Liberties Union), 171
Activists, Inc., 37, 40, 41, 43, 84–85, 90, 134
Addison, Walter J., 109
Agnew, Spiro T., 116, 157
Alexander Hamilton School, 28, 75
American Civil Liberties Union (ACLU), 171
American Concrete Institute, 67
American Friends Service Committee, *Report on Baltimore Civil Disorders, 1968*, 100
American Road Builders Association, 67
Ammon, Francesca Russello, 50
Anderson, Benedict, 166
appraisals. *See* housing appraisal
Architectural Forum (magazine), 9
Armor, John C., 160
Arthur Murray dance studio, 31
Augusta Building and Loan Association, 83
Axelrod, Joseph M., 95–96, 101, 105, 107, 109

Baltimore: activism for livability of, 92–93, 110–11, 166; "Black Butterfly" and "white L" in, 170; blockbusting in, 37–38; bottleneck, 59; as "Charm City," 166–69; downtown decline and proposals for renewal, 60–64, 76; financial constraints in 1970s, 161–62; history of, 16–17; immigrants in, 17; maps of, *vi*, *xiii*; poverty in, 169–70; public service cuts in, 169–70; race and population migration in, 161; riot in, 98–101; War on Drugs in, 170. *See also* Black Baltimoreans; expressways
Baltimore (magazine), 58
Baltimore Afro-American (newspaper), 11, 22, 26, 31, 47, 62, 101, 132, 134, 139–40
Baltimore Board of School Commissioners, 18, 20, 25, 26, 48–53, 93, 171
Baltimore Bureau of Recreation, 47, 49
Baltimore Business Council, 31
Baltimore city council, 9–10, 21, 27, 48, 52, 69–70, 72–73, 75–78, 80, 107, 110–11
Baltimore city officials, and housing situation in Rosemont and similar neighborhoods, 5–6, 59–60, 80, 126–28, 141, 147, 149. *See also* Baltimore city council; Baltimore Department of Housing and Community Development (HCD); code violations; residential segregation
Baltimore City Planning Commission, 71
Baltimore Conference of the Methodist Episcopal Church, 23
Baltimore Cossocks, 31
Baltimore Department of Housing and Community Development (HCD), 6, 10, 116, 122–29, 132, 135–42, 145–47, 149, 167–68
Baltimore Department of Planning, 66, 68–71
Baltimore Department of Public Works, 102, 105, 109
Baltimore Evening Sun (newspaper), 15

Baltimore Federal Savings and Loan, 40, 41, 90
Baltimore Housing Authority, 145, 147
Baltimore Magazine, 57
Baltimore Neighborhood Indicators Alliance, 171
Baltimore News-American (newspaper), 148
Baltimore Park Board, 47
Baltimore Plan for Housing Law Enforcement, 137–38
Baltimore Promotional Council, 166
Baltimore Salvage Depot, 168
Baltimore Sun (newspaper), 11–12, 15, 18, 21–23, 25–27, 33, 38, 41, 47, 48, 57–58, 67–69, 72–73, 75–77, 80–82, 84, 91, 94, 96, 99, 101, 103–4, 107, 110, 115–17, 122, 137–39, 142–43, 145, 149–50, 151, 156, 159, 160, 167, 170; "Picasso, Cats, and Gay Facades—That's Arty Tyson Street Now," 58
Baltimore Urban Renewal and Housing Authority (BURHA), 5–6, 81, 93–95
banks, 10, 33–37, 40, 42, 84, 119–21, 123, 135, 138–39. *See also* mortgages
Baradaran, Mehrsa, 36
Barclift, Dallas and Marian, 30, 44, 49
Barnett, Buddy, 142
Barre Circle, 167
Bay Haven Rod & Gun Club, 31
Bedford Holding Company, 40, 41
Bel Geddes, Norman, 8
Belmont Elementary School, 53, 70, 93
beltway, around Baltimore, 59
Belvedere Construction, 147
Berger, Jane, 31, 169–70
Berman v. Parker (1954), 49–50, 63–64, 77
Berry family, 25
Bethlehem Steel, 157, 161
Black, C. Warren, 59
Black & Decker Manufacturing, 156
Black Baltimoreans: blamed for having too many children, 50, 95; economic and class status of, 30–31; history of, 16–17; home financing available to, 7–8, 37; homeownership by, 37; housing options for, 7, 21–26, 33, 43, 70, 84, 90, 123, 134; middle-class, 8, 39, 46, 81; municipal employment of, 169–70; population growth in first half of 1900s, 25; poverty among, 169–70; violence against, 22–23
Black people: "blight" as code word for, 2, 6, 70; harmed or disadvantaged by white political and economic decisions, 1–2, 5–11, 16–28, 33–51, 60, 67, 70, 72–74, 80–82, 84–85, 93, 100–101, 119, 123–25, 130, 143, 148–49, 157–58, 163–65, 167, 171; poverty among, 120. *See also* Black Baltimoreans
Black Rosemont. *See* Rosemont neighborhood
blight: ascribed to Black Rosemont, 11; as code for "Black people," 2, 6, 70; highways as barrier to spread of, 2; as justification for public policy

benefiting white people, 5–6; meanings of, 2, 5–6, 64; in present-day Rosemont, 171; revitalization of, 68; urban renewal as response to, 63–64. *See also* slum clearance; urban renewal
blockbusting, 7, 9–10, 22, 33, 37–43, 90
Boucher, William, 76, 84, 130, 157, 162
Bowers, Herbert and Helen, 29, 46, 94–95
Boyer, Brian D., 148
Bradford, Calvin, 121
Bridwell, Lowell, 101
Brinkley, Douglas, 151, 152
Briscoe, Mary G., 86–88
brokers, 121, 123, 132, 135–37, 139
Brown, Bernard, 142
Brown, Lawrence T., 170
Brown v. Board of Education (1954), 28, 47, 49
Brownstein, Philip, 119
Bryant, Guy, 44, 46–48
Bryant Packing Box Company, 44, 46–48, 93, 148
Buchanan v. Warley (1917), 23
Buford, Fanny McConnell, 26, 70
builders/contractors, 120, 121, 123, 128, 139, 142, 144. *See also* roadbuilders
Bunch, Drusilla, 149
BURHA. *See* Baltimore Urban Renewal and Housing Authority (BURHA)
Butler, Bill, 76

Cadillac Construction Company, 147
California, 165
Callcott, Margaret Law, 17–18
C&P Telephone, 156
Caplan, Reuben, 78
Cardigans, Inc., 31
Carson, Rachel, 151
Carver Vocational High School. *See* George Washington Carver Vocational High School
central business district (CBD), 64
Chabon, Michael, 132
Charles Center, 64, 73
Cherry Hill, 134
Chesapeake Financial Corporation, 137, 147
Chicory (magazine), 77
Christian Science Monitor, The (newspaper), 169
Citizens' Planning and Housing Association, 103
City (magazine), 101
City of Baltimore Planning Commission, 71
Civil Rights Act (Fair Housing Act) (1968), 90, 119, 123, 134
Clements, Frank and Frances, 39, 117
code violations, 42, 68, 117, 122, 125–26, 134, 137–38
Cole, Albert M., 63, 68–69, 130
Colony Credit, 147
Columbia, Maryland, 131–32, 138
Committee for Downtown, 64

INDEX

Concentrated Code Enforcement Program, 125–26, 134. *See also* code violations
condemnation ordinances, and resulting corridors: city requirements for, 9–10, 52, 69, 72–73, 75–77, 105–6, 110–11; in Rosemont and surrounding areas, 9–10, 39, 52, 75–90, 102–6, *113*, 115–16, 123–30, 135, 137–38, 141, 148–50, 154, 156, 159–60, 166
Congress for Racial Equality (CORE), 81–82
Conley, Dalton, 7
Connolly, N. D. B., 4–5, 94–95
contractors. *See* builders/contractors
Corbett, Gertrude and Thomas, 15–16, 117, 171
CORE (Congress for Racial Equality), 81–82
corrupt, deceitful, and fraudulent practices, 11, 122, 126, 139–44, 147
County Loans, Inc., 127
covenants, restrictive, 23, 25, 36, 46
Coviello, Peter, 149
Crenson, Matthew A., 17
Crisis, The (journal), 19, 22
Cutler, Richard W., 164

D'Alesandro, Thomas, 47, 48, 68, 101, 104, 105–8, 110–11, 115–16, 129–30
Dalsheimer, Hugo, 59
Dashiell, Milton, 21–22
Davis, Ennis, 2
deed restrictions, 23
defaults. *See* foreclosures/defaults
Demarest, Michael, 169
Democratic Party, 17–18
Department of Transportation Act (1966), 154
department stores, 60–63
Dilts, James, 6, 11–12, 81, 84, 96, 101, 129, 149, 162–63, 166, 167
DiMento, Joseph F. C., 151
dollar-house program, 167–68
Doswell, James I., 75
Doswell Temple, 124–27
Dougherty family, 30, 49
Douglas, William O., 77
Douglass, Robert L., 107
Douglass Homes, 100
Downs, Anthony, 94
Dunbar Junior High School, 30

East Baltimore, 98–100, 109, 134
Eastern High School, 72, 154
Easterwood Park, 27, 47
East–West Expressway: eventual fate of, 153–63; financial benefits from effects of, 5, 10–11, 59–60, 80–81, 85–86, 93, 118, 123, 128, 135–49, 156–58, 160; neighborhoods wrecked by, 100; proposals for, 9, 69–71, 73, 92, 103; public hearings on, 72–73, 75–76, 106–11, 154, 156–58, 161; Rosemont impacted by, 9–10, 69–71, 73–75, 78, 80–82, 84–85, 89–90, 96, 100, 103–7; South Baltimore impacted by, 71–73; UDCT's alternative for, 101–2, 105–6. *See also* expressways; Highway to Nowhere; I-170
Edmondson Avenue, 25, 75, 86, 100, 134, 146
Edmondson Avenue Bridge, 15, 30, 49
Edmondson High School, 107
Edmondson Terraces, 23, 25, 31, 38–39, *39*, 71
Edmondson Village, 38
Edmondson Village Shopping Center, 60–61, 117
Eisenhower, Dwight D., 65
Ellis, Cliff, 151
Embry, Robert C., Jr., 116, 123–24, 128, 130, 139–43, 156
eminent domain, 49–50, 64, 77
Encyclopedia Britannica, 59
English-German School, 20
Enoch Pratt Free Library, 31
Environmental Monthly (magazine), 168
environmentalism, 151, 152, 158, 162
Equitable Trust and Maryland National, 40–41
Evans, Roy, 164
expressways: 3-A plan, 101–10, 130, 151, 153, 156, 159–60, 162, 167; 6-A plan, 110; 10-D plan, 71–76, 81, 95–96, *98*, 99, 100–106, 110, 116–17, 123, 125, 129–30, 132, 147, 154, 156, 160, 163; 1957 plan for, 65–71; 1960 plan for, 69, 71; Baltimore proposals for, 9, *55*, 59, 69–77, 110, 116; condemnation ordinances required for, 52, 69, 72–73, 75–77, 105–6, 110–11; environmental and social/historical regulations affecting, 151–54, 158, 162; federal aid for, 64–65; financial constraints on building, 160–62; GBC's advocacy for, 59–60, 64–65, 73, 76; as means of slum clearance, 66–67, 70, 73, 101; Moses and, 8, 66–67, 69–70; neighborhoods wrecked by, 100, 163–66; as popular sensation at New York World's Fair, 8; public hearings on, 72–73, 75–76, 106–11, *108*, 153, 154, 156–58, 161; public opposition to, 72–73, 92–93, 107–11, 151–59, 164; racial and class factors in planning of, 72–74; as urban planning tool, 2, 8–9. *See also* East–West Expressway; I-70; I-170

Fair Housing Act (Civil Rights Act) (1968), 90, 119, 123, 134
fair market value, 35, 38, 50, 75, 77–90, 128. *See also* property values
Fannie Mae (Federal National Mortgage Association), 35, 36, 121
Federal-Aid Highway Act (1956), 65, 76, 83, 152
Federal-Aid Highway Act (1973), 158, 163
Federal Bureau of Investigation (FBI), 142
Federal Highway Administration, 102, 105, 130, 153, 154, 156, 171

Federal Hill, 92, 153–54
Federal Housing Administration (FHA), 27, 34–37, 119–21, 127, 135, 138–40, 147, 148–50; *Underwriting Manual*, 35
Federal National Mortgage Association (Fannie Mae), 35, 36, 121
Federal Organized Crime Strike Force (FBI), 142
Federal Trade Commission, 147
Fells Point, 92, 153–54
FHA. *See* Federal Housing Administration (FHA)
Fields, Barbara, 16
FinanceAmerica Corp, 147
Finks, Estella "Peanuts," 31
foreclosures/defaults, 10, 11, 34, 42, 139, 146, 148
Fort McHenry Tunnel, 162
Francine's School of Dance, 31
Franklin Expressway, 67, 70
Franklin-Mulberry corridor, 28, 66–67, 69, 77, 92, 159
fraud. *See* corrupt, deceitful, and fraudulent practices
Frederick Douglass High School, 30
Freedmen's Bureau, 18
Freund, David M. P., 36
Futurama exhibit, New York World's Fair (1939), 8

Gallop, Rose, 104, 105–6, 138
G+E Contractors, 147
Gant, Danny, 82
Garreau, Joel, 16
GBC. *See* Greater Baltimore Committee (GBC)
General Motors Pavilion, New York World's Fair (1939), 8
George Washington Carver Vocational High School, 26–28, 47
GI Bill of Rights, 34–35
Glenn, Clement, 75–76
Globe Home Improvement Company, 127, 146
Glotzer, Paige, 19
Goldseker, Morris, 38, 40–41. *See also* M. Goldseker Company
Goldseker, Sheldon, 38, 40–41, 135
Government National Mortgage Association (Ginnie Mae), 121
Grady, J. Harold, 71
graft. *See* corrupt, deceitful, and fraudulent practices
Grande, Ottavio, 142–43, 144–45
Graves, Sterling, 3, 30, 49
Great Migration, 25
Greater Baltimore Committee (GBC), 59, 62–65, 73, 76, 156–57, 161, 162
Greater Rosemont, 23, 27, 84, 134. *See also* Rosemont neighborhood
Greiner Company. *See* J. E. Greiner Company
ground rent, 22, 39, 77, 79–80, 88

Gurda, John, 165
Gutman's department store, 60
Gwynns Falls Park, 3, 24, 27, 29, 46–47, 84, 154

Hale, Grace Elizabeth, 61–62
Hanchett, Thomas, 20
Harborplace, 168–69
Harlem Park, 77–84, 115, 154, 159–60, 166
Hauber, Douglas, 69, 71
Hawkins, W. Ashbie, 19, 22
Hawthorne, Nathaniel, 26
Hays, R. Allen, 122
HCD. *See* Baltimore Department of Housing and Community Development (HCD)
Hecht's department stores, 60, 61, 115, 157
Highsmith, Andrew R., 123
Highway Research Board, 67
Highway to Nowhere, 160. *See also* I-170
highways. *See* expressways
Hirsch, Arnold R., *Making the Second Ghetto*, 4–5
Hirshberg, Lewis, 19, 20
Hochschild, Kohn department stores, 60, 61, 62
Hogan, Larry, 170–71
Holdridge, Barbara, 154, 166
home improvement/maintenance, 8, 42, 51, 66, 78, 79, 81, 86, 117, 122, 142, 145–47, 167. *See also* landlords: neglect of properties by
Home Owners' Loan Corporation (HOLC), 34; Residential Security Map of Baltimore, 66
homeownership: by Black Baltimoreans, 37; for the poor, 120–21, 124, 127, 136, 148; in Rosemont, 8, 11, 29–33, 42–43, 46, 94–95, 97–98, 124–30, 143–49
House Committee on Banking and Currency, 122
Household Finance Corporation, 146–47
Housing Acts (1949, 1954), 63, 68
Housing and Urban Development (HUD) Act (1968), 10, 90, 119–22, 126, 134, 136–37, 140
housing appraisal, 78–79, 85–88, 125, 140–41. *See also* fair market value
housing prices: blockbusting, speculation, and, 33, 37–38, 121–22; discriminatory, 7, 22, 33, 36–38, 81; housing appraisal and, 85–88; in Rosemont neighborhood, 9, 11, 41, 85–88, 127, 138, 143. *See also* fair market value; housing appraisal; property values
housing rehabilitation, 11, 58, 68, 119–30, 132, 134, 138–40, 142–46, 149, 160. *See also* home improvement/maintenance
Howard, Leslie Carl, 149
Howard University Alumni Association, 31
Howard-Cramer provision, 158, 163
HUD. *See* US Department of Housing and Urban Development (HUD)
HUD Act. *See* Housing and Urban Development (HUD) Act (1968)

INDEX 233

Hunting Ridge, 91, 117
Hutzler, Albert D., Jr., 59
Hutzler's department store, 59, 60

I-70, 151, 154, 156, 159–60, 162, 163
I-83, 154, 162, 163
I-95, 154, 157, 158, 162, 167
I-170, 9, 75, 154, 156, 159–60, 162. *See also* East–West Expressway
I-595, 163
Imes, Thomas and Amelia, 40
improvement associations. *See* neighborhood (improvement/protective) associations
Inner Harbor, 92, 168–69
Interstate Division for Baltimore City, 77–91, 95, 101–5, 109, 115–17, 123–25, 127, 141, 143, 147, 153, 156, 158, 160, 162
Interstate Expressway Newsletter, 103
interstate highway program, 65
Isenberg, Alison, 61

J. E. Greiner Company, 71–73, 96, 157
Jack and Jill of America, 31
Jacksonville, Florida, 1–3
Jacobs, Jane, 151
Jacobs, Meg, 161
James Mosher School, 28
Jim Crow system: in Baltimore, 3, 16–24; in department stores, 61–63; in education, 18–20; in housing, 20–24; in Jacksonville, 1–2
John P. Rafferty Realty Company, 41–42, 85
Johns Hopkins hospital campus, 100
Johnson, Elzie and Maccabee, 41
Johnson, Lyndon B., 90, 119–20, 152
Johnson, Walter, 70
Jones Falls Expressway, 59, 67, 76, 100
Jude, George L., 156

Kadets of America, 31, 53
Kansas City, Missouri, 165
Kappa Alpha Psi, 31
Kappa Silhouettes, 31
Kappelman, LeRoy, 39–40, 127
Kappelman, Sarah, 127
Keelty Homes, 141
Kerner Commission, 100, 119
King, Martin Luther, Jr., 99

land-installment contracts, 41–42, 85
landlords: neglect of properties by, 26, 70, 100, 104, 125, 134; Rosemont properties owned by, 88, 102–5, 117, 126. *See also* slumlords
Landrum, Clarence and Elizabeth, 81, 82, 90–91, 117
Lapides, Julian, 107
Latrobe Homes, 100

Lauraville neighborhood, 23
Leakin Park, 69, 71, 92, 101, 151, 154, 157, 159–60
Leitch, Wilbur and Jessie, 40
Lethem, Jonathan, 45
LeViness, Charles, 59
Lewis, Tom, 65
Liem, Hugo, 109
Living for Young Homemakers (magazine), 58, 67–68
loans. *See* mortgages
Loewy, Raymond, 61
Louisville, Kentucky, 23
Lusk Reports, 41

M. Goldseker Company, 104, 134–35. *See also* Goldseker, Morris
Macht, Ephraim, 46
Maclin, Ruby and Thomas, 127–29, 134, 137, 143
MAD. *See* Movement Against Destruction (MAD)
Mahool, J. Barry, 21
Mandel, Marvin, 156, 157
Marchiel, Rebecca K., 121, 138
Marshall, Thurgood, 26
Martin, S. Lee, 135–37; advertisement sponsored by, *133*
Maryland Commission on Interracial Problems and Relations, 30, 41
Maryland Crime Investigating Commission, 100
Maryland General Assembly, 82–83, 101
Maryland Prime-O-Sash, 147
Maryland State Highway Administration, Interstate Division, 9
Maryland State Roads Commission, 59, 73, 75, 77, 83–84, 102, 107, 109
May Company, 59, 62, 115
McGuirk, Harry J. "Soft Shoes," 44, 48, 72–73
McKeldin, Theodore, 73, 82
McMechen, George, 21
Mencken, H. L., 6
Mergenthaler Vocational High School, 26–27
Mickle, Gwendolyn, 94
Mikulski, Barbara, 72, 109, 151
Miley, W. F., 79
Milwaukee, Wisconsin, 164–65
Milwaukee Journal-Sentinel (newspaper), 165
Minor, George, 140
Mitchell, Koritha, 51
Mitchell, Parren, 11, 42–43, 140
Montgomery Ward, 156
Monumental Life Insurance, 156
Moore, Wes, 171
Morelite Construction Company, 128, 139–42
Morgan, Mrs. S. B., 25
Morgan State College, 23–24, 30
mortgages: exploitative, 7–8, 10–11, 40–42, 84, 121–22, 134–35, 147, 170; federal rules regarding, 7,

mortgages (cont.)
    33; FHA and, 35, 147; foreclosures/defaults on, 10, 11, 34, 42, 139, 146, 148; guarantees and other incentives for lenders of, 10, 34, 120–21, 138–39; history of, 33–34; legislation to end discrimination in, 119–20; Section 235 and, 10–11, 120–27; segregated market for, 33–37. See also banks
Moses, Robert, Baltimore Arterial Report, 8, 66–67, 69–70, 162
Movement Against Destruction (MAD), 92–93, 107, 110–11, 118, 154, 157–60, 166
Movement Against Destruction v. Volpe (1973), 159
Mowbray, A. Q., 153
Mulberry Street. See Franklin-Mulberry corridor
Mumford, Lewis, 64
Murphy, Shelley, 57–59, 68–69

NAACP. See National Association for the Advancement of Colored People (NAACP)
National Advisory Commission on Civil Disorders. See Kerner Commission
National Association for the Advancement of Colored People (NAACP), 23, 26, 171; Legal Defense Fund, 26
National Commission for the Transportation Crisis, 109
National Environmental Policy Act (NEPA) (1970), 153, 159, 164
National Historic Preservation Act (1966), 152
National Housing Act (1934), 34
National Urban League, 7
neighborhood (improvement/protective) associations, 20, 21, 22, 27, 44
NEPA (National Environmental Policy Act) (1970), 153, 159, 164
New Deal, 33
New Haven, Connecticut, 165
New Michaels Permanent Savings & Loan, 39, 127
New Walbrook Bowling Center, 31
New York Times, The (newspaper), 131–32, 166, 168
New Yorker, The (magazine), 45
Nicholas, Dallas, 51–52, 95
Nixon, Richard, 152, 154
North Jacksonville Street Railway, Town and Improvement Company, 1–2
Novogrod, Leonard J., 59, 62

Oak Street Connector (New Haven, CT), 165
Odum, Alexander and Doris, 41
Old West Baltimore, 7, 19, 22, 26, 57, 66, 69, 99, 149. See also West Baltimore
Olmsted Brothers, 3
Olson, Karen, 17, 19
O'Neill's department store, 60, 61, 63, 64
OPEC oil embargo, 158–59
open-housing ordinances, 80–81

Operation Rescue, 122–23
Orleans Street Viaduct, 100
Orlinsky, Walter, 107, 109–10, 125, 156, 162
Orser, Edward, 38
Otterbein, 167
Owings, Nathaniel, 96

Parent-Teacher-Community Association, 53
Park Freeway West (Milwaukee, WI), 164–65
Patman, Wright, 122
Perman, Michael, 18
Piel Construction Company, 141
Pietila, Antero, 7, 37, 42
Pinn family, 30, 49
Pittsburgh Aluminum, 147
Poe, Edgar Allan, 109
Post Realty, 41
prices. See housing prices
Pride of Baltimore (ship), 169
Project Rehab, 122–23
Property Owners Association, 141
property values, 20–23, 33, 36, 80, 125. See also fair market value; housing appraisal; housing prices
protective associations. See neighborhood (improvement/protective) associations
public hearings, 72–73, 75–76, 106–11, 108, 153, 154, 156–58, 161
public housing, 93–95, 120, 124, 134, 137, 147–48
Purnell, Mrs. I. B., 24–25

R. H. Thomson Expressway (Seattle, WA), 163–64
R. L. Johnson (firm), 136
racial capitalism, 5, 51
Rae, Douglas W., 165
Rafferty Realty Company. See John P. Rafferty Realty Company
R.A.M. See Relocation Action Movement (R.A.M.)
R.A.M. Observer (newsletter), 85
Ranch Realty Company, 105
Rasin, Isaac Freeman, 17
Ray, James Earl, 98–99
Red Line light rail project, 170–71
Redd, Esther, 73, 108, 115–16, 130
redlining, 34, 36
rehabilitation. See housing rehabilitation
Reich, Larry, 160–61
Relocation Action Movement (R.A.M.), 80–83, 85, 90, 92, 107, 115, 124
replacement value, 82–83
Republican Party, 17–18
residential segregation: in Baltimore, 20–24; federal law against, 90; FHA guidelines for mortgages and, 35–36; historical integration preceding, 17, 19–20; legal enforcement of,

INDEX

21–23; open-housing ordinances and, 80–81; property values linked to, 20–23, 33, 36, 80; school segregation linked to, 3, 7, 18–19, 24–25, 28
restrictive covenants, 23, 25, 36, 46
Reuss, Henry, 119
Reutter, Mark, 65
R.H.I.A. *See* Rosemont Home Improvement Association (R.H.I.A.)
Rice, Samuel Joseph, 7, 24
roadbuilders, 2, 9, 11, 66–69, 72, 76, 81–86, 89, 96, 100–101, 106–7, 111, 115, 130, 151–52, 157–60, 162, 165
Roland Park neighborhood, 19, 23, 45–46
Romney, George, 122, 124
Rooks, Noliwe, *Cutting School*, 5
Rosemond, Mary (née Morgan), 1–4, 8–11, 30–33, 47, 49, 53, 71, 95, 106, 117–18, 170
Rosemont Area Studies (Urban Design Concept Team), 96–98, *98*, *99*, 102, 117
Rosemont Coalition, 124–25, 128, 135
Rosemont Home Improvement Association (R.H.I.A.), 30–31, 39, 44–45
"Rosemont Is Now" (workbook), 145–46
Rosemont neighborhood: Bentalou Street, *4*; condemnation corridor in, 9–10, 84–90, 97–98, 102–6, 110–11, *113*, 116–17, 123–30, 135, 137–38, 141, 148–50, 154, 156, 159–60, 166; creation of Black Rosemont, 3–4, 7, 24–28; deterioration of, 103–5, 116–18, *118*, *129*, 130, 143–50, 170–71; diversity of interests in, 124; drug trafficking in, 170; Ellamont Street, *52*; expressway map that wrecked, 6, 9, 11–12, 69–74, 118, 123, 129, 162–63, 166; factory built in, 46–48; Franklintown Road, *118*; homeownership in, 8, 11, 29–33, 42–43, 46, 94–95, 97–98, 124–30, 143–49; housing rehabilitation in, 123–30, 139, 142–46, 149, 160; Jim Crow system and, 16–24; kept ignorant of expressway plans, 71–73, 107; landlord-owned properties in, 88, 102–5, 117, 126; legacy of, 169–71; maps of, *vi*, *13*, *113*; middle-class character of, 8, 39, 46; North Rosedale Street, *129*; prices of homes in, 9, 11, 41, 85–88, 127, 138, 143; public housing in, 93–95, 124, 137, 147–48; public policy as cause of destruction of, 5–12; school planned for, 48–53; Section 235 and, 122–27, 129, 132–40, 143, 145–50, 160, 167; stability of, 8, 30–33, 45–46, 92, 94–97, 101, 106, 150; UDCT's study of, 96–98, *98*, *99*, 101–4, 117; white precursor to Black Rosemont, 3, 24–25, *25*. *See also* Greater Rosemont
Rosemont Neighborhood Improvement Association (R.N.I.A.), 45–46, 48–51, 53, 70–71, 92–95, 98, 101, 105–7, 109, 117, 118, 124, 130, 138, 148, 154, 170
Rosemont Sales Program, 128, 135–36, 148
Rosemont Vacant House Program, 123–25, 128–30, 133–36, 138, 142, 147–48

Rosenfeld, Eddie, 57–58, 67
Rothstein, Richard, 67
Rouse, Bill, 59
Rouse, James, 131–32, 137–39, 168
Rouse Company, 41, 132, 137–38, 143, 146, 148

salvage, 167–68
Samuel DuBois Cook Center on Social Equity, Duke University, 42
San-Dee construction company, 139, 142
sanitation services, 81, 94, 117, 124, 170
Saturday Evening Post (magazine), 37
Save Tyson Street Committee, 68
savings and loan associations, 40
Schaefer, William Donald, 75–76, 156, 157, 160, 162, 168, 169
school segregation: in Baltimore, 18–20; and condition of Black schools, 26; and overcrowded Black schools, 27–28, 49; residential segregation linked to, 3, 7, 18–19, 24–25, 28; and school conversions, 3, 7, 24, 27; and "separate but equal" principle, 26; unofficial, by exclusion of transfers, 49
Scotland, Fern, 31
Seattle, Washington, 163–64
Second Commercial Use District, 46, 48
Section 235 lending program, 10–11, 120–27, 129, 132–40, 143, 145–50, 160, 167; advertisement related to, *133*
segregation: in department stores, 61–63; economic profit from policies enforcing, 5; of parks and swimming pools, 47. *See also* Jim Crow system; residential segregation; school segregation
"separate but equal" principle, 26
Shelley v. Kraemer (1948), 36
Sherwood, John R., 52, 76
Sierra Club, 151, 154
Silver, Harrison, 165
Simmons, Johnnie and Larene, 41, 85
Skidmore, Owings, and Merrill, 96
slum clearance, 50, 57, 63–64, 66–67, 70, 73, 101
slumlords, 66, 123, 137
Somerset Court Homes, 100
South Baltimore, 71–73, 92, 107
speculators, 40–43, 50–51, 66, 84, 89–90, 103–5, 119–20, 122, 126, 134
Stanley, William and Estelle, 41
Stark, Alexander, 101, 107, 110
Starr, Blaze, 166
State Building Supply Co., 147
State Home Remodeling Co., 146
Stewart's department store, 60, 62
Stonewall Democratic Club, 44
Straw Man, Inc., 41, 127
Study for East-West Expressway, 69, 71

suburbs: Black people's movement to, 30; economic drain on downtown initiated by, 60–61; segregation in, 19, 23; white people's movement to, 19, 24–25
Sugar Hill neighborhood (Jacksonville, FL), 1–2
supplemental payments, 83–86, 88–90, 127, 162
swimming pools, 47

Taylor, Brian D., 161
Taylor, Keeanga-Yamahtta, 10, 120, 121
Terry, George, 125, 128
Thomsen, Roszel C., 26, 27
Thorp Credit, 147
Thurber, James, 6
Time (magazine), 169
Tinley, Sidney H., 137–39
Topaz Realty, 40
Tots and Teens, 31
Trainor, Richard, 109
Truman, Harry S., 67
Tulip Club, 31
Tyler, Mrs. E. B., 24
Tyson, Carolyn, 157, 158, 166
Tyson Street, 57–58, *58*, 66–72, 130, 167

Urban Design Concept Team (UDCT), 96–98, 101–4, 110, 116–17, 151–52; impact of 10-D expressway through Rosemont, *99*; representation of 10-D expressway through Rosemont, *98*
urban homesteading, 167
Urban Land Institute, 67
Urban League, 25, 31
urban renewal, 50, 63, 68, 93, 97, 100, 101, 130, 131. *See also* blight; slum clearance
US Bureau of Public Roads, 95–96, 102
US Congress, 66
US Department of Housing and Urban Development (HUD), 122–25, 138, 143–44
US Department of Transportation, 65, 106, 152
US Supreme Court, 23, 154
U.S.S. *Constellation*, 166

Veterans Administration (VA), 35, 37
VOLPE. *See* Volunteers Opposing the Leakin Park Expressway (VOLPE)
Volpe, John A., 110, 116, 154
Voluntary Home Mortgage Credit Program, 36
Volunteers Opposing the Leakin Park Expressway (VOLPE), 154, 166; brochure, *155*

Walbrook Improvement Association, 27
Wall Street Journal, The (newspaper), 168
Walter, C. Edward, 109
Washington, DC, 165–66
Washington Post, The (newspaper), 44, 122, 134, 168, 169
We Moms, 31
We Wives, 32, 53
We Workers Social and Civic Club, 31–32, *32*, 49, 53
Weingroff, Richard, 158, 163
Weintraub, Melvin, 139
Welch, Agnes, 12
Wells, John and Ada, 77–84, 115
Weschler, Stu, 108, 111
West, Samuel, 21
West Baltimore, 3, 15–16, 20–24, 27–28, 44, 81, 96, 134, 142, 170. *See also* Old West Baltimore
Western Cemetery, 101, 109–11, 116
Western Electric, 156
Western Maryland Railway, 46
white supremacy, 6–7, 18
Whitestone Baptist Church, 44, 48
Wiles, Joseph and Esther, 29–30, 49, 93–94, 102, 104, 148
Williams, Archie, 95
Williams, Rhonda Y., 94
Wilson, Harry B., 139
Winichakul, Thongchai, 166
Wolf, Jerome B., 84
World's Fair (New York, 1939), 8

Yale Daily News (newspaper), 165
Yale Law Journal, 148

zoning laws, 23, 46, 48, 94, 148

www.ingramcontent.com/pod-product-compliance
Lightning Source LLC
Chambersburg PA
CBHW022050290426
44109CB00014B/1048